M000166833

WORKING
WITH THE
BEREAVED

THE SERIES IN DEATH, DYING, AND BEREAVEMENT

ROBERT NEIMEYER, CONSULTING EDITOR

FORMERLY THE SERIES IN DEATH EDUCATION, AGING, AND HEALTH CARE

HANNELORE WASS, CONSULTING EDITOR

WORKING
WITH THE
BEREAVED

Multiple Lenses on Loss and Mourning

SIMON SHIMSHON RUBIN,
RUTH MALKINSON,
AND ELIEZER WITZTUM

Routledge
Taylor & Francis Group
New York   London

Routledge
Taylor & Francis Group
711 Third Avenue
New York, NY 10017

Routledge
Taylor & Francis Group
27 Church Road
Hove, East Sussex BN3 2FA

© 2012 by Taylor & Francis Group, LLC
Routledge is an imprint of Taylor & Francis Group, an Informa business

Printed in the United States of America on acid-free paper
Version Date: 20110525

International Standard Book Number: 978-0-415-88165-4 (Hardback) 978-0-415-88166-1 (Paperback)

For permission to photocopy or use material electronically from this work, please access www. copyright.com (http://www.copyright.com/) or contact the Copyright Clearance Center, Inc. (CCC), 222 Rosewood Drive, Danvers, MA 01923, 978-750-8400. CCC is a not-for-profit organization that provides licenses and registration for a variety of users. For organizations that have been granted a photocopy license by the CCC, a separate system of payment has been arranged.

Trademark Notice: Product or corporate names may be trademarks or registered trademarks, and are used only for identification and explanation without intent to infringe.

Library of Congress Cataloging-in-Publication Data

Rubin, Simon Shimshon.
    Working with the bereaved : multiple lenses on loss and mourning / Simon Shimshon Rubin, Ruth Malkinson, Eliezer Witztum. -- 1st ed.
        p. cm. -- (Series in death, dying, and bereavement)
    Includes bibliographical references and index.
    ISBN 978-0-415-88165-4 (hardcover : alk. paper) – ISBN 978-0-415-88166-1 (pbk. : alk. paper)
    1. Bereavement--Psychological aspects. 2. Loss (Psychology) 3. Cognitive therapy. I. Malkinson, Ruth, 1938- II. Witztum, Eliezer. III. Title.

BF575.G7.R83 2012
155.9'37--dc23   2011018664

Visit the Taylor & Francis Web site at
http://www.taylorandfrancis.com

and the Routledge Web site at
http://www.routledgementalhealth.com

For my unmet siblings, Rachel and Yisroel Rubin,
and their mother, Sara Krauthammer,
killed 1943 in the Holocaust
—SSR

To the memory of my beloved parents
Nahum Bogin and Shoshana Nerfin-Bogin
—RM

For the memory of my dear parents
Shmuel (1914–2001) and Yafa (Sonia) (1922–2000) Witztum
—EW

Contents

SECTION I   CHOOSING LIFE AFTER LOSS

SECTION II   THE TWO-TRACK MODEL OF BEREAVEMENT: CONTINUING BONDS AND CONTINUING WITH LIFE

SECTION III INTEGRATING VARIOUS THERAPEUTIC APPROACHES WITH INSIGHTS FROM THE TWO-TRACK MODEL OF BEREAVEMENT

SECTION IV EXPANDING HORIZONS: CULTURE, CLINICAL CHALLENGES, AND FACILITATING RESILIENCE

Series Editor's Foreword

For the better part of the 20th century, bereavement research and practice could be fairly described as falling principally within one of two broad trends. On the one hand, following the pioneering work of Sigmund Freud, writers and analysts in the psychoanalytic tradition posited elaborate and sometimes esoteric dynamics of inner processes as mourners resisted coming to terms with the hard reality of loss, eventually withdrawing emotional energy from the lost relationship in order to reinvest in living relationships. On the other hand, more general medical and psychiatric authors and practitioners concentrated on documenting the overt symptomatology of grief, and especially with the advent of psychopharmacology, its amelioration. By contrast to these two dominant traditions, serious attempts to integrate the two faces of grief work were rare. As a result, generations of bereaved people, if they consulted a professional at all, often confronted a choice between protracted personal therapy focusing on their unconscious dynamics regarding the loss and medical attempts to mitigate their (chiefly depressive or anxious) symptomatology. Common to both approaches was a presumption of patient passivity, insofar as little attention was paid to the active agency of the bereaved themselves in dealing with the death and its consequences, either as individuals or as families.

Much has changed in the past few decades, however. Models of grieving as an active process of coping with separation have grown in number and sophistication, as have the substantial empirical literatures on issues of attachment, meaning making, psychological trauma, complicated grief, and a host of other topics of direct relevance to bereavement intervention. Indeed, the authors of this book are themselves lively participants in this burgeoning area of conceptual and clinical work, having drawn on their own consultation with the bereaved as well as a growing research base to posit a genuinely integrative theory of grief: the Two-Track Model of Bereavement (TTMB). Guided by this helpful heuristic frame, clinicians are led not only to take stock of the myriad *biopsychosocial consequences* of loss for clients' daily lives (reflected, for example, by struggles in emotional, cognitive, interpersonal, and work domains), but also to consider their ongoing *relationship to the deceased*, as reflected in often complex attempts to maintain contact with their loved ones while also buffering the painful evidence of their absence.

After briefly reviewing pioneering contributions to bereavement studies, Rubin, Malkinson, and Witztum explore the thorough interpenetration of trauma and bereavement, noting that the former is not limited to its impact on the emotions, belief systems, and behaviors addressed under the track concerned with biopsychosocial functioning, but indeed extends to various features that complicate the relationship to the dead. Among these are the ways in which the traumatic imagery that typically accompanies violent death, as well as relational traumas like betrayal or conflict, can contaminate the very memories of the deceased that might otherwise give solace. As the authors share with the reader case study after case study, it becomes more and more clear how inadequate traditional models are in capturing the nuances of post-loss adaptation and its myriad challenges. Rather than simply deactivating one's attachment to the deceased, the "work of mourning" is found to consist both in regulation of the multifaceted disruption in biological, psychological, and social functioning occasioned by the death and in renegotiation of one's constructive relationship to the deceased, drawing on personal, familial, religious/philosophic, and cultural supports for reengaging life as it now presents itself.

For me, the heart of the book is the convincing, clinically rich portrayal of psychotherapy with the bereaved, going beyond facile vignettes to explore the nuances of actual cases, in all their reality and recalcitrance. In these core chapters the reader will step into that fruitful liminal space in which clinicians may prompt clients through the use of imagery and metaphor, spiritual beliefs and practices, letter writing and chair work to reestablish, renegotiate, and sometimes partly relinquish their bonds with the dead. Sorting through tangled legacies of past losses and conflicted relationships in psychodynamic work, promoting adaptive interpretations of grief and survivorship in cognitive behavioral/rational emotive therapies, and realigning family relationships in systemic work all contribute to a robust depiction of grief therapy, not as a stand-alone specialty, but instead as an empirically informed refinement of general frameworks for practice. The book closes with an advocacy for suicide and crisis intervention in the earliest phases of loss when a subset of the bereaved show great vulnerability, and with a welcome attention to cultural diversity in mourning rituals as displayed by different ethnic or religious communities in the United States and Israel.

In sum, *Working With the Bereaved: Multiple Lenses on Loss and Mourning* offers truth in advertising; it is a thorough and thoughtful handbook for working with both the symptomatic and relational challenges of grieving, one written *by* intelligent clinicians *for* intelligent clinicians. I hope that it will offer a trove of concepts and methods that enhance your practice with grieving clients, as it will enhance mine.

Robert A. Neimeyer, PhD
Series Editor

Preface

This book is competing for your time and attention. The potential reader considering a book referring to loss and bereavement in its title has entered the first circle of curiosity. What will justify the decision to read on? The authors, all seasoned readers themselves, sought to write a book that would be interesting, informative, and useful for a wide swath of clinicians. Those of you who proceed will be the judge of that.

This book is written for clinicians by clinicians. It is written by people who are not strangers to loss and bereavement for people who should not be strangers to loss and bereavement either—even if they experience themselves as such. Many of the things we have written will interest anyone who wishes to learn more about bereavement. Nevertheless, despite the temptation to write a book for "Everyman," we have chosen to write for "Every-clinician" and to do so in a way that is designed to be appropriate for widely varying theoretical, personal, and clinical orientations and experience levels.

No human being is a stranger to love, attachment, and life with others. No human remains a stranger to loss, loneliness, and death. Our personal and professional lives have allowed us to take on the challenge of helping others live more fully in the transitional space that exists between love and loss, attachment and loneliness, and life and death. Our intent is to produce a book that will be of interest and of use to clinicians in the fields of mental health as well as other persons interested in the area. We have made liberal use of clinical material throughout the book. This facilitates communication, maintains interest, and is closest to much of what we do as psychotherapists.

Having addressed the *what* and *how* questions (what we attempt to do and how we do it), there remains the *who* question. *Who* has written this book? The formal aspects of that question are easiest to answer. We are a clinical psychologist, social worker, and psychiatrist who maintain active psychotherapy practices while also serving as academic and clinical faculty. We have written independently and together on a range of issues related to bereavement as well as to other aspects of mental health. More detail about the formal aspects of who we are can be found on the About the Authors page as well as on the Internet.

We invite you to continue on with us and enter additional circles of curiosity. The book is composed of four sections: Section I: Choosing Life After Loss; Section II: The Two-Track Model of Bereavement: Continuing Bonds and Continuing With Life; Section III: Integrating Various Therapeutic Approaches

With Insights From the Two-Track Model of Bereavement; and Section IV: Expanding Horizons: Culture, Clinical Challenges, and Facilitating Resilience. In the Appendix, we include the full Two-Track Bereavement Questionnaire (TTBQ2-70). Designed for clinical and research use, the TTBQ2-70 has value as a screening tool, and as a measure of pre- and post-treatment effectiveness. The measure is accompanied by a short commentary. The chapter titles further clarify the nature of the topics we address.

Acknowledgments

As this book is an amalgam of the life experiences of the authors forged in the crucible of their personal, intellectual, and therapeutic experiences, it makes sense to acknowledge some of those experiences. Many forces have served to temper the book and to influence the way in which we understand loss and bereavement and share that with you the reader. We do this first in the plural, speaking as one, and then we continue on to speak in our own individual voices as the singular beings we all are.

Professionally, we acknowledge our own teachers, our clients, our supervisors, and our supervisees for the education they gave us. From all of them, we learned a lot about the human face of loss and how to communicate what we know, and are still learning, to ourselves and to others. The commonalities and the singularities of bereavement are striking. Both poles of interpersonal loss deserve our attention, our understanding, and our respect. Humility in the face of the pain and longing of bereavement is something that one learns and relearns over time. Respect for human resilience—for the ability of people to cope, grow, and develop—is something more fully appreciated in the context of the therapy relationship. The unique conditions of psychotherapy allow for a category of interpersonal connection, and emotional intimacy, in a framework that encourages the sharing of private thoughts and feelings. To be a psychotherapist is to be accorded a privilege and a sacred trust. To listen, to hear, and to help bereaved clients is to accomplish what we are expected, and have been allowed, to attempt. Our abilities and our tools are not unlimited, but our basic humanity should never lag behind either. This, too, has been taught to us by our teachers, our students, and our clients.

We have been very fortunate in the realm of colleagues. First and foremost, our ability to work together over a span approaching a quarter century has been a source of professional creativity and personal satisfaction. It is said that the whole is greater than the sum of its parts, and that is our subjective appraisal of our joint work. Our circles of colleagues extend much farther and wider than the three of us. The International Work Group on Death, Dying and Bereavement, more commonly known to its members as the IWG, has connected us with a fascinating array of leaders in the field.

To our publishing team at Routledge, Senior Editor Dana Bliss, Associate Editor Anna Moore, and Project Editor Iris Fahrer, and to series editor and friend Robert Neimeyer, we extend our thanks and appreciation. They are a professional and personable group. We wish to thank the Witztum families for permission to use original artwork by their mother. We thank those assisting us in Israel, Meyrav Blizovski, Mertyn Malkinson, Michal Rubin, and Galia Witztum.

At this point, the individual authors add their individual thanks and acknowledgments.

I acknowledge my debt to my two parent countries and cultures, the United States and Israel, for giving me wonderful traditions and challenges. From time to time, I have been able to share a sliver of my own thoughts on those influences on, and their interplay with, my professional work in both ethics and bereavement. I have been fortunate to have the support of my colleagues and students in the Department of Psychology and at the International Center for the Study of Loss, Bereavement and Human Resilience at the University of Haifa. Finally, I thank my wife Lisa, our children, and their families—Abraham; Sara, Yehuda, Naomi and Joshua Halper; Jonah and Annabella; and Michal—for being who they are.

Simon Shimshon Rubin
Haifa

Writing the acknowledgment concludes a unique journey filled with people who were a source of inspiration and support as the book was moving toward its final form. In addition to being thankful for working as a threesome, a growth experience for me, I would like to thank my colleagues and students for the inspiration and support they provided throughout the writing. I wish to express special thanks to my husband, Mertyn, whose patience and support were invaluable all along the way. And finally I would like to thank my dear children, Yael, Dan, and Guy, and their families, who continue to educate me about evolving relationships.

Ruth Malkinson
Rehovot

I would like to thank my colleagues and friends for their inspiration and help over the years. Professors Haim Dasberg and Onno Van der Hart deserve special mention in that regard. Closer to home, I wish to especially thank my children, Galia, Dan, and Uria, and my brother Menachem and his wife, Nilly, for their help and support in difficult times.

Eliezer Witztum
Jerusalem

About the Authors

Simon Shimshon Rubin, Ph.D., is a full professor of clinical psychology and director of the International Center for the Study of Loss, Bereavement and Human Resilience at the University of Haifa in Israel. He is chairman of the Postgraduate Psychotherapy Program at the Department of Psychology based there as well. Dr. Rubin is active as a clinician, consultant, researcher, and teacher. He has lectured and published extensively on bereavement, ethics, and training in psychotherapy. Over the course of his career, Dr. Rubin has been a visiting professor at the Northwestern and Harvard University medical schools; board member of the International Work Group on Death, Dying and Bereavement (IWG); chair of the clinical psychology program at the University of Haifa; chair of its University Ethics Committee; director of the Israel Ministry of Health's Haifa Child, Adolescent and Family Clinic; and senior clinical psychologist at Michael Reese Medical Center in Chicago, Illinois. Professor Rubin's Web site can be viewed at http://psy.haifa. ac.il/~rubin.

Ruth Malkinson, Ph.D., is adjunct senior lecturer at the Bob Shapell School of Social Work, and the School of Medicine, Tel Aviv University. She is the founder and director of the Israeli Center of REBT (Rational Emotive Behavior Therapy). Dr. Malkinson is also a core member of the International Center for the Study of Loss, Bereavement and Human Resilience at the University of Haifa. She is a past president of the Israeli Association for Couple and Family Therapy. Dr. Malkinson is a member of IWG (International Work Group for Death, Dying and Bereavement) and consults, lectures, and conducts workshops nationally and internationally on these subjects. She teaches and practices individual and family therapy along the life cycle. Her most recent book is titled *Cognitive Grief Therapy: Constructing a Rational Meaning to Life Following Loss* (2007).

Eliezer Witztum, M.D., is a full professor in the Division of Psychiatry, Faculty of Health Sciences, Ben-Gurion University of the Negev. He is director of Psychotherapy Supervision at the Mental Health Center, Beer Sheva and senior psychiatrist at the Community Mental Health Center of Ezrat Nashim Hospital in North Jerusalem.

Professor Witztum's areas of expertise include cultural psychiatry, the history of psychiatry, trauma and bereavement, strategic and short-time dynamic psychotherapy, and the treatment of pedophile sexual offenders.

Professor Witztum has published more than 200 scientific publications. He coauthored (with D. Greenberg) *Sanity and Sanctity* (2001) and collaborated (with Aryeh Kasher) on *King Herod: A Persecuted Persecutor: A Case Study in Psychohistory and Psychobiography* (2007). His recent Hebrew language books include *Spirit, Loss and Bereavement* (2004); *Genius and Madness: The Complicated Relationship Between Creativity and Psychopathology* (with V. Lerner, 2008); and *To Bear a Child: Psychological Aspects of Fertility Problems and Their Treatment* (with Z. Birman, 2010).

The authors have published numerous articles together and coedited the following books: *Loss and Bereavement in Jewish Society in Israel* (1993) and *Traumatic and Nontraumatic Loss and Bereavement* (2000).

Section *I*

Choosing Life After Loss

Figure S1.1   James Guthrie, A Funeral Service in the Highlands. © Culture & Sport Glasgow (Museums).

Section I opens with two introductory chapters. The first chapter sets the stage and begins the theme of the struggle to return to full life after loss. It touches upon what makes this field so difficult to work in for many people. Case examples discussed include the biblical story of Jacob mourning for Joseph, the son he presumed dead, as well as more contemporary examples. The chapter closes with theoretical and historical issues in the field centered on the work of three of the "founding fathers" of the field, Freud, Lindemann, and Bowlby.

The second chapter presents an overview of five themes that frame much of the discussion and thinking about loss. To cite the first, the question "Is there right and wrong in the bereavement response?" is addressed. The way this theme is developed has less to do with "answers" and more to do with understanding the context of the question and its connection to how people think about loss. The remaining themes are also considered with attention to context as well as content. They address the centrality of interpersonal relationships in bereavement, potential for change and growth following loss, how to facilitate adaptive grieving, and the relevance of ethics for the field.

1

Love—and Loss—and Life

*T*he life thread of human interconnection brings with it the certainty of loss through death. Despite the variation in circumstances and their significance, bereavement will come to us all. The emotions accompanying bereavement are often painful. Sadness, longing, profound unease, guilt, and feelings of losing one's mind are but a few of the emotions that may overwhelm family members as they respond to the death of a loved one. And yet, over time, most of us experience the loss of a loved one and continue to live a full and productive life with acceptance of loss becoming part of it. For the clinician encountering people who have suffered the loss of a significant other, perhaps the most basic question we ask ourselves regarding bereavement is which responses deserve our intervention skills and which do not? Responding to even this "relatively straightforward" question requires us to acknowledge that the responses to such questions are embedded in a veritable matrix of assumptions and epistemological ways of thinking about human behavior. In the next chapter, we address some of the current assumptions and controversies that precede questions of assessment and intervention, which take up the major part of this book. Prior to that, however, we begin with aspects of the therapists' own attitudes to loss before we address the phenomenology of loss as experienced by bereaved individuals. Ultimately, it is the therapists' own attitudes to loss that frame and organize the personal experience of how they approach the encounter with the bereavement of another.

ENTERING THE FEARED REALM
WITHOUT BEING TRAPPED THERE

Separation, loss, and death are painful, frightening, and emotionally threatening. From time immemorial, the individual's encounters with loss and death have been met within a framework of resources and meaning structure designed to support those experiencing the death of significant persons. The individual's own psychological experience of loss is strongly mediated by the meaning framework of the familial, cultural, and religious-spiritual resources that help organize the experience. The sustained attention to helping those who experience the death of a loved one, separated physically from the deceased in the form of burial and mourning rites, is a part of every faith tradition. The need to attend to this part of human experience merely underscores how significant an event and process the death of another sets in motion.

All living things die. During the time that people are alive, the impact of their existence may be known to others or not; it may be great or small, but we believe it is never null or absent. For those closest to the deceased, the impact of their loved one's death can be assessed and categorized in many ways. In many respects, that is what this book will address. The impact of loss is so great because our connections to those closest to us are so important. Loss and bereavement are ultimately about love and connection. One can be traumatized by being exposed to the death of a human being whom one does not know. But one can only truly and deeply grieve and mourn someone with whom one has a connection.

In our individual and combined experience encountering, teaching, and treating bereavement, we have noted time and again how difficult it is for some clinicians to acknowledge the universal significance of this topic. Most of the time, at best, cursory attention is given to loss and bereavement during training. Rarely is the area approached as an experience that is a central part of human existence and so ubiquitous as to require that all clinicians have basic competence in this aspect of the human encounter.

Clinicians' own feelings (their "countertransference") are operant in many areas of experience. Some topics are avoided by many. For example, working with victims of sexual abuse, and particularly child sexual abuse, is difficult for many therapists, but working with perpetrators is seen as significantly more difficult and avoidable. Whereas a therapist may avoid intentionally choosing such clients in one's practice, one can never know in advance whether such history will reveal itself in what seemed to be initially a client to whom this history did not apply. At least some familiarity with the impact and consequences of such experiences equips the therapist with the ability to encounter the complexity of what people bring with them unbeknownst to the therapist. Similarly, working with the terminally ill is something that some are drawn to and others avoid (Berzoff & Silverman, 2004).

Yet no one can ever know whether one's clients will become seriously ill and bring that issue to bear into a therapy relationship. In the case of loss and bereavement, the necessity of being familiar with the topic, even for those who are not themselves drawn to the topic, is even more necessary, for all living persons will both lose significant others and be the cause of a bereavement response for those who love them. And thankfully, because people are important to each other, their loss matters. We do not minimize how painful, upsetting, life wrenching, and tragic the event of death can be. All of this contributes to why the field of bereavement work is typically so anxiety provoking to so many. At the same time, however, the most adaptive responses to bereavement are about finding ways to renew and reorganize connections to oneself, to the deceased, and to the interpersonal and greater surroundings of one's world.

The trauma of forced separation from a loved one is the stuff of nightmares for young and old alike. Yet the reality of human adaptation to loss and death is one of survival, adaptation, and a mix of scar tissue and renewed growth. There are many pathways in which humans respond to the physical separation from others and yet continue to benefit from the history and essence of their connection. That fact, as well as helping persons cope with the deleterious impact of less adaptive responses to loss, will reverberate throughout the book.

All living things die.
   One can only truly and deeply grieve someone with whom one has a connection.

A CASE OF LOSS

Throughout this book, we focus on the therapist's encounter with loss and bereavement and how to assist clients. Parallel to that theme runs the idea that the natural course of bereavement is not always salutary. We turn to the Bible's portrayal of one particularly painful bereavement and its "solution" for the pain of loss depicted.

The biblical figure of Jacob stands out as a powerful case history of the impact of child loss and bereavement for many reasons. From close attention to research as well as intervention with bereaved parents, the details of Jacob's response to the purported death of Joseph convey one picture of what today we would call complicated bereavement. The story is told in the book of Genesis about Jacob's favoring his son Joseph. The recipient of great love and affection from his father, Joseph is not sufficiently sensitive to the negative family dynamic this perpetuates. Hated by his brothers, Joseph is sold by his brothers to human traffickers who sell him off to servitude and slavery. The dynamics of the plot relevant to us follow from Jacob being presented with the bloodied coat of many colors that was Joseph's and his natural assumption that Joseph has been killed by wild beasts.

> 37:34 And Jacob rent his garments, and put sackcloth upon his loins, and mourned for his son many days.
> 37:35 And all his sons and all his daughters rose up to comfort him; but he refused to be comforted; and he said: "Nay, but I will go down to the grave to my son mourning." And his father wept for him. (Jewish Publication Society [JPS], 1962)

The biblical story of Jacob's grief spans a period of many years during which he is inconsolable. Head of a clan, father to 13 children and to grandchildren, we are told time and again that Jacob's focus is on his "deceased son," and his description of himself is a perpetual mourner destined to continue mourning until his own death. Only one thing can change that, and that is understood by Jacob to be impossible, and that would be a reunion with Joseph. The story continues and, viewed from the perspective of today, seems to be some sort of unethical psychological experiment utilizing deception to make its point. The story is designed to show us the impact of child loss for some—and its "only" cure. The impact of the event, the loss of Joseph, and its amelioration can be seen best when a solution is found for Jacob's depression and grief.

> Genesis 45:26 And they told him, saying: "Joseph is yet alive, and he is ruler over all the land of Egypt." And his heart fainted, for he believed them not.
> 45:27 And they told him all the words of Joseph, which he had said unto them; and when he saw the wagons which Joseph had sent to carry him, the spirit of Jacob their father revived.
> 45:28 And Israel [Jacob] said: "It is enough; Joseph my son is yet alive; I will go and see him before I die." (JPS, 1962)

The impact of child loss, and its ability to affect the bereaved, can be devastating, and its effects are often lifelong. In the biblical story, we are told that Jacob is inconsolable and that his spirit only revives when he learns that Joseph lives. Although it is far from clear that Jacob would meet recent DSM (*Diagnostic and Statistical Manual of Mental Disorders*) proposed criteria for complicated grief, pathological grief, or prolonged grief disorder, there are many indications of his ongoing suffering (Prigerson, Vanderwerker, & Maciejewski, 2008; Rubin, Malkinson, & Witztum, 2008). It is clear from the story that despite all his ongoing familial connections, Jacob's bereavement exacts a great cost from him and from his extended family. In the remainder of this book, we seek to formulate and communicate to the clinician reader, useful and fundamental understandings of bereavement and intervention following loss that have conceptual, clinical, and personal meaning for therapists and clients alike.

> The biblical story of Jacob describes prolonged grief and mourning for Joseph and Jacob's inability to respond appropriately to his other children.
> The psychological cost to the individual and to the family following loss can be chronic and devastating as has been known since ancient times.

CONTEMPORARY BEREAVEMENT

The effects of loss can be profound, but for the most part, these effects vary dramatically in duration and magnitude. Predicting the effects of bereavement has been quite difficult and suffers from controversy regarding what those effects are and how they are to be understood. The lifelong effects of some losses, and the seemingly transient effects of others, have been a source of consternation as well as inspiration for writers, clergy, physicians, and scientists. In this opening chapter, our goal is to introduce the experience of loss and to highlight some of what has gone into the modern psychological approach to this field. We would like to introduce the reader to an understanding of the experience of loss and its aftermath by taking things we have learned from the bereaved and constructing a composite portrait of a bereaved young man. Although these are not the words of a specific individual person, everything included is faithful to the themes and examples we have encountered in our research and clinical work. The circumstances allowing our speaker Joe, the youngest of three boys, to share this information are as follows: Joe enrolled in an elective course on loss and bereavement. The course required him to narrate why he had signed up for the course and to dictate his reasons into a digital recorder. The following are his words:

I was 14 when my mother died of cancer. No one ever told me that she was ill. I mean we knew, but we never talked about it at home. There were days when I ate at Gramma's because Mom was away for "vacation." Then she would come back home and life went on as usual, as if nothing was wrong. Then one day my father called us together and said: "Your mother is dead, she did not suffer." I started crying and went to my room where I sobbed all night, and told myself it wasn't true, that my dad was lying. The following morning I woke up ready to go to school but was told that I didn't have to and could stay at home. My principal suggested that I see the school counselor but I turned the idea down because I saw no point in talking about it. Mostly because it was inconvenient. I had no one to talk with. Neither Mom nor Dad spoke with us about her illness when she was sick. None of us did really. I do recall that he seemed very businesslike when telling us about Mom's death, like he was talking about whose turn it was to take out the trash. Looking back I guess he didn't know what to do. He had three sons and two were teenagers. He remarried a year after Mom died. I guess it was his thinking that it was important to continue with life. Perhaps he even thought that my stepmom would care for us and that would be like he was caring for us. I was very confused and felt very lonely. Mom's stuff, the furniture she liked, even the sofa where she used to watch TV with us were taken out of the house when I was at school. It was almost as if she never existed. It was like, like, as if that was his way of saying that life goes on and that it didn't pay to live in the past.

Ten years later I felt "stuck" in college. I thought maybe it was the subject, you know, like math and business. I went for job counseling and they sent me to the counseling center for therapy. I didn't understand why. Therapy was about grieving for myself, my mom, and the family. After about a month, when I kept saying I didn't remember much, my therapist told me to check with other family members. My father said to put it away and move on. My brothers said they didn't remember much either. They said they would write me from where they lived (out of town), but they never did. I wanted to understand all about my mother's death and what I went through. I connected with my aunt (my mother's sister), who we saw infrequently. She had helped out at our house too when Mom was sick. She helped me recall events from when Mom was sick. Turns out I remembered more than I thought I did, and it started coming back to me. There was a lot. I remembered the afternoon about a month before she died, when she was going to go on "vacation" again. We all were going to a picnic in the park in the spring. My brothers were kicking a ball and my mother, who broke her leg, was in a wheelchair and her sister was pushing. She looked so old and tired. But I was ashamed of her. I didn't want any of my friends to see her or know that she was my mom. I wanted to disappear so I walked far behind, all by myself. I didn't come close so as not to be part of "them." My dad was at work. He was never there. Remembering it felt like it was happening again. This was hard. I felt like crying when I remembered it. My therapist helped me see how angry and how scared I was. I felt so bad. I felt so guilty—her own son running away from her 'cause she looked so sick, she looked really scary. I cried (pause) [tearing up], I hated my mom for not being like the other mothers. And I felt like she thought it was better not to talk about it. And my dad, too. You know it destroyed the family. Yeah. My brothers moved away as soon as they hit college age. Before that, they were always "out" doing stuff. I was alone. My father's marrying again—didn't help you know. We never took to her. She knew it too.

My stepmother is always reminding my dad what a wonderful woman she is, taking on three kids that were not her own. Boys too. Sometimes, it felt, and this is crazy, but it felt, like, like my mom had gotten back at us, you know, for not caring enough that she had died. I had to work on some of this stuff. I eventually went to her grave to ask for her forgiveness. I thought she was OK with it too. I also had to work on forgiving myself, which is harder, and my dad, which is even harder. I thought about how "grave"—funny word, huh— how serious her condition had been, and how courageous she was. I mean she knew she didn't have much time left. She did her best to continue with routine life in order to spare us suffering. She was of German descent, not the kind of person to talk about feelings very much. I think talking and remembering helped me to reach some resolution. Both with my mother and myself. My life changed you know. I left math and decided to study social work. I stopped being so resentful of Dad's wife. I mean I confronted him for not talking with us or explaining Mom's condition. He said, that was his way, and maybe it was wrong, but that is his way. I know he cares. But all those years, he never calls her "my wife" or "your mother" but calls her by her first name, Paula. He still thinks about her, I know he does. Looking back, the most unbearable part for me was lack of communication and lack of information. I felt stuck and dammed up for many years, like I was waiting for something to change, and nothing did. Then finally, it did. Like everything was in black and white as in the old movies, and now, after a year of talking about all this, like the color was back in. Not everywhere, but in most places. Like I got my mother back. And even my father and his wife, like she is scared of life too. Afraid that after all she did for us, that we don't care about her. She ain't Mom, but she did the best she could. And maybe that is worth keeping in mind. We all do the best we can. And that is all that we can do. My mom used to tell us that about trying our best in sports and school and not worrying about how it turns out. I guess she knew something important. Like that tombstone in Jerusalem that says, "We do what we gotta do and then we go,"* but it isn't what we gotta do, it's what we can do.

The words of Joe convey a lot in a very short space. Condensed in this narrative is a story of coping with illness and impending death. There is information about the importance of communication and about potential risks to some coping styles and family communication styles. The handling of impending death and the way loss is handled afterward have the potential to affect the bereaved for years to come. And revisiting and reconnecting with the emotions, memories, and thoughts surrounding the death and its aftermath can have powerful and life-changing effects as well. Making sense out of loss and its impact is a task for each human individual and each human society.

The story of Joe presents a picture of response to loss that does not allow for open expression of the grief or the feelings, thoughts, and questions that the death

---

* John Shortlidge's (1928–1986) tombstone epitaph in the Protestant Cemetery in Jerusalem.

of a parent or family member triggers. The importance of resuming
loss is something that all cultures address in their culture-specific wɑ
later in the book (Grisaru, Malkinson, & Witztum, 2008; Rubin & Yɑ
2004). There are times, however, when the rush to return to life exɑc
interferes with the very goal that is aimed for. In the case of Joe, the situ   ᴜ ᴜɴᴇ
that reflects what Bowlby (1980) describes as the response to loss for an adolescent
and his family when conditions are not optimal. The attempt by all the family members of Joe's nuclear family to avoid the impeding loss and its impact upon their
lives results here in a constriction of life, love, and familial bonds. Returning to the
story of the loss of his mother and engaging with the memories and experiences of
the loss and its impact allow Joe to grieve for his mother and open up Joe to being
able to accept himself, his mother, father, and stepmother. Actual stories and case
reports in the literature embodying the features in Joe's narrative are by no means
rare in the field of bereavement and loss. Finding the right balance of engagement
and distance from the experience of loss is a daunting task. Nonetheless, avoiding
dealing with the experience altogether is, as many in the field would assert, a particularly perilous route to take in the attempt to continue with life.

In recent years, the importance of recognizing "resilience" and resilient
responses following loss has reentered the discussion on the impact of bereavement (Bonanno, 2009). Depending on one's perspective, it would be quite possible
to think about and classify Joe (especially in the eyes of other family members) as
the one person in his family who eventually is unable to adequately deal with the
death of his mother. At the same time, all the other family members might be classified as responding adequately and without difficulty to life after the loss—as one
might expect from "resilient persons." Many clinical as well as research paradigms
following outcome to loss for as long as 5 years after a death would also miss Joe,
unless some areas of his academic, social, emotional, or biological behavior suggested difficulty and dysfunction. And that would be unfortunate.

As we shall demonstrate repeatedly throughout this volume, addressing
bereavement response and aftermath without particular attention to the nature of
the organization of thoughts, memories, and feelings associated with the deceased
is to risk missing one of the most fundamental features of interpersonal loss.
Bereavement from a psychological point of view is not only how we live and function after loss from the view of the individual survivor's ability to navigate and
function in the world; bereavement is equally about how we reorganize the relationship to someone important to us who is no longer living. Because that person's
existence was important to our psychological well-being (in the present as well
as in the past), there is a need to strike a balance between letting go of what can
no longer occur, for example, the physical interaction involved in spouses' sexual
intimacy, and the maintenance of the sense of significance and value that spouses
communicate to each other and which is not dependent on live interaction.

To better understand some of the ferment in the field of bereavement research
and intervention today, we believe it necessary to thread one's way through a jungle
of ideas, data, and perspectives to come through the experience safely. To do so,
we shall attempt to balance the wisdom and passion of the clinician perspective
with the rigor and skepticism of the research scientist so as to integrate the thick

and rich narrative of the consulting room with the cool objectivity of the research center. To do so, we continue with a discussion of loss and grief in the situation where the bereaved allow themselves a painful but less defended journey through the experience than that described by Joe.

When confronted with the loss of a loved one, one's shock and a sense of disbelief may delay the earliest awareness of the event. When the shock wears off, however, the more prominent emotions experienced may be a powerful mix of anxiety, depression, anger, helplessness, and guilt (Siggins, 1966). There are alternative theories as to what these emotions express (Bowlby, 1980; Furst, 1967). Perhaps at a minimum, it may be said that they all reflect the response to the inability of the bereaved to protect either the self or one's close relations from the realities of death and that, following death, it is not even possible to maintain the pre-loss bond to those we love. Our inability to control fate, together with the permanent severance of contact with a loved one, attacks simultaneously two foundations of human strivings: the wish to be with one's significant relations and the wish to be able to affect and influence one's surroundings (Bibring, 1953). Deprived of those we love, and deprived of the ability to affect the world we live in, it is no wonder that the loss of a loved one is so devastating in its impact (Janoff-Bulman, 1992; Parkes, 1975; Parkes & Prigerson 2010; Raphael, 1983).

As a result of the dislocation produced by loss, the bereaved is immersed in emotional crises. The routine of life has been dislocated. At the most basic physiological level, somatic homeostasis has been upset. Sleep difficulties, eating disturbances, and difficulties with concentration and thinking often emerge. These responses may be so pronounced so as to lead to excessive use of medications—physician prescribed or otherwise—to allay the pain and anxiety that sweep over the bereaved. While somatic routine is so disrupted, the social network is being disrupted as well. In spousal loss, for example, the partners may fill functions for each other and connect each other to different social circles and support networks. As a result of loss, however, these networks and relationships may be disrupted and the comforting elements of the relationships involved may be lost or withdrawn. Even when the relationships remain in place, the bereaved may limit their beneficial and comforting impact by pushing those relationships away. Interpersonal ties may seem virtually meaningless for the bereaved. The prism through which a bereaved views him- or herself and the world is characterized by a fundamental bias: that there is no value to a life without the deceased who was so loved.

How deeply, for how long, and in what ways the response to loss should manifest itself are indeed the fundamental questions of the bereavement literature.

Taking a broader view of bereavement outcome, the observation of change and continuity following loss involves much. For it is also the manner in which the bereaved remembers, internalizes, and maintains continued psychological involvement with the deceased that is central to bereavement outcome. People remember, imagine, accompany, and separate from their loved ones in their internal psychological world in ways that mirror the nature of how ongoing relationships to living people are represented and maintained in the psychological world. At levels of conscious and unconscious psychological organization, every individual has a complete set of mental representations associated with significant people (Orbach,

1995). The loss of a relative destabilizes the memories and feelings regarding the deceased and their meaning for the bereaved. As time passes, there will be changes in what is remembered and experienced, but these features will remain at the core of bereavement. We shall return to the importance of the relationship to the deceased, involving the memories, thoughts, and feelings associated with him or her, throughout this volume (Bowlby, 1980; Klass, Silverman, & Nickman, 1996; Malkinson, Rubin, & Witztum, 2000).

> The case of Joe illustrates coping styles of avoidance of emotion in a family and contrasts it with a more open dialogue.
>
> Resilience is not equivalent to an absence of difficulties. It also implies a way of retaining an emotional relationship to the deceased.
>
> How deeply, for how long, and in what ways should one respond to loss are the fundamental questions of the bereavement literature.

THE CONTRIBUTIONS OF FREUD, LINDEMANN, AND BOWLBY

The theoretical and clinical insights of three psychiatrists have been seminal and continue to influence our current thinking regarding loss and bereavement. The work of Sigmund Freud, Eric Lindemann, and John Bowlby stimulated much of what later was to evolve in this field.

Sigmund Freud (1856–1939)

Surprisingly much of clinical literature has involved a connection to the impact of loss. This often did not occur in a premeditated fashion but reflected the realities of clinical practice. The fascinating story of Bertha Pappenheim, known as Anna O., stimulated some of the earliest understandings of unconscious processes. This case revolved around Josef Breuer's treatment of a woman who suffered from symptoms of "hysterical neurosis" in response to the progressive illness and death of her father (Breuer & Freud, 1895/1955). Much has been learned since then, and much of what was accepted as true, even for psychoanalysis, has changed in the ensuing decades (Mitchell & Black, 1995). Nonetheless, the validity of the idea that how people respond to the emotions and experiences surrounding loss has significant and powerful implications for their health and psychological functioning has remained axiomatic and empirically validated. Furthermore, today, as in the past, the bereaved's narration of her or his experience of the events and accompanying emotions surrounding traumatic events is deemed important. For many clinicians, irrespective of theoretical orientation, the telling of the trauma story to others and to oneself is understood as being one of the most critical therapeutic axes to recovery and integration (Herman, 1992). This narration is a cornerstone of much of psychological diagnosis and treatment in general, and more so of the treatment of the bereaved in particular (Langs, 1976; Schafer, 1992; Spence, 1982).

In "Mourning and Melancholia" (1917/1957), Freud reported on the essence of the bereavement process and compared it to clinical depressions (major affective disorder). A penetrating observer of the human condition, Freud focused on the emotions felt by bereaved persons. The emotions of loss included painful depression; a dramatic drop in interest in matters associated with others and the outside world; loss of the ability to love; and a lack of interest in things that do not relate to the deceased. The bereaved is virtually totally absorbed in mourning the loss. Freud stressed that this process had a clearly defined goal. Going beyond the description of the clinical condition, Freud postulated that the aim of the response to bereavement was one that would free the bereaved from his or her previous commitment to the relationship with the person who had died. Thus he presented the psychological processes of grief and mourning as part of an adjustment and healing process following loss. When the goal of relinquishing the commitment to the deceased was accomplished, the bereaved would have completed the mourning process and would be free to invest anew in relationships with others.

In the "work of mourning" (in recent years, this has been referred to as the grief work hypothesis), Freud describes how the bereaved vividly recalls and relives memories and associations regarding the deceased during the psychological mourning for that person. Part of the overwhelming focus on the person who is dead, a "working through" of the implications of the loss is understood as a process taking time. The bereaved reminisces and emotionally connects to memories and experiences involving the one who has died as a milestone on the path to dismantling involvement with him or her. The bereaved gradually absorbs the finality of the death. This awareness combines with recognition that the deceased can no longer supply basic life needs in the real world. Successful completion of the mourning or grief process allows the living person freedom from bonds to the deceased and heralds a letting go of the connection. At its terminus, the bereaved will have reclaimed the necessary emotional energy (libidinal energy) that will allow for investment of this emotional capital in new relationships.

Tracing the history of the bereavement field, we can appreciate that a number of Freud's ideas were accepted by the majority of those working in the area. Among the ideas receiving wide acceptance are the following:

1. Bereavement is a form of emotional absorption or working through of loss characterized by components of an intrapersonal (intrapsychic) process occurring within the persona of the bereaved.
2. The recognition and acceptance of the finality of loss is one goal of the loss process.
3. Accepting the unrelenting permanence of loss generally follows an emotionally painful process, which requires time for its impact to be fully appreciated.
4. There are both conscious and unconscious aspects to the mourning process.

5. Appreciation of the way in which the deceased is represented and organized in human experience involves a complex combination of memories, emotions, and experience, which deserves our attention in any consideration of the process and outcome of loss.

Freud's contribution to the study of loss was an important one. Yet the extent of Freud's influence was such that the understanding of his work also had negative implications for theory and practice. Freud's stature served to hamper the empirical investigation of his clinical insights and too often resulted in undue veneration of his texts within the psychoanalytic tradition. Some have asserted that his work was interpreted at variance with his intent (Siggins, 1966). For example, the view that successful adjustment to loss resulted in a total emancipation from the deceased and a full acceptance of the irreversibility of the loss held sway for quite some time. This view led some to exclude children from the ability to accept loss and led others to see any continuing emotional involvement with the bereaved as a maladaptive response to loss (Wolfenstein, 1969). We have irrefutable proof that Freud himself understood an ongoing involvement with memories of the deceased as a natural and even desirable feature that existed alongside and after the mourning process. This attitude is powerfully addressed in his letter to his colleague, Ludwig Binswanger, who had recently lost his child which prompted the following response from Freud:

> April 12, 1929
> My daughter who died would have been thirty-six years old today … Although we know that after such a loss the acute state of mourning will subside, we also know we shall remain inconsolable and will never find a substitute. No matter what may fill the gap, even if it be filled completely, it nevertheless remains something else. And actually this is how it should be. It is the only way of perpetuating that love which we do not want to relinquish. (E. L. Freud, 1961, p. 386)

Although the psychoanalytic paradigm was predominant well into the 1960s, the specific attention to bereavement within that conceptual framework received relatively little attention. Too often, the psychodynamic literature addressed loss in the context of discussions on depression, its contribution to psychopathology, and the significance of child development for later coping with loss (Bibring, 1953; Fenichel, 1945; Klein, 1940). The importance of attention to the impact of bereavement in its own right, as a significant branch of clinical and theoretical interest, continued to suffer from neglect.

Freud's 1917 description of the psychological mourning process emphasized the decathexis, or withdrawal of libidinal energy, from the deceased so it could be invested in a new relationship.

This formulation has unduly influenced the professional mental health field and has stressed a severance of connection to the deceased.

Freud correctly emphasized the significance of the relationship between the bereaved and the deceased.

ERIC LINDEMANN (1900–1974)

At the same time that psychodynamic and psychoanalytic psychiatry focused on the internal psychological struggles occurring deep within the psyche, clinical psychiatry was beginning the investigation of bereavement from an empirical point of view. Particularly influential was Eric Lindemann's article on the symptoms accompanying acute grief and how to focus clinical intervention in response (Lindemann, 1944). Lindemann was born in Germany and studied medicine, neurology, and psychology there before immigrating to the United States in 1927 (Caplan, 1975). While a psychiatrist at Massachusetts General Hospital and at Harvard Medical School, he translated his experience as a practicing psychiatrist to the observation and understanding of the impact of various bereavements. Responding to the horrible aftermath of the Boston nightclub fire at the Coconut Grove establishment, he was exposed to a group of individuals who had been suddenly and traumatically bereaved. Thus he based much of his work with this population on clinical experience and was assisted, but not restricted, by theory. His paper, "Symptomology and Management of Acute Grief," described a group of 101 bereaved individuals to assemble a descriptive ordering of responses to loss. Working with observation, diagnosis, and clinical acumen, he reported on a syndrome of responses that accompany the initial reactions to sudden loss. Having worked with a relatively large group of bereaved people, and because the work was closely tied to empirical phenomena, his writing was utilized by a range of disciplines and theoretical approaches.

Lindemann's description of the acute response to the loss included attention to the following: the sense of unreality; the focus on the imagery of the deceased; difficulties in interpersonal relationships; somatic difficulties (such as appetite change), tension, and restlessness; emotional responses, including guilt, aggression, and impatience with others; and a general loss of functioning in areas where previously the bereaved had functioned. Among some of the bereaved in his sample, a number of these responses were extreme and overwhelming.

As others who came before and who were to come after him, Lindemann returned to stress the concept of the "work" in grief. This included the importance of freeing oneself from an overly strong link to the deceased, renegotiating adaptation to the life environment, and the formation of new interpersonal relationships. Lindemann described difficulties in post-loss adjustment, and proposed that short-term interventions of 8 to 10 sessions could be sufficient during the initial acute grief period. The grief period was defined as lasting in the range of 4 to 6 weeks. Over the years, Lindemann's focal attention to this period within the response to loss, along with a paradigm for intervention, proved central to what became known as *crisis theory* (Parad, 1966).

Lindemann's landmark studies and empirical work helped bring the field of loss and bereavement into the modern era.

He focused on traumatic grief and on short-term interventions.

John Bowlby (1907–1990)

Undoubtedly, the individual whose body of work significantly and systematically transformed the field of loss was John Bowlby. The British-born psychoanalyst Bowlby developed attachment theory as a developmental and emotional structure for understanding the developing individual and the individual's management of interpersonal relationships across the life cycle. Relationships and relationship styles were understood to reflect aspects of behavior in interpersonal relationships as well as tendencies to psychological organization of experience within the individual. With a matrix for thinking about the nature of relationships within the individual, the theoretical framework for understanding the individual's response to the death of another was given a solid footing and rooted firmly in the tapestry of the individual's interpersonal relationships.

Succinctly stated, some highlights of this perspective are useful. Starting from the crucial importance of the mother–child bond for the individual child's development, Bowlby went on to a comprehensive theory emphasizing both intrapsychic and interpersonal relationships (Bowlby, 1969, 1973, 1980). In this theory, Bowlby postulated that people have a need, most apparent in times of danger or stress, to be close to the important attachment figure. As the maturation process unfolds, however, the same proximity function is achieved by connecting to the inner mental representation of significant others who serve as attachment supports. These characteristics are central and integral to the development and function of the individual throughout life.

For the same reasons that the psychological experience and organization of relationships are central to the individual's physical and psychological well-being, the threat to these relationships take on cardinal importance. A threat to closeness in childhood, such as an actual separation of some duration, triggers what is commonly referred to as *separation anxiety*. The individual will try to reduce this harbinger of danger by attempting to rejoin the significant other. As people mature, much of this tendency to regain closeness escapes awareness and functions from within the psyche as an unconscious dynamic. Only a small part of this generally emerges as interpersonal behavior and interaction, although psychological experiments have been devised to demonstrate this very process in adulthood (Mikulincer & Shaver, 2007, p. 20). Across the life cycle, a portion of the need to seek safety by proximity to secure attachment figures will remain as the wish to regain closeness to the significant figures of childhood and their later counterparts in some mixture of symbolic and literal fashion (Cassidy & Shaver, 1999; J. Sandler & Sandler, 1978; Stierlin, 1970).

Bowlby, Ainsworth, and virtually all of the developmentalists and clinicians working with attachment theory have identified and characterized a variety of attachment styles that characterize persons (Mikulincer & Shaver, 2007; Oppenheim & Goldsmith, 2007). While all persons form attachments and those attachments are central to people's physical and psychological well-being, the organization of those styles varies. In addition to the adaptive "secure" attachment style, there are insecure attachment forms, namely, anxious-ambivalent and avoidant attachment styles, which function to deny, dismiss, or otherwise minimize the free-flowing attachment to significant others.

In situations of loss and death, there is a convergence of the wish to be close to the person in the flesh and the wish to become close to the mental representations associated with him or her. When death occurs, a set of responses is set in motion that seems well designed to bring about a physical reunion with that significant other in many of the normal situations where that significant person had been alive and accessible. When it becomes clearer to the bereaved that there is no avenue by which to change the situation and connect to the deceased, the import of loss is apprehended. A collapse of the defenses against this sad reality, and an inability to resist the disorganization that often follows, results in depression. The sense of helplessness is also tied up with the realization that one is powerless to return the deceased. Arising from the ashes of this powerlessness is a reorganization of how one will live after loss. With the recognition and a degree of acceptance that death has irreversibly claimed the significant other, the change demanded by that reality can be undertaken.

The humanity, rigor, scope, and firm connection to human experience were central to Bowlby's written work. Bowlby succeeded in translating and transforming the rich complexity of psychoanalysis into a new and understandable framework with many opportunities for empirical study. By avoiding many of the pitfalls of metapsychology (J. Sandler, Dare, & Holder, 1972), Bowlby combined empirical, ethological, intrapsychic, and interpersonal approaches to emphasize the following: (a) the importance of actual as well as psychologically accessible relationships within the person for the development and functioning of the individual across the life cycle, and (b) threats to the connection with significant others of the inner and outer worlds of the individual, which are triggered by significant separations in general and by death in particular. In the case of death, the threat triggers the loss response.

Together with Colin Murray Parkes, a major figure in his own right, Bowlby (1980) conceptualized the loss process as traversing a set of four recognizable stages: (1) shock and numbing when the individual is struggling to make sense of the fact of the loss; (2) the search for reunion with the deceased and being attuned to reminders of him or her; (3) disorganization expressed in the erosion or collapse of previous ways of being with the self and the other; and (4) a reorganization of one's inner and outer life, to some extent, which allows the bereaved a way to live adaptively with the changed realities of life. These stages are not meant to be taken as a linear series of stations or a universal blueprint for the successful management of the bereavement response. The move away from stage theory is strong but by no means complete (Holland & Neimeyer, 2010; Maciejewski, Zhang, Block, & Prigerson, 2007).

We suggest using the "stages" of bereavement as representative heuristic constructions that highlight individual aspects of the response to loss. Ultimately, there is a great deal of overlap and fluctuation in how the bereaved responds to loss. The stages set forth here structure and assist in the narration of the distribution of various elements in the response to loss. The relative proportions and weighting of the features of each of the stages generally shift over time. The value of attention to them, however, is constant. Recognizing the wide variation among individuals in their responses to loss while also recognizing the limitations of stage theories of human behavior is important for theoreticians and clinicians alike.

Freud, Lindemann, and Bowlby are three clinicians whose writings related to loss and bereavement remain relevant and seminal to much of what modern clinicians and researchers are working on today. This is not to say that their contributions are universally accepted as valid and supported by current research. Sometimes the exact opposite is true. Current research and thinking may stand in opposition to the work of Freud, Lindemann, and Bowlby. At the very least, we can recognize the gaps between the tools and information available to experts today and that which was available to them in their respective generations. Yet even when these gaps are evident, the writings of these pioneers provide stimulation and a focus for our evolving understanding of the field in ways that continue to benefit from their place in the intellectual and clinical history of our field.

> Bowlby's work on attachment and loss continued the significance of the relationship to the deceased for normal development and for bereavement.
>
> Bowlby and Parkes's stage theory of bereavement was influential and described stages of shock and numbing, searching, disorganization, and reorganization.
>
> Contemporary theory is assisted by the phenomena described in stage theories but has moved sharply away from the implication that people progress through stages in bereavement.

CONCLUDING REMARKS

In this opening chapter, we have invited the reader to look to the human experiential encounter with loss and bereavement as well as history relevant to the evolution of the field. The interpersonal interconnectedness of the human encounter underlies the significance of bereavement and is central to its full appreciation. This will emerge in greater detail and with clinical relevance as we proceed. We now turn to a number of important issues that preoccupy many working in the field from both clinical and research perspectives.

2

Current Perspectives on Bereavement

What are the most important things that should inform the clinician working with the bereaved? This chapter contains a summary of our answer to that question. Here we address the topics and controversies that characterize current knowledge and practice in the field of loss and bereavement. Many of the issues and themes addressed here reverberate throughout this book and are the product of advances in theory, research, and intervention work. Those interested in understanding these issues more fully will do well to refer to the referenced articles, chapters, and books that give them the fuller exposition they deserve. Our goal in this chapter, however, is to allow the reader an overview of what to look for in other places in this book to better appreciate the dynamism and sense of excitement surrounding the field of loss and bereavement today. The chapter is divided into five sections based on the following themes: (1) right and wrong in the bereavement response, (2) the centrality of interpersonal relationships, (3) the potential for change following loss, (4) facilitating adaptive grief and bereavement, and (5) ethics and bereavement.

IS THERE RIGHT AND WRONG IN THE BEREAVEMENT RESPONSE?

Is it possible to speak of right and wrong in the bereavement response? Although this may sound overstated, the reality of both societal and clinical approaches to the loss response is that people are typically making many judgments about what is right and wrong in the response to loss (Rubin & Schechter, 1997; Wikan, 1988). Societal responses allocate various responses to being classified as proper, fitting, and normal or as excessive, extreme, abnormal, and the like. Researchers and clinicians make many of the same types of decisions, although the degree to which they base themselves on statistical data or clearly defined categories specifying what is meant vary tremendously in practice (Stroebe, Hansson, Schut, & Stroebe, 2008). The terms used by the professionals are many and have often joined words such as *normal, pathological, prolonged, complicated, traumatic, absent, delayed,* and *incomplete* to the terms *grief, mourning,* and *bereavement* (Horowitz et al., 1997; Malkinson et al., 2000; Parkes, 2006; Rubin et al., 2008). In addition to these terms, the field of bereavement has also considered how negative outcome to loss may manifest itself in virtually every form of physical and emotional diagnosis and thus make use of the terminology already in place.

The consensus among researchers, practitioners, and the bereaved themselves is that *there is no one right or universal way to experience and respond to loss.* Peoples and cultures differ in many ways, and respecting those differences has led many in the field to search for pluralistic approaches to considering the ways in which people respond to the loss of a loved one (DeSpelder & Strickland, 2008). Thus, although loss and bereavement are universal experiences for all humankind, the ways in which they affect people and how they are responded to are increasingly understood to be highly variable (Bonanno, Boerner, & Wortman, 2008). All of those dealing with loss should be careful to avoid giving the impression that there is a "right" way to grieve. The literature suggests that there are varied adaptive ways to experience and process loss, and it is also clear that no one way works for all persons. Without a doubt, decades of research and clinical experience have contributed to a multivariate understanding of loss and one that is open to a variety of distinctions.

The response to the loss of significant figures by death is influenced by multiple factors characterizing who is the bereaved and who is the deceased (Stroebe, Folkman, Hansson, & Schut, 2006). Among the more striking or prominent of these factors are the gender of the bereaved, the type of formal kinship relationship, the age and stage of life at the time of loss, and the sociocultural context within which the bereavement is experienced and the cultural beliefs and framework operant (Goss & Klass, 2005; Weiss, 2001). Although bereavement is viewed as a universal experience, there is a large body of data and experience to indicate that there are a number of response patterns in bereavement. Cultural differences account for some of the variation in the response to loss; and because of the wide variations in how cultures shape and interpret bereavement, the bereavement process, and the desired outcome, culture emerges as a major factor to be taken into account (Rosenblatt, 2008).

Taken together with the fact that bereavement is always an individual experience for a particular human being and relationship, it is easy to appreciate that the perception of right or wrong in bereavement reflects interpretive perspectives that benefit all parties when the assumptions they reflect are clarified (Kasher, 2004; Yasien-Esmael & Rubin, 2005). In the final section of this book, we will focus on culture very directly; but throughout the book, we touch upon it where relevant.

Numerous other variables are at work as well and influence what coping and response styles serve adaptation to loss under particular conditions. For example, when specifying what the conditions of the bereavement are, it is important to consider the pre-loss situation, the circumstances of the loss (Rynearson, 2006), the bereavement setting and such things as degree of financial and social support (Vanderwerker & Prigerson, 2004), the personality structure of the bereaved (Wijngaards-de Meij, Stroebe, Schut, Stroebe, Van den Bout, Van der Heijden, et al., 2007), and other conditions. Whereas gender has been specified, questions regarding the contributions of race, culture, social class, marital variables, time since loss, social support, current family, and so forth remain to be considered. The specification of these variables contributes to the recognition that the empirical picture of the loss response is really never a simple one. Research, theory, and clinical practice are all served by attending to these features.

The point we wish to make here is that whether considering classes or nomothetic groupings of persons who respond to particular bereavements, or whether one addresses idiopathic or individual responses to loss, the contextual factors are highly relevant and should be reported and described.

Moving away from the rough categories of right and wrong still leaves us with the need to understand what underlies the choice of outcome perspective—that is, what is considered to be "normal and abnormal" in the response to loss. In other words, are we justified in using terms that privilege and stigmatize ways of responding to loss? Although not identical with the point raised previously, there is a degree of overlap.

Of concern to society are the many forms of negative health outcomes of both a physical and psychological type that may result from loss. In speaking of the majority of bereavements as involving significant depression and changes in living, Freud (1917/1957) stressed how most of this was considered normal in the response to loss during the initial grief period. For many years, those who did not show these significant departures from their previous life functioning were considered to be responding in maladaptive ways. In recent years, there has been more awareness of the tremendous range of response in biopsychosocial functioning. One such example is the empirical work of Bonanno and colleagues, who have made a case for a consideration of a variety of trajectories that follow bereavement. Thus the proportion of persons that come through the loss response without demonstrating noticeable distress, depression, or anxiety has been demonstrated as a viable response pattern (Bonanno, 2004).

The significance of findings identifying persons who appear to respond to loss with biopsychosocial functioning not negatively affected lent support to earlier critiques such as those of Wortman and Silver (2001), that questioned assumptions about the course of loss. The upshot was a clearer charge to bereavement professionals and researchers to demonstrate what, in earlier periods of the development of the field, had been assumed to be axioms. Thus, if a psychological mourning process characterized by the sadness and "work of mourning" (where the bereaved are emotionally involved with memories and emotions concerning the deceased as part of the hypothesized mourning process) was assumed to be a *sine qua non* of adaptive response to bereavement, the request was to "prove it." The quest for empirical data to demonstrate such principles and to qualify the particular contours of when such principles might apply was joined. With the particulars of many such "clinical principles" not yet settled, many may wonder if there are clear parameters of normal or adaptive grieving and how are they distinguished from the not "normal." The answer lies, of course, in part as to what, when, and how the criterion is being measured.

As is true in much of Western psychiatry, since the publication of the *DSM-III* in 1980, and the *DSM-IV* after it, the emphasis has been on defining clear empirical criteria for the medical-psychiatric classification of disease or pathology. Without going into too much detail, the important issue at hand remains what to say about bereavement when the individual is suffering but does not meet criteria for a formal disease entity, or even when he or she does meet all formal criteria.

It is not surprising that the question of whether to include a grief-related diagnosis in *DSM-V* that addresses maladaptive responses to bereavement and labels them as problem grief responses has raised questions and divergences among those working in the field (Prigerson et al., 2008; Rubin et al., 2008). The first issue to be considered is whether any diagnosis of grief-related difficulties is detrimental to bereaved persons and should be avoided. On this question, the protagonists who resist the diagnosis stress the tremendous variation in bereavement response and the ubiquitousness of grieving, which make it more a dimension of life experiences than a diagnosable mental health or medical pathology. On the other hand is an impressive array of protagonists who marshal sophisticated statistical methodology and compelling empirical data to support their arguments for inclusion (Parkes, 2006; Prigerson et al., 2009).

A second controversy arises regarding what are, and what should be, the criteria for defining some bereavement as maladaptive and requiring professional attention. Some argue that the degree of difficulties in biopsychosocial functioning may be sufficient to quantify grief as maladaptive, prolonged, or pathological. Others argue that it would be a mistake to quantify bereavement as a separate entity as long as the response is similar to other recognizable entities such as major depressive disorder (Schaal, Elbert, & Neuner, 2009). While the self-help movement champions the value of bereaved persons sharing and communicating directly with each other, many persons with that orientation also resist a health care or medical vantage point that would study the problems that may follow loss of a loved one. At the same time, mental health and other health care professionals who are involved in systematic assessment, treatment, and research bring a professional perspective that allows them to make a contribution to discussions about what is individual variation, and what are maladaptive responses, following loss.

Our position is that all of us, professionals, nonprofessionals, and bereaved alike, are stakeholders in the discussion and sit around the same table. When it comes to contemplating loss, sharing perspectives and knowledge is the most adaptive way to proceed (Rubin et al., 2008). We would all do well to recognize that persons sometimes respond to bereavement in maladaptive ways, with low-end estimates ranging from 5 to 15% and different criteria producing even higher percentages. The suffering and difficulties associated with bereavement occur in multiple domains of biopsychosocial functioning and show up in a variety of studies targeting different criteria. At the same time, it is important to keep in mind that not only biopsychosocial dysfunctions or difficulties are relevant to the measurement of loss outcome. A major domain of bereavement (as distinct from depression, anxiety, and PTSD [post-traumatic stress disorder]) that examines the post-loss presence of difficulties in the relational realm and bond to the deceased has implications for the conceptualization of what constitutes maladaptive responses following loss as well as therapeutic considerations. We shall direct our attention to this in the next section.

> There is no one right or wrong way to experience and respond to loss.
>
> Factors influencing response include circumstances of the loss, kinship, gender, culture, identity of the bereaved and identity of the deceased.
>
> Terms such as normal, pathological, complicated, and prolonged grief and mourning reflect adaptive and maladaptive responses to loss as measured on specific variables.
>
> Estimates of the percentage of people responding maladaptively to bereavement run between 5 and 20%.
>
> Currently, the need for a specific medical diagnosis reflecting maladaptive response to grief is a controversial topic.

INTERPERSONAL RELATIONSHIPS ARE CENTRAL TO BEREAVEMENT

The loss response in bereavement is set in motion by the information that a valued person has died. First and foremost, loss occurs at the interface of the individual and his or her relationship with another. In other words, the loss of a flesh and blood connection to another is what we mean by the term *bereavement*. True, there are indeed many losses that affect people powerfully, but the prototypical bereavement is the loss of a close kinship relationship. There is much to be learned by not obscuring this. For if you think about it, bereavement in such circumstances can mean very different things. It may reflect the sundering of the realities of day-to-day living, such as a couple living together and spending much of their time together. Yet it may reflect the death of one person whose interpersonal connection was strong but has also been transformed by many factors. Such bereavements may be mediated by years of physical distance, changing roles and life demands, and the realities of living apart. Here, the response to loss of parents separated from their adult children by time, oceans, and maintaining minimal contact may overlap strongly with the response of parents living in the same neighborhood as their adult children. In all of these situations, the loss response in bereavement involves the actual death of another, but the psychological manifestations of what that death sets in motion within the surviving person may have little to do with current patterns of behavior and contact.

In the case of understanding bereavement, once the significance of the interpersonal has been grasped, the nature of the relationship to the deceased rightfully takes its place as a major domain of interest. Why should one respond so strongly to the death of another that one barely has any contact with today? Why do some persons respond with overwhelming grief to speak incessantly of the deceased and others with no apparent faltering of their ability to function and no change in what they discuss with others? In recent decades, John Bowlby's work on interpersonal relationships has served as a theoretical and empirical organizer for many working in the field (Bowlby, 1969, 1973, 1980; Mikulincer & Shaver, 2007, 2008; Rubin & Katz-Dichterman, 1993).

From an attachment framework, the questions around loss echo Bowlby's trilogy of books. Broadly speaking, they address the following questions: Why and how do people form relational bonds, how do people manage short- and long-term physical separation, and how do people adapt to the death of another? A number of important directions and current advances in this area are now at work here. The first direction reflects the attempts to understand how bereavement unfolds for different kinship relationships (such as spouse or child) at different stages in life (younger or older persons) as mediated by the nature of the attachment bond (the types of attachments that influence how the bereavement will be experienced). When we study how bereavement is mediated by various styles of attachment and object relationships, the focus is on how the attachment style affects bereavement outcome. Attachment styles have been variously characterized to describe secure attachment, as well as variations of insecure attachments, classified as ambivalent and anxious, avoidant and anxious, and minimizing or dismissive. On the basis of characterizations, the assumption generally made is that attachment influences the response to bereavement rather than the bereavement experience influences the nature of one's attachment style. In many cases, the distinction is less clear and may be bidirectional. In this area, some of the most relevant questions extend to how persons who have formed particular secure or less secure attachment bonds with the deceased (be they to parent, partner, or child) respond following loss of that particular person (Fachler, 2009).

Attachment is increasingly important in the study of how bereavement impacts upon the individual and family. Although we have presented these emphases as two approaches to the study of the interaction of attachment and bereavement, the extension of the paradigm asks the question from both ends: What is the influence of bereavement on attachment, and what is the influence of attachment upon bereavement, and how do these influences interact to magnify or mitigate the impact of loss?

Looking broadly, many disparate theoretical approaches take into account the significance of interpersonal relationships and the human bonds that comprise so much of the life space of individuals irrespective of theoretical bias. How interpersonal relationships buffer the bereaved and what aspects exacerbate the adaptation to loss interest them all.

Death does not sever the relationship with the deceased; thus today we refer to the "continuing bonds" paradigm as predominant in loss. The general acceptance of the Continuing Bonds Paradigm is a welcome development in the theoretical and clinical understanding of bereavement (Klass et al., 1996). The idea that death does not sever the relationship to the deceased but transforms it took hold so that today, one can say that the continuing bonds perspective is highly influential upon the professional public (Stroebe, Gergen, Gergen, & Stroebe, 1992). The theoretical conceptualizations and empirical data supporting this viewpoint made a strong case for the ubiquity of the ongoing relationship to the deceased by the bereaved years after loss. Particularly striking were indications of the ongoing relationship to the deceased in cases of loss involving the parent–child bond (Klass, 1988, 1996; Rubin,

1981, 1992, 1996; Silverman & Worden, 1993) and developing children (Balk, 1996; Hogan & DeSantis, 1996). The ongoing relationships of children to their deceased parents and siblings provided a dramatic alternative to the more typically studied situations of spousal loss. Although many in the field have adopted this continuing bond perspective in their conceptualization of what the typical trajectories of loss and mourning are, the "decathexis" model advanced by Freud has proven surprisingly resistant to modernization and integration with the newer approach (Freud, 1917/1957; Malkinson et al., 2000).

Developments over the past 2 decades reflect a reality where the ubiquity of the ongoing relationship and bond with the deceased is often assumed in the case of close kinship relations. Clinicians and researchers consider in greater detail the kind of bonds that may be beneficial and those that may be problematic in the adaptation to loss and life following loss (Field, 2006; Malkinson, Rubin, & Witztum, 2006).

The acute phases of grief and mourning generally subside over time, but an ongoing reworking of loss and the relationship to the deceased continues (Malkinson, 2007). Sometimes, as, for example, in the case of child loss, the triggers for reworking are linked to the external features such as developmental milestones of others in or out of one's own family (Rubin & Malkinson, 2001). No less potent are the developmental milestones of the bereaved themselves that serve as occasions to take stock of what is newly recognized as having been lost. These join together with the reworking of aspects of the loss that had previously been recognized (Gaitini, 2009; Horowitz, 2006; Lampert-Tsamert, 2007; Malkinson & Bar-Tur, 2000, 2004–2005).

In bringing to a close the interpersonal significance of loss and the importance of the type of bond with the deceased, it now becomes unthinkable to ignore the ongoing nature of the relationship to the deceased—that is, the continuing bond—when considering bereavement outcome. Therefore, it becomes imperative to approach interpersonal loss and bereavement as best understood as involving two domains of the bereaved's experience: The first domain tracks the overall manner in which life is lived, while the second domain tracks the specifically relational features of the connection to the deceased. While we shall go into much greater detail and explanation about this distinction when we present Rubin's Two-Track Model of Bereavement (Rubin, 1999) in Section II, there is an intuitive component to this distinction that can be grasped succinctly as well. Given that bereavement, grief, and psychological mourning are related to the death of a significant other person, there are two basic questions any clinician can and probably should ask: (1) What is the current status of the impact of the loss upon the bereaved's day-to-day living? (2) What is the current status of the ongoing relationship to the person who has died? The answers to these questions will generally vary at different time points following the bereavement in the case of the typical grief response. When difficulties are present, however, the responses to these questions may be quite surprising and range from "no response whatsoever" to serious dysfunction and preoccupation with the deceased.

The experience of bereavement stems from the death of a loved one. The heart of the bereavement response over time reflects how the bond to the person who has died undergoes transformation and how the bond's significance for the bereaved changes over time. Whether or not changes in the relational bond to the deceased are accompanied by changes in the biopsychosocial functioning of the bereaved is highly relevant. And yet, it is not the same as asserting that functioning is a direct reflection of the current status of the post-loss bond to the deceased.

The significance of the relational bond in bereavement as described in the Two-Track Model of Bereavement has also been taken up by Stroebe and Schut (1999) in their Dual Process Model (DPM) of coping with loss. They emphasize the coping following loss and see it as oscillating between the tasks the bereaved must cope with, which have a restorative focus, and a loss focus which involves separating from the deceased. The Two-Track Model of Bereavement (sometimes referred to as the TTMoB or the TTMB) takes the approach that coping following loss is but one feature of response to loss and can focus us, too narrowly, on the stressors and coping associated with the initial period accompanying bereavement rather than the life-cycle perspective we advocate. The ongoing nature of the relational bond to the deceased for the most significant kinship relationships, such as parent, child, spouse, and sibling, impact the entire life course of the bereaved and deserve attention well beyond the coping associated with the initial grief and mourning. The implications of this are discussed more thoroughly in the next three chapters of this book.

> Interpersonal relationships are at the core and heart of bereavement.
>
> In current thinking, the relationship with the deceased is transformed, but not ended, following death.
>
> What is the current impact of the loss on the bereaved's meeting with the world?
>
> What is the bereaved's current experience of the deceased and the death story?
>
> The Two-Track Model of Bereavement and the Dual Process Model of Coping with Bereavement both emphasize the importance of relationship to the deceased.

THERE IS SIGNIFICANT POTENTIAL FOR CHANGE FOLLOWING LOSS

Loss is a major catalyst for change in the bereaved. In addition to the need to reorganize the relationship to the deceased, there are potential challenges to one's worldview, to the significance of priorities in life, to one's view of oneself, and more. In this section we consider bereavement for its impact on one's worldview and meaning structures, and for the potential of the loss experience to result in deterioration, as well as the potential to stimulate growth in the aftermath of death.

The bereaved's need to make sense of what happened and what it can and should mean for life after loss is a powerful feature of the response to the death of someone important to us. Meaning making following bereavement has always been central to systems of religion and culture. Many of the rituals as well as the significance of ritual following loss are part of what shapes the response and the outcome to loss. The 19th and 20th centuries brought with them changes and challenges to traditional frameworks of meaning that only continue to multiply in this century. The modern and postmodern challenges to previous individual, familial, cultural, ideological, national, religious, interpersonal, societal, and moral views of life have resulted in a cacophony of possibilities and a kaleidoscope of individual constructions of their worldviews. The fractured and multifocal points of view that are inherent to Western civilization are generally felt most acutely during times of crisis and change. When previous ways of living and understanding life are challenged, the search to find meaning that often results is a search to create and find meaning simultane- ously. Victor Frankl's book *Man's Search for Meaning* was part of the sustained trend attending to the dimension of meaning making (Frankl, 1959/1984; Yalom, 1980).

Within psychology, the importance of meaning making as an overarching theme has been carried forth by the constructivist tradition (Kelly, 1955; Neimeyer & Mahoney, 1995). Particularly following tragedy, trauma, and loss, the significance of attributing, constructing, and finding meaning are important to the recovery and adjustment process. For some theorists, the sense that the world has lost its meaning is a reflection of the depressive processes and overwhelming preoccu- pation with mourning the deceased that saps the ability to appreciate the many aspects of the world that retain their valence (Freud, 1917/1957). In recent years, however, bereavement has begun to be viewed as an event that may attack the very foundations of one's basic worldview in ways that extend far beyond the specific nature of the death itself (Kauffman, 2002). Not only is bereavement a highly per- sonal experience requiring reorganization of the relationship to the deceased, it is a trauma that changes the way in which one experiences his or her way of seeing the world and the self-in-the-world (Janoff-Bulman, 1992). The constructivist position of Neimeyer, based on the pioneering work of George Kelly, emphasizes the fact that people are continually preoccupied with making meaning of their lives and surroundings. When a loss occurs, the impact of the loss affects how the survivor interacts with his or her self and with the surrounding world (Nadeau, 2008). Not surprisingly, the role of religious and spiritual traditions and frameworks have also been included in the examination of meaning reconstruction and meaning mak- ing (Paloutzian & Park, 2005). Psychological research on the ability of bereaved to make meaning of their losses has provided support to the assumption that when the meaning of the loss is not integrated by the bereaved, post-loss adjustment is affected negatively (Holland, Currier, & Neimeyer, 2006).

In addition to recovery—with the implication that people can return to what they had been before the loss, at least on some dimensions—the potential for growth and positive change following bereavement has emerged as a focus of study as well. As part of the broadening of the understanding of the response to loss that includes the search for meaning following loss but is not identical with it, clinicians and researchers have paid greater attention to positive aspects of the loss experience.

The focus on growth emphasizes positive changes in the organization of self that accompany loss. Tedeschi and Calhoun (2004) suggested that events that frac- ture one's assumptive world, including beliefs about control, predictability, and benevolence, motivate a search for new meanings. Davis (2008) has reported on how the concept of meaning making can be differentiated from the idea of post- loss growth. Thus it is possible to describe specific as well as general changes that characterize the bereaved and that may include changes in the way the bereaved thinks about him- or herself following the loss that do not involve a major attack on self or meaning structure per se.

In our opinion, it seems that oftentimes, the growth perspective is too little concerned with the relational aspects of the post-loss connection with the deceased. Change may revolve around how the post-loss reorganization of life and growth is directly and indirectly connected to the connection with the deceased. For example, when a bereaved parent establishes an organization that has as its goal to battle against the disease, accident, or circumstances that claimed his or her child—there can be both individual growth and growth most intimately tied to the connection with the deceased. The various pathways for these connections is deserving of additional research. At the same time, the emphasis on growth, however, does serve to underscore that loss can bring with it an opportunity to improve and add skills, abilities, insights, and personality attributes. Rising to these challenges and transforming oneself in large and small ways is part of coping with life change and adversity. The direction that these changes will take, and the individual's method of organizing them, will vary among the bereaved. The positive and often heroic struggles against adversity that stimulate growth are present in many domains of living and are present in the struggle to live after significant interpersonal loss as well.

> Loss is a major catalyst for change and not just for "recovery."
>
> For some persons, a degree of chronic grief and mourning will be a permanent aspect of the change that they have undergone. This is not necessarily "maladaptive."
>
> Positive growth is an element of that change that can accompany response to loss—including among those who continue to mourn their loss months, years, and decades later.
>
> The basic questions remain—How has the bereaved changed in general, and how has the bereaved's relationship to the deceased changed?

HOW CAN WE FACILITATE ADAPTIVE GRIEF AND BEREAVEMENT?

Do therapy and counseling help everyone? Throughout the book runs the theme of how to facilitate adaptive grief and bereavement for adaptive living. Some of this can be accomplished in the nature of responses to loss, and sometimes it appears that counseling and psychotherapy can assist the bereaved. But is there evidence to support the claims of psychotherapy, support groups, and so forth? And what social conditions can be attended to and improved to help the bereaved? Those points are addressed here. Do psychotherapy and other intervention programs help the bereaved respond to loss? Who does and who can benefit from intervention and treatment in the aftermath of a loved one's death, and what is the evidence for this? In today's world, which increasingly asks for documentation of the benefits and risks of intervention procedures, the formal investigation into the effects of bereavement support, counseling, intervention, and psychotherapy programs are of particular interest (Sandler, Wolchik, Ayers, Tein, Coxe, & Chow, 2008)

Recent reviews on these topics reflect a significant degree of controversy. On the one hand, a number of meta-analyses of outcome studies have consistently shown that the effects of "bereavement interventions" administered to the general population of bereaved persons have, at most, moderate effects (Currier, Neimeyer, & Berman, 2008; Wittouck, Van Autreve, De Jaegere, Portzky, & van Heeringen, 2011). At the same time, these same studies strongly document the efficacy of intervention for persons suffering from complicated, prolonged, or traumatic grief (Jordan & Neimeyer, 2003). On the basis of current literature, it appears that providing some form of counseling or psychotherapy for all the bereaved and all bereavements has been shown to be ineffective (Schut, 2010). When bereavement intervention is targeted for particularly difficult bereavements, such as those involving child loss, suicide, or conditions of external violence and trauma, the relevance and power of psychological interventions emerge strongly (Rando, 1993). Hoyt and Larson have stepped forward to challenge the view that therapeutic interventions can be ineffective in many cases and disputed the suggestion that it could be deleterious (Larson & Hoyt, 2007, 2009). The controversy will stimulate clearer thinking and research over time, and we shall all benefit from that. We believe that objectively classified traumas as well as subjectively perceived traumas increase the risk of maladaptive responses to loss (Rubin et al., 2008). If interventions are examined for their impact on well-being, their ability to shorten the period of suffering, and their ability to facilitate positive change, we expect that the discussion regarding efficacy will show more effects than those focused on maladaptive responses alone.

At the level of social support, there are also many features that can enhance or dampen the provision of support for the bereaved (Stroebe, Zech, Stroebe, & Abakoumkin, 2005). Those that interfere with adaptive response to bereavement have sometimes been referred to as "disenfranchised losses," and they deserve our attention (Doka, 2002). The processing of loss and bereavement is an interesting blend of personal and interpersonal interaction. The importance of social support—of sharing one's grief and being supported by one's community—appears repeatedly as a feature that assists adaptation to loss. The ability to share and interact with loss can assist in the reworking of the life narrative and can serve to encourage and reconnect the bereaved to his or her own grief, to the fuller appreciation of who the deceased was and could have been, and also to the ongoing living fabric of one's connections to one's fellows. In recent years, researchers and clinicians have emphasized how certain losses, such as those that do not permit and or encourage public or socially sanctioned grief, can interfere with the ability to experience, process, and incorporate the loss into one's life narrative. Following Doka and colleagues, we refer to these losses as *disenfranchised losses,* from the idea that they are less recognized by society, and therefore, the individuals' grief and mourning are impacted negatively as well.

Disenfranchised losses include the loss of "secret" or hidden attachments, as may be found among persons who have or had an ongoing romantic relationship to a person married to someone else. Similarly, a single-sex pair relationship may be hidden and rejected by one's family and social circle, increasing the likelihood that grieving may not be expressed by the bereaved or supported by those close to him or her. Disenfranchised grief, however, has levels of acceptance or rejection. For example, the loss of a pregnancy or the death of a sibling in childhood may be losses that are not responded to by the interpersonal environment with sufficient support, and again, the bereaved may feel estranged from his or her own self, from the deceased, and from the surrounding environment.

Emotional, historical, religious, and political circumstances can also serve to disenfranchise grief. Here there can be an active refusal or damper on toleration of one's grief by the community that one is a part of. For example, American soldiers serving in Iraq, Afghanistan, and other controversial postings may be exposed to grief in the loss of comrades in arms at the same time that their countrymen denigrate their sacrifice and are not accepting of themselves or their stories. Such distancing of the bereaved serves to impede the internal dialogue and social acceptance that are so central to the general bereavement process.

> Psychotherapy and other intervention programs have been shown to help the bereaved respond adaptively to loss—when complications of grief and/or risk factors (i.e., suicide) are present
>
> More research is needed to support our expectations that a broad range of interventions can contribute favorably to well-being, shorten the period of suffering, and facilitate positive change,
>
> Disenfranchised losses as well as traumatic losses are prime candidates for intervention.

ETHICS AND THE FIELD OF BEREAVEMENT ARE LINKED

Attending to the ethical dimensions and implications of our work is a requirement for all working in the field. Sustaining an ethical perspective in all things connected with bereavement is important (Margolin & Witztum, 2003; Rubin, 2010, May 2010). The ethics of clinical work and the ethics of research have become increasingly codified so that those seeking information on the topic can find it more easily (Balk & Cook, 1995; Cook, 2001). There are ethical dimensions to the field of bereavement that are basic to human endeavor. Other aspects of the ethical dimension of our work are less well understood and need specification (Koocher & Keith-Spiegel, 2008). In the former category would fall such issues as making sure that counseling, intervention, and research always be conducted in ways that protect the vulnerable participants. Equally important is attention to information dissemination to ensure that that the information we share in our publications and on the Internet is accurate and presented honestly. In the second category of less well understood ethical aspects of professionals fall a number of considerations that have emerged in recent years with the growing attention to health care and research ethics in general, and bioethics in particular (Beauchamp & Childress, 2001; Emanuel, Grady, Crouch, Lie, Miller, & Wendler, 2008). In this category would fall such things as the responsibility of bereavement researchers to include minority as well as majority persons in their studies and the importance of full disclosure to prospective participants in our research or clinical work as to the nature of what they are being asked to do and what we will be doing with the information we obtain from them.

To this list, we would add that in our disagreements and disputes, it is important to respect the moral and professional authority of both sides to state and uphold their views (Beutler, 2009). Viewing some of the more partisan points of view that have attacked the legitimacy of those holding opposing views under the guise of ethics has done harm to the growth of our field. There are multiple perspectives on what constitutes the scientific study and practice of bereavement research and intervention. The significance of evidence-based methodology in redrawing how we approach various intervention strategies has major implications for health care in general, and bereavement intervention in particular. At our current state of knowledge, we would caution against sweeping attempts to make permanent and irreversible decisions about bereavement trajectories and interventions. Although we believe that gathering evidence regarding the effectiveness of intervention is terribly important, we are not in favor of excesses of the type in which an overly narrow, evidence-based framework is championed as the gold standard and the legitimacy of other ways of examining the effectiveness of intervention is rejected. We have arrived at an interesting point in the evolution of our study and knowledge of loss, and the ethical requirements of our work require us to continue to study and assess the varieties of loss and the varieties of loss intervention with an awareness of our limitations. Limiting harm and doing good are well-regarded maxims in health care, and all interventions need to pay heed to those parameters and to the need to document their impact in both positive and deleterious ways.

The ethical dimensions of our work deserve our active attention.

The ethical principles of respect for autonomy, beneficence, non-maleficence, and justice are relevant for both intervention paradigms and research studies (Beauchamp & Childress, 2001).

CONCLUDING REMARKS

We take leave of these introductory chapters and invite the reader to continue on to learn more about theory, research, and intervention following bereavement. The topics and issues raised so far will continue to interest us in the coming chapters. It is possible to revisit this chapter after having completed the rest of the book and to allow it to serve as a summary as well as an introduction. For the time being, however, let us turn to the Two-Track Model of Bereavement as a means of learning more about the processes of responding to loss and ways to understand, measure, and intervene following loss.

Section *II*

The Two-Track Model of Bereavement: Continuing Bonds and Continuing With Life

Figure S2.1   "The Cholmondeley Ladies," from the British School, 17th century. © Tate, London, 2011.

Section II contains four chapters introducing and developing the understanding and clinical application of the Two-Track Model of Bereavement. This way of looking at bereavement was initially developed as a result of research and interviews with bereaved mothers who had lost infants to sudden infant death. The Tate Galleries' picture of two sisters who gave birth captures much that resonates with the historical genesis of the model (Rubin, 1981, 1984) as well as the independence and interdependence of the domains under study. Like two sisters, or like two mothers with their individual children, the intent is to help compare, contrast, and consider the connections between biopsychosocial functioning and connection to the deceased. Chapters 3, 4, and 5 address bereavement as well as the interface of trauma and bereavement with case material included in each chapter. Chapter 6 summarizes and highlights clinical work with the model. Assessment and therapy issues are illustrated by a number of supplemental materials that can be used by the practitioner. Our writings on this model are informed by many years of research, teaching, and clinical work with this way of thinking about loss and bereavement.

3

Introduction to the Theory and Clinical Applications of the Two-Track Model of Bereavement

*I*n this chapter, we enter into an in-depth consideration of the Two-Track Model of Bereavement. Our primary focus remains on clinical application, and we address theoretical and practical issues with that goal uppermost in mind. As will become clearer over the course of this chapter and the next, the structure of the model provides a degree of clarity for this field with its simultaneous focus on both biopsychosocial responses to loss and the nature of the ongoing relationship bond to the deceased. After a brief overview of background and history, we concentrate on the clinical utility of the model.

The evaluation of psychological well-being and functioning is something that most people do intuitively. Following bereavement, referral to mental health clinicians and counselors is either done to prevent the development of difficulties or to ease difficulties once they have arisen. The fact that clinicians, both individually and as a group, generally see people who are having difficulties has pluses and minuses. On the one hand, it leaves them with expertise in understanding and working with such individuals. On the other hand, it often means that the clinicians lack parallel expertise in understanding what bereavement looks like in populations that do not seek or receive treatment. Research that supplements the clinicians' direct experience can do much to expand one's perspective and counterbalance clinician bias in that regard. The Two-Track Model of Bereavement is suited for the clinician seeking to evaluate and intervene if necessary. It is helpful for the clinician evaluating research and for the researcher seeking to identify areas of particular significance in the consideration of the possible impact of bereavement. The use of a conceptual framework that includes conceptions of dysfunction, but extends beyond it, allows for a wide-angle view of the continuum of human response to interpersonal losses.

It is well recognized that there is typically a powerful impact to significant interpersonal loss. In the wake of loss generally follows a process of adjusting, accommodating, and assimilating these changes. Many factors will influence the nature of the individual's response to loss over time. Of particular interest to all is what features and dimensions of change we should be considering. For clinician and client alike, often it is the presence of strong distress or dysfunction, or the anticipation of such features, that prompts the search for assistance and support.

> The evaluation of psychological well-being and functioning is something that most people do intuitively.
> The presence of strong distress or dysfunction or the anticipation of such often prompt the search for assistance and support.

The following case presentation fits this pattern (Rubin, 1999):

> Tanya called to ask for an appointment as soon as possible. Her friend, a social worker, had made the referral to a clinician with expertise in grief because Tanya's mother had died 3 months prior after a long illness. A successful professional woman, Tanya had descended suddenly into dysfunction following her return from a vacation abroad. She was awakening at 3:30 a.m., experiencing bouts of anxiety, and verbalized that [she] was afraid that she was going to have a mental breakdown. She had abdominal upset, experienced bouts of weepiness, and other somatic complaints. She herself did not associate this response with any cause.

Temporally, Tanya manifests significant behavioral dysfunction on biological-somatic, psychological, and functional lines. These responses are sufficiently severe for her and those around her to be very concerned about them. Although she does not link her difficulties to any cause, those around her see her response as connected to the loss of her mother.

Prior to a more comprehensive evaluation, it is reasonable to postulate that this severe dysfunction response is connected to her recently experienced bereavement. A fuller evaluation and exploration are warranted. At the present time, however, the difficulties in biopsychosocial functioning are of sufficient magnitude and the distress is so great that professional assistance presents itself as a first-line response. Overt distress and dysfunction that are manifest to both the bereaved themselves and to the social support system are what most people think of as the painful response to loss. Sometimes, even a relatively short and focused grief response will be characterized by features that we associate with negative experience of loss. Expression of one or more of the following are common: sadness, hopeless and depressive feelings and ideation, anxiety, guilt, helplessness, the feeling that connection to the world has been lost, and a sense that life has lost its meaning. When such responses are brief, of moderate power, and self-limiting, the need for professional assistance is questionable. The longer and stronger the response is, however, the more likely that clinicians and lay people will see the need for monitoring or intervention (Rubin & Schechter, 1997). This is true even relatively early in the response to loss.

Interpersonal loss is inextricably linked to many difficult, fearsome, and transformative aspects of one's existence. Although one cannot go through the death of a significant other unchanged, this is not to say that the changes are always dramatic, overt, and recognized by the bereaved themselves. The challenge of loss relates to concrete concerns connected to the most basic of human needs, such as food, lodging, and social connections. In young families, the loss of income, downward social mobility, changed surroundings, and difficulties at work or school often accompany the death of a spouse and parent (Sandler et al., 2008).

At the psychological level, in the case of highly significant attachment, kinship, and friendship relationships, loss brings an additional class of responses. These include preoccupation with the loss event and the ramifications of the loss for the survivor's psychological future. For example, death may come to bring to salient awareness the fragility of the interpersonal environment and social web, thereby shaking the bereaved's sense of safety and security. Even more deeply, the death of a significant other upends something that is not rooted in the self alone, but rooted in the other and our connection to him or her. This sets in motion a focus on the person who has died with the intent of reconfiguring our sense of the other, our connection to him or her, and, ultimately, our connection to ourselves. Donald Winnicott, the British psychoanalyst and pediatrician, wrote extensively on the importance of transitional space, phenomena, and objects for human development (Winnicott, 1971). In the area of interpersonal relationships, the blurring of boundaries between self and other in our most significant relationships accurately reflects the fuzzy state of bereavement—where what is lost is both something of ourselves and yet it is the loss of another, someone else, at the same time.

Not surprisingly the experience of loss for the bereaved may contain any number of cognitive and emotional responses connected to the changes set in motion by the death. But it is not the external features of one's changed life that are the key to much of bereavement intervention work. The deeper aspects of the implications of loss relate to the person who died and what that person's presence, and absence, meant and will mean for the bereaved. Changes in the degree of material support available, the social matrix, changes in the experience of self, and potentially radical changes in the multiple levels of involvement with the deceased follow bereavement. At the same time that there may be a host of emotional responses involving the anxiety, pain, and other emotions aroused by loss, the bereaved is responding consciously and unconsciously to the changes in life that loss has set in motion. As concretely and adaptively as possible, the bereaved is seeking to deal with the changes that require attention. Psychologically, however, it is not the life tasks alone that preoccupy the bereaved. A reorganization of the meaning and nature of the previous, current, and, ultimately, future relationships with the way the memories of the deceased are organized within the bereaved is central to many understandings of what the psychological process of grief and mourning is all about (Bowlby, 1969, 1973, 1980).

From the psychological and relational point of view, the two-track paradigm of loss was constructed to assist the clinician and researcher with a model of "normal" life that makes room for the significance of a particular relationship. The ongoing relationship to the deceased may exist emotionally and behaviorally to the relative exclusion of other relationships, or it may be one relationship among many. The focus on this relationship does not ignore the question of how the grievers are managing their lives. The concern with biopsychosocial function and life engagement remains. But the significance of the single relationship which is specifically and particularly considered to the exclusion of all other relationships—that second track—is familiar in loss. A mirror image of such preoccupation is sometimes found in the early stages of a love relationship—where the preoccupation with the loved partner can be overwhelming. In the relational track of the Two-Track Model of Bereavement, the bond with the deceased is given the attention it warrants. That then has far-reaching implications for understanding bereavement and intervention following loss.

> Interpersonal loss is inextricably linked to many difficult, fearsome, and transformative aspects of one's existence.
>
> In our most significant relationships, bereavement reflects an imprecise state where what is lost is both something of ourselves and someone else—simultaneously.
>
> The two track paradigm in loss was constructed as a model of "normal" life that makes room for the significance of a particular relationship.
>
> The relational track of the Two-Track Model of Bereavement gives the bond with the deceased the attention it warrants.
>
> The mirror image of acute grieving can be found in the early stages of a love relationship—where the preoccupation with the loved partner can be overwhelming.

HOW THE TWO-TRACK MODEL OF BEREAVEMENT CAME INTO BEING

The Two-Track Model of Bereavement was advanced by Simon Shimshon Rubin in the late 1970s and early 1980s. The intent was to create a scaffolding that would capture more fully the complexity of the response to interpersonal loss across the life cycle. As a doctoral student trying to make sense of the literature scattered in different areas, Rubin had concluded that distinct bodies of clinical and research literatures were relevant to a comprehensive study of the impact of bereavement (Rubin, 1981).

The first body of clinical and research literature considered the separation from the deceased as the heart of the response to loss (Freud, 1917/1957). In accord with the psychodynamic and interpersonal approaches to loss, this framework considered the effects of loss through the prism of a weakening or change in the tie to the deceased. In the absence of the bereaved's return to earlier levels of functioning following grief, it was assumed at that time that there is a continuing difficulty in the "working through" of the loss toward the severing of the relationship. This was understood to mean that the process of renegotiation of the relational tie with the deceased had not been completed—particularly with regard to accepting the reality of death and the forced separation from the deceased. Difficulties in function were understood to reflect the incompleteness or derailment of that separation process. The range of symptomatic response was broad and included anxiety, somatic, and psychiatric manifestations. Alternatively or additionally, cognitive, affective, and interpersonal difficulties might be manifest as well. Despite the variation in the symptom picture, the precipitant and maintaining cause was assumed to lie in the difficulty of achieving successful "separation" from the deceased (Rubin, 1984b; Stroebe, Gergen, Gergen, & Stroebe, 1992; Volkan, 1981). Although the ideas of separation and severance of the bond with the deceased would give way to the ideas of reworking and maintaining bonds, the focus on relationship was the key. Theory, clinical observation, and intervention experience each contributed to this conceptualization, and the value of modifications of the relationship to the deceased in bereavement remain active to this day. The centrality of the relationship to the deceased, and the ongoing bond with him or her, was clear. During those years, a number of researchers were beginning to sow the seeds for a paradigm shift regarding what was normative in maintaining the bond to the deceased. This emerged from encountering the phenomenon of the maintenance of the connection to the deceased. For example, the ongoing relationship and continuing bonds in child loss were being observed repeatedly (Klass, 1988). This was reflected in Rubin's research and clinical experience as well as can be seen in the following quote:

> In their own way, the bereaved mothers made clear that the process of resolving the experience of loss was far different from withdrawing all interest from the memory of the lost child. The reactions elicited by stimuli were dynamic in their impact and current in their interface with other aspects of living. ... Mrs. D. lost her firstborn child some five years previously. She was a thirty-two-year-old woman who had two children living at home with her, but admitted to thoughts of Tom, her dead son. Stimuli triggering these thoughts were varied. "Sometimes when I meet a few of the neighborhood children who would have been Tom's playmates, or when I meet a Tom who is five years old—I think of my son again. Not as he was then, but as he might have been had he lived." (Rubin, 1984a, p. 351)

The second worldview on loss, however, had a decidedly different perspective. This way of understanding bereavement drew from a predominantly empirically oriented perspective associated with stress and life change. This approach viewed the "outcome" of the bereavement experience as a biological, behavioral, cognitive, and emotional process fundamentally similar to the response of individuals to any other situation of crisis, trauma, and stress (Crisp & Priest, 1972; Malkinson et al., 2000; Rubin, 1981; Rubin, Malkinson, & Witztum, 2003; Schut, DeKeijser, van den Bout, & Stroebe, 1996).

In the years before the explosion of interest in PTSD, and prior to the Web-assisted information age, important aspects of this literature seemed to be scattered in different areas of inquiry. Much of the stress literature of the time was focused on short-term outcomes to a variety of stressful events, including, often, an interest in the contribution of stress to varieties of psychopathology. Researchers and clinicians associated with understanding life change and stress were relatively unconcerned with the significance of the bond to the deceased and its meaning for recovery from loss. Instead, the extent of change and difficulty following loss were assessed in their own right, relatively devoid of context. Measuring the various components of day-to-day functioning following loss was part of the mapping of the response to a particular category of stressful events. Although it was possible to estimate the extent to which the bereaved continued to suffer the aftereffects of the stress of bereavement in their various life activities, little thought was given to the relational component of the experience (van der Kolk, McFarlane, & Weisaeth, 1996).

These two disparate approaches to the experience of bereavement had little opportunity for engagement. Although each approach had merit and value for its contribution to the understanding of loss, the predominance of either one to the exclusion of the other had serious drawbacks. A combination of the two held the most promise. Armed with this understanding, Rubin adopted and began to argue for a bifocal approach to bereavement. In a series of theoretical and research articles, Rubin was careful to preserve the unique perspective of each but worked with both of them in tandem. In this way, the utility and significance of their individual contributions remained, but adopting a double perspective allowed for the synergism of the separate viewpoints to be harnessed. The first decade of publications based on the two-track model of bereavement advocated for an overarching framework incorporating both the relational and the stress perspectives, while expanding and broadening their use (Rubin, 1984b, 1985).

Overall, bereavement was understood as an event with potential for highly significant life change. The individual's adaptation to bereavement often manifested serious disruption followed by a stabilization and recovery of homeostatic functioning. These occur at the level of the individual as a biologically based organism, and at the level of the individual as a sentient, thinking, and feeling person. A similar disruption of continuity also occurs in the relationship bond to the deceased, and there, too, a type of homeostasis will be reached. To consider the bereavement trajectory from both perspectives simultaneously promised to enrich the clinical and scientific understanding of adaptation to loss.

The title of the 1981 article describing bereavement from this perspective stuck, and since then, it has been referred to as the Two-Track Model of Bereavement (Rubin, 1981). The model addresses the principal domains of the bereavement process and directs attention to both the bereaved's functioning *and* the quality and nature of the psychological relationship bond to the deceased. One benefit of this approach allowed for the study of response to trauma and loss as complementary and supplementary processes. Track I of the model considers how one was functioning in an approach that went beyond mere psychopathology and dysfunction. Directing our attention to a variety of domains of life function, the biopsychosocial sweep of human adaptation more fully captured the response to loss and will be discussed further in the next section. Track II of the model highlights the importance of a broad perspective on the significance of the relationship to the memories, feelings, and experience vis-à-vis the deceased. Significant interpersonal attachments are highly meaningful. They are important for the way in which the individualized self is constructed and experienced while, at the same time, they are also important for the construction of the social engagement network or web of relationships that contribute to one's sense of placement, security, and connectedness (Attig, 1996; Berzoff, Flanagan, & Hertz, 2007).

The model laid the groundwork to allow clinicians and researchers to address bereavement with an encompassing perspective. Thus, a range of bereavement losses, occurring under varying conditions, with varying combinations of external and intrapersonal stressors, at any time frame chosen, could be studied by considering the nature of the bereaved's functioning and the nature of his or her organization of, and relationship bond to, the deceased.

> The Two-Track Model of Bereavement (1981, 1999), was proposed by Simon Shimshon Rubin.
>
> The model combined the insights of the psychodynamic and interpersonal view of loss that emphasized the relational bond to the deceased with the more empirically oriented perspective associated with stress, trauma, and life change.
>
> The first decade of publications on the Two-Track Model of Bereavement provided theoretical and empirical support for the framework incorporating both the relational and life stress perspectives.

The Two-Track Model of Bereavement included the following main features:

1. The bereavement response should always be conceptualized as occurring along two main axes, each of which is multidimensional. The first axis, or track, is reflected in how people function naturally and how this functioning is affected by the cataclysmic life experience that loss may entail. The second axis is concerned with how people are involved in maintaining and changing their relationships to the deceased. The bereaved themselves may not always appreciate the extent, or be aware, of the nature of this relationship and their investment in it, or of their consequences. Nonetheless, this component is critical for appreciating what the human bereavement response involves across the life cycle.
2. The implications of the Two-Track Model of Bereavement are relevant for theory, research, clinical work, and counseling intervention. One can always ask to what extent the bereaved's response along each of the tracks of the model is addressed and understood at any point in the life cycle and at any time point following the loss.

The clinical implications of the model derive directly from the focus on both the functional and the relational aspects of the response to loss. The extent to

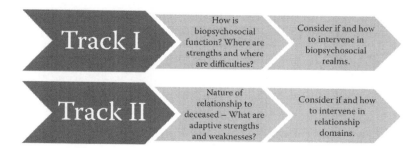

Figure 3.1   The twin tracks of bereavement.

TABLE 3.1   An Overview of the Two-Track Model of Bereavement

Track I: Biopsychosocial Functioning	Track II: Relationship to the Deceased
1) Where are the difficulties in biopsychosocial functioning? 2) Where are the strengths and growth manifest?	1) What is the state of the desire to reconnect with the deceased affectively and cognitively? 2) What is the nature of the ongoing relationship to the deceased? Is the death story integrated?
1) Anxious affect	1) Reconnection wishes and longing for the deceased
2) Depressive affects and cognitions	2) Imagery, memory, and physical experience of deceased
3) Somatic concerns	3) Degree of emotional involvement and closeness vis-à-vis the deceased
4) Indications of traumatic response (e.g., PTSD)	4) Strength and frequency of positive perceptions and affects associated with the deceased
5) Familial relationships	5) Preoccupation with loss event, the deceased, or both
6) General interpersonal relationships	6) Strength/frequency of negative perceptions and affects associated with thinking of the deceased and the relationship
7) Self-esteem and self-system	7) Presence of conflict surrounding the deceased, the relationship, the loss event, or all of these
8) General meaning structure	8) The loss trajectory: Rather than "stages" of loss, reconfigure them to represent features of response to loss (e.g., shock, searching, disorganization, and reorganization)
9) Work or similar roles	9) Upset of self-system vis-à-vis the deceased
10) Investment in life tasks	10) Progress toward memorialization and transformation of relationship with deceased

which interventions deal with either one or both domains of the response to loss is one benefit of the binocular lenses of the Two-Track Model of Bereavement. Schematic visual representations of the model in clinical use and relevant texts are contained in Figure 3.1 and Table 3.1. A more complete presentation on how to assess loss using this model in clinical practice follows the briefer presentation seen here in Table 3.2.

Track I addresses functioning and assesses the individual's adaptive and disrupted life functioning (see Table 3.1). The two basic questions addressed here are how problematic are the responses and where are the areas of growth and adaptation. The loss event and the experience of interpersonal loss are examined here for their impact. The ranges of domains include affective-cognitive, intrapersonal, social-interpersonal, somatic, and psychiatric indicators as well as the experience of self and the organization of meaning systems. Each of the 10 domains listed has received attention in the literature and figures prominently in response to bereavement. For example, the anxiety and depressive components of the response to loss are central to most clinicians' assessments of individual functioning (Blatt, 2004). Somatic and psychological-psychiatric components are important aspects of one's functioning as well as sensitivity to disruption following major life events such as bereavement. Attention to stress reactions and PTSD is relevant to this category (Raphael & Martinek, 1997). The nature of the bereaved's interpersonal interactions has relevance far beyond questions of the degree of support available (Rubin, 1993). Both inside the family and in other relationships, much is to be learned from attention to these domains. One's self-system and experience of self address many issues that include the bereaved's sense of cohesion and integration as well as who she or he is after the loss (Golan, 1975).

Meaning in life and how the bereaved integrate past and present thoughts and emotions in this area are important in the sense of connectedness to a worldview, people, and meaning matrices that can be used to sustain the bereaved. The state of the bereaved's religious and/or other meaning framework is important for understanding the extent to which the bereaved may have been disconnected from fundamental belief networks that provide critical inner emotional support (Durkheim, 1897/1997; Neimeyer, Keese, & Fortner, 2000). The ability of bereaved people to be invested in work and things that extend outside of their own grief and mourning is a critical feature in identifying those who are stymied by their loss and those who have reentered, somewhat, the stream of life (Wikan, 1988). As is true for the bereaved's ability to manage interpersonal relationships and work, the ability to invest in life tasks in a balanced fashion is one of the major benchmarks for understanding the response to loss (Rubin et al., 2000; Worden, 2008).

Track II is focused on the psychological construction and relationship regarding the deceased (see Table 3.2 in chapter appendix.). The first question we ask is to what degree is the relationship to the deceased sought out and focused on by the bereaved? There may be a painful yearning for the deceased and the wish to rejoin him or her. Perhaps the only thing of interest is thinking or talking about the deceased, or there may be an avoidance of thinking about the relationship, or any combination of the two. From the point of view of when and how the lost person is experienced and how it feels, we are asking about the process, or flow, of the bereaved's experience. There is another aspect as well: the content or organization of the cognitive and affective psychological memories and construction of, and vis-à-vis, the deceased. These elements reflecting the content of the relationship from Table 3.1 are summarized in the following paragraphs and in Table 3.3. Here too, the organization is broken down into 10 subareas that capture the salient features of the interpersonal relationship to the deceased that go toward the question of who and what the bereaved represents. This is very different from asking about the experience of distress or yearning the bereaved reports.

Having gauged the strength of the wish to connect and be reunited with the deceased, we turn to the understanding of who the deceased is and what he or she represents for the bereaved. The first consideration is the nature of the imagery memory and physical sense that is involved in the imagery, sensations, and memories that the bereaved can and do experience or long to reconnect to. What degree of emotional closeness and distance from them is present? The affects reported as well as the content of the memories and thoughts set the stage for understanding the present relationship to the deceased and how he or she is represented for the bereaved. Closely following this is the importance of understanding the positive and negative affects associated with memories of the deceased. The degree of preoccupation with the person of the deceased as well as with the loss event is important to explore when considering the management of the relationship bond to the deceased. Although the two are often intertwined, they represent very different things, and their specifications have different therapeutic significance.

From a different angle but still central to the relational bond, it is important to consider the extent of positive perceptions of the person and the relationship on the one hand, as well as to determine the degree of active and veiled conflict connected to the deceased, the relationship, and the mode of death. These provide a layered picture of the nature of the bereaved's experiential, cognitive, and emotional construction of the person of the deceased, the loss event, and the relationship.

The problems inherent in stage theories of bereavement have led many bereavement specialists to criticize their use and to avoid them (Holland & Neimeyer, 2010). Our own position on them is similar, but with a variation and a twist. We reconfigure the classic stage theories of the progression of bereavement into a paradigm that addresses the most salient feature of each "stage" as an independent dimension for evaluation throughout the bereavement experience and as a reflection of the nature of the bereaved's construction of the loss experience. For example, features of the Bowlby–Parkes paradigm lead us to address and evaluate the loss experience as a single matrix across time (Bowlby, 1969, 1973, 1980; Parkes, 1986). Thus the following aspects are considered: (a) shock and trauma, (b) the degree to which imagery and primed-ness to locate the deceased are present, and (c) the state of depression and disorganization in the organization of the experience of the loss and the narrative regarding the deceased. At the same time, however, (d) features of the response reflecting the bereaved's progress on the vector of reorganization of the relationship and of the meaning of the loss are included in this exploration. Next we consider how the self-system vis-à-vis the deceased addresses the extent to which thinking about the deceased leads to varieties of experiences intertwined with the deceased (e.g., I feel guilty whenever I think of the deceased or I feel good when I think about how she loved me [Horowitz, Wilner, Marmar, & Krupnick, 1980; Malkinson et al., 2000; Rubin, 1985, 1996; Sadeh, Rubin, & Berman, 1993; Silverman, Baker, Cait, & Boerner, 2003]).

Finally, the memorialization process and the way in which the bereaved may have transformed the relationship with the deceased into something additional can speak volumes regarding whether the processes involved in the reorganization of the relationship are generally progressing or stymied over time. Understanding if and how the deceased is being memorialized is highly relevant to understanding the progression of the bereavement response over time.

The ways in which the bereaved may have taken on tasks or changed in ways that reflect an identification with elements of the bereaved's life or an involvement with the nature of the death are relevant for our understanding of the nature of functioning. Clearly, in cases where the bereaved assumes interests or behaviors that characterized the deceased, one can appreciate that this has implications for the nature of the relationship to the deceased. From the point of view of function, however, when these types of identifications and modes of finding closeness to the life and person of the deceased become overly powerful and rigid, they may interfere with other elements of processing the loss experience in negative ways.

It is not uncommon that the bereaved become involved with concerns or activities that may seen to interfere with the grieving and mourning at one phase of loss and may be part of the expression of memorialization at a later stage. For example, a focus on finding the cause and person responsible for the death may interfere with focusing on the more personal aspects of the loss early on. When this process continues for some time, however, the bereaved may change the nature of the involvement from punitive goals or blame-finding and transform this into a search for ways to ensure that further such deaths are prevented.

In the appendix to the chapter, we present the clinical observer with a number of tables containing the questions that we find useful in the examination of the variables of both Track I and Track II. This is followed by illustrations of an optional scoring method that can be utilized to score and organize the data in clinical work for those interested in a clinician numeric summary of the bereaved's responses to loss.

In this category of memorialization and transformation, we are interested in understanding how the loss has been transformed into something that serves to remember and honor the person of the deceased but may extend beyond the particular focus on the deceased into a broader involvement with other elements of the outside world. In that way, the web of social connections and hierarchies of meaning disrupted by the bereavement may be reconfigured in ways that connect to the processes of responding to loss. These reweavings of one's life express both the individuality of the bereaved and the uniqueness of the deceased and his or her mode of death (Pollock, 1989; Rubin, 1985; Silverman, Nickman, & Worden, 1992).

We return to the case of Tanya and apply the framework of the Two-Track Model of Bereavement to the initial presentation of her difficulties in treatment (Rubin, 1999).

Tanya was the 44-year-old woman who came for therapeutic consultation and entered therapy because of difficulties in her ability to function. Her concerns, combined with strong distress, collapse of her regular routine, and high level of activity, were striking. A glance at the application form suggested she was no stranger to loss and bereavement. As mentioned before, the most recent of her losses was the death of her mother several months prior to her symptomatic outbreak. Her mother's death had followed an ongoing battle with cancer that had raged for a year. Tanya had selflessly nursed her mother through the progressively worsening illness. She had left no time for herself or her own pursuits. During the year of her mother's terminal illness, she juggled many roles inside and outside the family. She continued to fulfill her job responsibilities with the same level of involvement as she had before. At the same time, she was a good wife to her husband, an involved mother for her children, a dutiful daughter to her own father, and an active caregiver and nurse to her failing mother. These behaviors seemed self-evident to her.

> I am the only surviving child of my parents so of course the burden falls on me. My sister died suddenly when I was 15, and it was up to me to care for both of my parents and to fill the void left in their lives. I have been similarly occupied for the past 30 years.

Prior to the current crisis in her life, Tanya described herself as an active and competent professional woman who worked in marketing with notable success. She and her husband entertained a great deal and led an active life with a wide network of friends. All of this had totally stopped given the changes in her emotional life and the "onset of the 'd-word' thing—I can't even say the word."

Having obtained an idea of the problematic nature of her biopsychosocial functioning, the recent death of her mother invited exploration as well. To what extent would it be reasonable to link her current difficulties with the death? As an integral segment of the initial intake sessions, Tanya was asked about her mother's death and the overall relationship with her mother in the more distant past as well as the more recent past. The questions seemed almost irrelevant to her. At present, she was minimally introspective. Both now and in the past, she had spent little time thinking about what made her and others in her family behave as they do. Although the information she gave on her family of origin was relatively sparse, it was significant. She conveyed a picture of interpersonal tensions and conflict with her mother as features of her home life growing up. Tanya gave examples of the conflictual relationship with her mother and portrayed her as a strong-willed woman who typically got her way in the home by force of personality. Whatever Tanya conveyed, however, was overshadowed by her preference not to talk about any of these things. To her they seemed irrelevant. What emerged from the exploration of the circumstances of her mother's death and the aftermath was that she had not been open to grieving for her mother. Rather than utilizing the *Shiva* mourning period, Tanya had immediately immersed herself in a bout of activity. Doing things rather than feeling things had assumed priority in the days and weeks following the loss of her mother.

Further exploration of her family of origin gave more information about the relationships. Tanya described her relationship with her father as "not easy." She described her parents' relationship as strained and attributed it to patterns characteristic of "the older generation." Tanya noted that her father had generally done what his wife had wanted and was dominated by her. She found it "surprising that he does not feel free and liberated, but now complains to me that he is alone and expects me to take care of him."

Listening to her limited descriptions of her relationships with her parents led to a comparison with other relationships. Although generally not able to provide much detail of things in the past or of her own emotional life, Tanya was a reliable informant when it came to describing concrete activities and the content of her relationships with her husband, children, and friends in the present. These were described quite differently and did not reflect the tension or difficulties described in her family of origin.

Given the location of difficulty in the family of origin, and in the response to loss most specifically, it was important to learn more about the latter. Although the loss of her mother figured strongly as the precipitant of her distress, Tanya's loss of a sister during adolescence was explored.

She explained that her sister had been killed suddenly in an automobile accident, and as a result, life had totally changed for her (Davies, 1999). She described the necessity of her "being strong" to take care of her parents, and how proud she was that she did not cry at the funeral but was on top of the situation. For the next several years, she was the liaison with the outside world, as her mother did not leave home to go out. Her father had been withdrawn as well.

> **REFLECTION**
>
> Reviewing the state of Tanya's current life situation made it clear that there were many features of her response that suggested acute distress. Although there were hints of a complicated relationship to her recently deceased mother, the avoidance of conscious mourning for her death and her wish to return to functioning as soon as possible suggested that the relational track would need attention in the course of this intervention. The biopsychosocial difficulties present at the time of consultation were striking. Tanya was suffering intently right now, and in order to mitigate her suffering and symptoms, an immediate focus on the functioning aspects of her life was necessary. The clinician evaluation of her response is scored according to the Two-Track Model in Table 3.6 in the appendix at the end of the chapter.

The initial sessions with Tanya provided both history and a window into her current experience. Tanya's distress and anxiety were pronounced during the two initial sessions that were held the same week. She felt a constant need for reassurance. This interfered with her ability to share much detail of her past. Obtaining even the rudimentary history proceeded fitfully and in spurts. In between, Tanya wished for reassurance and to be told many things. She wanted to be told that her condition was not unusual or serious and that her husband would not have to put up with this for long. She wanted to know that she would soon return to function as an adequate mother and professional and that she was going to get over her problematic condition soon. Figure 3.2 portrays Tanya's own treatment goals.

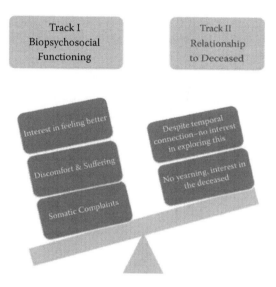

Figure 3.2   Tanya's interest in various goals of therapeutic intervention.

The meeting outlining the treatment plan was held within a week of the initial session. Therapist SSR began by sharing with Tanya his understanding of her situation and condition. The assessment of her condition was phrased in a manner intended to be both honest and supportive. The evaluating therapist (SSR) talked about her depression as generally being self-limiting and that her situation was a temporary one. At the same time, it seemed that in contrast to her sense that there was no reason for the change in her functioning and what she was now experiencing, that seemed not to be the case. From the therapist's perspective, what she was going through seemed linked to the loss of her mother and her sensitivity to that loss. The therapeutic challenge was to try to enlist her in the search for meaning to her depression. She was content to see it as due to some unknown unreasonable biochemical quirks of life. A contrasting view was offered.

SSR suggested that emotional pain could be thought of as similar to physical pain. Typically, pain was understood as a message that something was wrong. One needed to look for what required attention and not rush off to ameliorate and anesthetize the pain and thus ignore the message that something needed attending to. If this perspective held true in her case, the onset of her depression and pain could well be related to the relationship with her mother and with her mother's death. Given her assumption that she was responsible to act for the benefit of so many others, it would not be surprising that some of her own needs might not have received the attention and care that were important. A therapeutic intervention might very well lead to discussion of the losses she had experienced. The death of her mother, as well as that of her sister, were significant events in her life that had multiple meanings and reverberations that would be important to explore. But before therapy could address the meanings of her losses and her way of handling such things, it would be critical for her to return to adequate functioning. It was very important that she not feel so totally overwhelmed, anxious, and unhappy. Helping her find the ability to feel more hopeful and relaxed were very important. To do so, therapy would spend a large part of the focusing on the problems and questions that she already had and on ways to help her feel better.

We discussed the possibilities of a time-limited therapy framework and contact. Somewhat reluctantly, she agreed that referral to a medically oriented psychiatrist with expertise in psychotropic medication was indicated. A twice-weekly therapy meeting for the initial month of treatment was agreed on, as well as reevaluation of the intensity of the sessions to be jointly determined at that time. The initial meetings with Tanya were sufficient to establish a working relationship that she found sympathetic and energizing, and treatment began. Tanya agreed to the contract and entered into the treatment slightly more relaxed in the knowledge that she had a place where she could share concerns, ask questions, and receive support in her quest to return to functioning. Although initially skeptical about the need to discuss the loss of her mother and sister, she was willing to spend time on those aspects of her life even though she was not sure they would prove to be of any value.

CONCLUDING REMARKS

Throughout the remainder of the book, we will be addressing bereavement from the bifocal perspective of the Two-Track Model. Before we address the issues of trauma in the next chapters, we will summarize a few things about the case material considered so far. The case of Tanya is important for several reasons. First, it serves to remind us of the difference between the clinician's understanding and formulation and that of the client. Second, despite her significant difficulties, the issue of parent loss for older adults is not generally considered to be a seriously disruptive loss. Joining with the client, hearing her pain, and making sure to meet her where she is experiencing pain is important. Third, the presenting situation illustrates the importance of attending to the great distress experienced by some of our clients and the need to bring them into an emotional zone that they can tolerate and that will allow them to work and do some of the relational work. Other aspects of interventions that may be suggested will be something we will return to in the chapters on therapy as well.

CHAPTER APPENDIX

In Table 3.2 we illustrate the kinds of questions that may assist the clinician in understanding the range of areas that are important to explore in the investigation of the biopsychosocial response to loss and bereavement. In Table 3.3 we illustrate the kinds of questions that may assist the clinician in understanding the nature of the relationship to the deceased, its characteristics, and how the relational track of the model is manifest in practice. In Tables 3.4 and 3.5, we give the scoring key for clinician scoring and range of scores. In Table 3.6, we provide the clinician score for Tanya at the beginning of treatment.

TABLE 3.2   Track I: Biopsychosocial Functioning

1. **ANXIETY** – Thoughts and feelings: What are the degree and frequency of these, what triggers and what mitigates these responses?

2. **DEPRESSION** – Thoughts and feelings: What are the degree and frequency of these, what triggers and what mitigates these responses?

3. **SOMATIC CONCERNS** – What is the current state of such basic homeostatic processes as appetite, sleep, sexual drive, and general health concerns?

4. **TRAUMATIC RESPONSES** – Degree and duration. Consider if criteria for various disorders are met, particularly PTSD or Acute Stress Disorder.

5. **FAMILIAL RELATIONSHIPS** – What is the nature of the current relationships to spouse, parent, children, siblings, and extended family? What has changed, and which are positive and which are negative changes? Consider patterns of interpersonal interactions, which include sensitivity to others and ability to adequately maintain (via give and take) relationships.

6. **GENERAL INTERPERSONAL RELATIONSHIPS** – Explore relationships with colleagues, friends, neighbors, etc. What has changed? Which are positive and which are negative changes? Consider patterns of interpersonal interactions (e.g., sensitivity to others, ability to adequately maintain relationships).

7. **SELF-ESTEEM and SELF-SYSTEM** – What has changed, and which are positive and which are negative changes? This includes the sense of self as helpless, unimportant, or worthless, alone, as well as competent, unshaken, and stimulated to grow.

8. **GENERAL MEANING STRUCTURE** – What has changed? One's view of the world, its value, religious worldviews, etc., may be affected (e.g., "My faith is unshaken and guides me," or its opposite, "I no longer can believe in a god" or "Life has lost its meaning for me").

9. **WORK** – Can the individual manage to function adequately to meet the demands of the workplace? Or better than adequately?

10. **INVESTMENT IN LIFE TASKS** – Has the individual managed to direct resources to various aspects of life beyond the basic requirements of existing? What are they, and how are they utilized? This is one of the places to look for growth, positive change, and resilience.

TABLE 3.3   Track II: Relationship to the Deceased

1. **RECONNECTION** – What is the nature, character, and strength of the wish to reconnect with the deceased? Are the longings and yearnings significant? Constant? Not present? To what extent is the finality of the death accepted?

2. **IMAGERY AND MEMORY** – What is the degree, content, and nature of what is remembered regarding both the deceased and the relationship to the deceased? How broad is the sweep of the relationship remembered? In some cases, this may be constricted or restricted to the period surrounding the death event rather than allowing access to the life course of the deceased and serve to interrupt the connection to the deceased.

3. **EMOTIONAL CLOSENESS** – What is the degree of emotional closeness and involvement that is experienced and communicated about the deceased and the relationship to the deceased?

4. **POSITIVE PERCEPTIONS AND AFFECT VIS-À-VIS THE DECEASED AND THE RELATIONSHIP** – What positive perceptions and affects are present when client is thinking about the deceased? What are the things that stimulate positive feelings with regard to the deceased, and when are they experienced? To what degree is the deceased idealized and recollected as an ideal figure and/or as having had an idealized relationship with the bereaved? Respect and love for the deceased, joy at having known him or her, satisfaction around specific events are among the positive affects. Often, understanding these affects is a matter of inference, based on careful listening to the story of the bereaved.

5. **PREOCCUPATION WITH THE LOSS EVENT, THE DECEASED, OR BOTH** – What is the degree of time and experience invested in thinking about the loss or the lost person? Are there things that precipitate and mitigate the preoccupation?

6. **NEGATIVE PERCEPTIONS AND AFFECTS VIS-À-VIS THE DECEASED AND THE RELATIONSHIP** – What negative perceptions and affects are present when thinking about the deceased? What are the things that stimulate negative feelings with regard to the deceased, and when are they experienced? Anger, painful sadness, guilt, and distress are among the negative feelings associated with the deceased.

7. **CONFLICT** – To what degree is the deceased recollected as a problematic figure and/or having had a particularly problematic relationship with the bereaved? Also look for second-order conflict when the relationship to the deceased is a source of interpersonal conflict with others.

8. **FEATURES OF THE LOSS TRAJECTORY** – Reconfigure the understanding of "stages" of loss as *dimensions* of the response to loss (Rubin, 1992). In the Bowlby–Parkes stage model this might be addressed as follows: What are the indications communicating the experience of shock and disbelief (searching for, and openness to, reminders of the deceased)? What is the current experience of disorganization in life without the living presence of the deceased? What is the state of the reorganization of the relationship and continuing bond with the deceased, and how is it integrated into the life story of the bereaved?

9. **UPSETTING IMPACT UPON SELF-SYSTEM** – To what extent does the bereaved experience feelings of lower self-esteem (e.g., "He was the better one and I survived," or guilt over actions involving the relationship or the loss) in contrast to positive feelings (e.g., "She loved me and valued me and when I think of her, I feel strong and centered within myself")?

10. **MEMORIALIZATION AND TRANSFORMATION OF THE LOSS AND DECEASED** – How is the deceased memorialized in conventional and personal ways? From the details of gravestones and ash scattering to memorials, Web sites, and any number of ways that serve as tributes to the one who died, this allows the bereaved additional freedom to "give" and "care" for their loved one after death. The more problematic variations on this are the cases where the actions involved disproportionately serve to interfere and divert affect and attention from mourning and adapting to the loss of the deceased.

TABLE 3.4   Scoring Option for the Clinician

Track I: Biopsychosocial Difficulties		Track II: Relationship to the Deceased
Attend to: Where are the difficulties in biopsychosocial functioning? Where are the strengths and growth manifest?		Attend to: What is the state of the desire to reconnect with the deceased affectively and cognitively? What is the nature of the ongoing relationship to the deceased?
Track I assesses problems: 1 low—5 high		Track II assesses variable strength: 1 low—5 high
_ 1. Anxious affect	_	1. Strength of reconnection wishes and longing for the deceased
_ 2. Depressive affects and cognitions	_	2. Degree of presence of imagery, memory, and physical experience of deceased
_ 3. Somatic concerns	_	3. Degree of emotional involvement, closeness vis–à–vis the deceased
_ 4. Indications of trauma/ PTSD	_	4. Strength/frequency of positive perceptions and affects associated with the deceased
_ 5. Familial relationship difficulties	_	5. Degree of preoccupation with loss event, the deceased, or both
_ 6. General interpersonal relationship problems	_	6. Strength/frequency of negative perceptions and affects associated with thinking of the deceased
_ 7. Self-esteem and self-system problems	_	7. Presence of conflict surrounding the deceased, the relationship, and the loss event
_ 8. Difficulties with general meaning structure	_	8. The loss trajectory: Rather than "stages" of loss, reconfigure them to represent features of response to loss. These are shock (S), searching (Se), disorganization (D), and reorganization (R).
_ 9. Problems in work or similar roles	_	9. Upset of self-system vis-à-vis the deceased
_ 10. Problems in investment in life tasks	_	10. Effective progress toward memorialization and transformation of relationship with deceased

TABLE 3.5 Scoring Key for Clinician Rating

None to low	Mild	Moderate	Strong	Very strong	Not scoreable, insufficient information
1	2	3	4	5	NS –

On Track I—All items are scored on a 5-point scale where 1 is none to low and 5 is very high to extreme. (In addition, one can make the notation of NS (not scoreable.) A score of 3 is at midpoint—below this, the variable may be affecting the individual but it is not necessarily a focus of concern; above the midpoint, it should be a focus of intervention or continued monitoring and assessment.

On Track II—All items are scored on a 5-point scale where 1 is none to low and 5 is very high to extreme. On Track II, the numbers are similar but the interpretation of high and low scores changes with the variable. The meaning of the scoring requires interpretation on both the clinician's and the bereaved person's part.

TABLE 3.6   Tanya's Score by Clinician at End of Evaluation Prior to Therapy

	Track I: Biopsychosocial Functioning		Track II: Relationship to the Deceased
	Difficulties were manifest in virtually all of the 10 vectors of biopsychosocial functioning. Strengths: Her history suggested that she had many with good prognostic potential.		No reported desire to reconnect with the deceased. Ongoing relationship to the deceased suggested conflict and avoidance.
4.5	1. Anxious affect	1	1. Strength of reconnection wishes and longing for the deceased
4.5	2. Depressive affects and cognitions	1	2. Degree of presence of imagery, memory, and physical experience of deceased
4.5	3. Somatic concerns	1	3. Degree of emotional involvement, closeness vis–à–vis the deceased
4.5	4. Indications of trauma/PTSD	2	4. Strength/frequency of positive perceptions and affects associated with the deceased
3	5. Familial relationship difficulties	1	5. Degree of preoccupation with loss event, the deceased, or both
3	6. General interpersonal relationship problems	2	6. Strength/frequency of negative perceptions and affects associated with thinking of the deceased
3	7. Self-esteem and self-system problems	3	7. Presence of conflict surrounding the deceased, the relationship, and the loss event
3	8. Difficulties with general meaning structure	1 S 1Se 3D 1R	8. The loss trajectory: Rather than "stages" of loss, reconfigure them to represent features of response to loss. (These are shock, searching, disorganization, and reorganization.)
3	9. Problems in work or similar roles	1.5	9. Upset of self-system vis–à–vis the deceased
3	10. Problems in investment in life tasks	1	10. Effective progress toward memorialization and transformation of relationship with deceased

4

Clinical Theory and Practice at the Interface of Trauma and Bereavement

*I*n this chapter, we revisit the concept of traumatic bereavement. The massive and ever-burgeoning literature on trauma, post-traumatic stress, and its deleterious impact on functioning are the stuff of media reporting, popular culture, and professional interest (Reyes, Elhai, & Ford, 2008; Wiseman & Barber, 2008). The literature on stress and trauma draws from a broad spectrum. At one end are the research findings drawn from basic sciences involving biology, neurochemistry, and neuroanatomy. At the other end of the spectrum are research findings drawing from the social and medical sciences, including sociology, clinical and social psychology, and psychiatry. The sheer mass of information and interest in trauma and post-trauma, along with the tremendous human suffering characterizing those who suffer the aftereffects of traumatic events, make clarifying basic understandings of this field a must for clinicians.

Working with the framework of the Two-Track Model of Bereavement, we consider how usage of the terms *trauma* and *bereavement* can clarify as well as confuse our understanding of interpersonal loss. We shall distinguish bereavements that occur under conditions of external trauma involving the deceased and those that occur under conditions of external trauma involving the bereaved. In the next chapter, we shall address various types of relational traumas that are intertwined with the continuing bond with the deceased. We shall illustrate our discussion of the concepts of trauma and loss from the theoretical and empirical perspectives by considering intervention that illustrates the potential difficulties as well as potential positive effects of both trauma and bereavement. The implications for what might be considered features of Track I (including PTSD-like symptom cluster following loss) and what might be considered features of Track II (the relational aspects of a loss) are addressed specifically with regard to case material. Their significance in cases that might otherwise be considered "purely" trauma will further clarify our way of looking at the interface of loss and trauma.

In keeping with most of those working in the trauma field, we pay particular attention to the variation in circumstances of loss as a source of trauma and difficulty. By doing so, the objective circumstances of the loss impacting the bereaved, the deceased, or both parties are given their due. However, we believe that subjective elements in the loss experience of the bereaved, as well as elements concerned with the organization of the relationship to the deceased, are a clinically significant source of traumatic disruption following bereavement (Gildin-Kellerman, 2010). Ultimately, considering what has been transformed by the bereavement experience along the twin axes of Tracks I and II can help the clinician better conceptualize the nature of the difficulties and the intervention options that might best serve the bereaved.

TRAUMA AND BEREAVEMENT

The terms *trauma* and *bereavement* are often joined together, both in common speech and in professional discussion. The frequent use of the terms in combination is present in the professional literature where there is growing attention to a category of loss referred to as "traumatic bereavement" or "traumatic grief" (Malkinson et al., 2000; Prigerson & Jacobs, 2001). This may seem to imply that there is also a distinct type of nontraumatic bereavement to be sharply separated from the traumatic kind. Although we have used the terms *traumatic and nontraumatic loss* and *bereavement* (Malkinson et al., 2000), we believe that bereavement and trauma interact to form a mixture whose psychological and behavioral expression are difficult to predict. When bereavement occurs under external conditions of life threat, it brings together the causal events, as well as the life experiences, physiological responses, and varied symptomatic responses that vary in their manifestations.

For clinicians and clients alike, it is useful to specify the location of the trauma in bereavement context. "What here is traumatic?" is the relevant question to be asked. Sometimes this is almost self-evident and would reflect the objective external trauma surrounding or accompanying the bereavement. For example, death under terrible circumstances witnessed by virtue of the bereaved being present would be one instance. Alternatively, death not directly witnessed but involving particularly violent and unusual bereavements would fall under this category as well (Rynearson, 2002). Terror attacks, suicide, homicide, and natural disaster are types of loss that are intertwined with external trauma. Not all individuals respond to these bereavements similarly, but it is clear that the external circumstances of horror increase the risk for dysfunction and symptomatic difficulties in the bereavement response (Neria, Gross, Litz, Maguen, Insel, Seirmarco, et al., 2007; Rynearson, 2002).

At the same time that we acknowledge the symptom picture following loss under conditions of external trauma, we believe it should not be the only criterion for determining which bereavements are traumatic. In other words, going beyond symptoms of trauma, as well as external circumstances considered potentially traumatic, has advantages. The complexity of the issues involved in specifying the traumas of bereavement is insufficiently reflected in the theoretical and intervention literatures (Rubin et al., 2008; Shear & Smith, 2002; Silverman,

Johnson, & Prigerson, 2001; Stroebe, Schut, & Finkenauer, 2001). Among the clinical models that do focus on this is the work of Rynearson (2001), which is informed also by his understanding of the importance of pre- and post-loss relationships to the deceased.

Some of the causes of what has been slow to evolve in the dialogue of the fields of trauma and bereavement may stem from competing trauma and bereavement perspectives that often appear to vie for primacy in the discussion of the traumatic bereavement hybrid (Green, 2000; Rando, 2000). Indeed, one may view the varying emphases of the relatively independent developmental lines of the trauma and bereavement literatures as part of a struggle to achieve conceptual and therapeutic domination where none is necessary (Rubin, 1984b; Rubin, Malkinson, & Witztum, 2000). Thus, the literatures and representatives of each field may shade the approach to the phenomena of trauma and bereavement in ways that emphasize either the loss (bereavement) or the trauma (stress) framework. This is unfortunate, because ultimately a combined, bifocal, and balanced trauma–bereavement perspective provides the best promise for adequately responding to the challenges posed by the complications of trauma and bereavement (Brom & Kleber, 2000; Horowitz et al., 1997; Rubin, Malkinson, & Witztum, 2000).

We now present the case for a multichannel approach to the phenomenon of trauma interfacing with bereavement. We do this by highlighting the importance of attending to the objective circumstances of the loss while not neglecting the significance of the relationship to the deceased. This way of looking at the effects, as well as the causes operant in what can be understood as the traumas of bereavement, has implications for both research and intervention. Ultimately, we seek to challenge ourselves and our colleagues in both the trauma and the bereavement fields to better integrate the multiple perspectives where possible and, eventually, to better define the operant components requiring our attention in the various traumas of bereavement where this is warranted as well. To achieve this, after clarifying a few basic concepts with regard to trauma, we continue with our examination of the Two-Track Model of Bereavement (Rubin, 1984b, 1999) to demonstrate the advantages of a double focus on loss and trauma in ways that parallel the focus of function and relationship present in the model. Keeping in mind functioning and its derivatives, on the one hand, and attending to the nature of the emotional, cognitive, and psychological relationship to the deceased, on the other hand, yield an inclusive view of the response to loss alongside trauma. This is a more sensitive approach than that of either a narrow trauma or narrow bereavement perspective alone could provide (Malkinson, 2001, 2007a; Malkinson et al., 2000; Rubin, 1999).

The terms *trauma* and *bereavement* are often joined in common speech and in professional discussion.

   Bereavement and trauma interact to form a mixture whose psychological and behavioral expression are difficult to predict

   It is useful to specify the location of the trauma in bereavement context. "What here is traumatic?"

> A combined, bifocal, and balanced trauma–bereavement perspective adequately responds to the challenges of complications of trauma and bereavement.

Let us turn to a case that will sharpen our thinking on these matters.

CASE PRESENTATION
(Daie & Witztum, 1991; Rubin et al., 2003)

Sam, a 25-year-old man from a traditional Jewish-Iranian family, was called up for reserve duty during the Israeli occupation of Lebanon. He was serving a month's tour of reserve duty when a car bomb was detonated near his armored personnel carrier. The force of the explosion killed two of his comrades seated on either side of him although he was not injured. Immediately after the explosion, Sam responded with optimum function. He radioed his base unit, helped evacuate the wounded, and only after relief forces reached the area did he allow himself the luxury of fainting. Sam received emergency treatment at the front line, and within 2 days, his mental functioning and physical functioning were restored, with the exception of a functional paralysis of his left leg. Shortly thereafter, his unit was demobilized, and he was referred for psychotherapy to a military outpatient clinic for further treatment 2 weeks after this traumatic event.

Given his exposure to life threat, he had been exposed to the sights, sounds, and experiences associated with objective external trauma. He thus met criteria for exposure to events that may provoke an acute stress response (Briere, 1997; A. Y. Shalev, 2002) that can solidify over time to receive the diagnosis of post-traumatic stress disorder (PTSD).

When speaking initially to the mental health team that was to treat him, Sam defined his main problem as paralysis of his leg following the attack, which caused him difficulty at work. He expressed concern that his income would be affected, and he would be unable to support his family. Sam went on to explain that he felt depressed, suffered from nightmares about the explosion, and experienced sexual impotence.

Sam's response was diagnosed as acute stress disorder (and later, when he met criteria for it, as PTSD). The formulation of Sam's psychological response to the explosion included a somatic response reflecting what has been described as a conversion reaction. His depression and recurrent nightmares about the event were consistent with a response to a traumatic life event (American Psychiatric Association, 1994).

Although eligible for disability payments, Sam was unwilling to consider any compensation payments. He explained that rather than be supported by society for what he had done, he felt that he deserved punishment because he "was to blame for the death of his friends." He explained that they had protected him with their bodies and "died instead of me." The notion that he was to blame and that his comrades had died to save him was reminiscent of the survivor guilt often seen in civilian and military casualty situations (Erikson, 1950). Yet Sam's particular way of discussing what had happened was seen as evidence of the disruption he had suffered in the near-death event, and it was assumed that it would remit in the context of a general intervention focused on the trauma of exposure to life threat.

Intervention Plan One

Determining what intervention to apply emerged naturally from the understanding of what had caused the response. The idea that life threat triggered a traumatic response suggested that Sam was experiencing a psychophysiological reaction to the loss of his sense of safety and control. A short-term intervention strategy based on emphasizing health, returning self-control, mastering anxiety, and encouraging function was instituted. The short-term strategy stressing adaptation was based partly on the client's positive emotional resources and prior high functioning. The treatment goals included the restoration of functioning to Sam's leg and his return to normal life as quickly as possible. Addressing the traumatic life threat would also affect the hyperarousal and flashbacks (including intrusions of the event and nightmares). This approach would be subsumed under the Track I formulation of the Two-Track Model of Bereavement. The chapter appendix contains the clinician assessment scale for this phase of treatment (see Table 4.1 in the chapter appendix).

For now we return to the theoretical discussion, but we shall pick up the story of Sam a bit later in the chapter.

TRAUMA

The terms *trauma* and *traumatic* are so familiar that their specificity is often lost. In everyday speech, we associate them with those things that are potentially painful, wounding, and of great magnitude. Understanding what one means by the term *trauma* in professional usage is similarly plagued by the confounding of various aspects of the experience of disruption inherent in trauma. The use of the term *psychological trauma* involves overlapping domains, which include such areas as the objective aspects of the stress event, the subjective appraisal of that event (or series of events), and the individual's acute and chronic response to the stress (Weathers & Keane, 2008, p. 658). Despite a long history of somatic expression of response to psychological trauma, which resulted in terms such as *railway spine, soldier's heart, shell shock*, and the like, eventually, the psychological origin was more sharply recognized and addressed (Kinzie & Goetz, 1996; Witztum & Kotler, 2000).

In its original formulation, PTSD originated from Kardiner's (1941) descriptions of traumatic neurosis. It was later made into a diagnostic criterion based on empirical data and on considerations of a conceptual structure. In the words of Breslau (2002), "The intent here was to offer an objective measure of trauma sufficient to cause PTSD and to bracket that class of traumatic events from other stressful experiences and PTSD from other responses to stress" (p. 34). Put another way, "Distinguishing traumatic stressors from other serious but more common life stressors (e.g., bereavement, chronic illness, job loss, marital conflict, and motor vehicle crash) implied that the valence of the stressor would overwhelm the adaptive capacities of most people" (Lasiu & Hegadoren, 2006, p. 73).

The description of the stressor event, however, known as the Criterion A feature of the *DSM-IV*, was adopted to differentiate responses by the screening out of events that were not deemed sufficiently stressful. If the stress event passes muster, three clusters of response are defined as characterizing the full-blown post-traumatic response. These are (1) intrusion where the event continues to pre-occupy and often torment the individual, who cannot avoid memories, images, and other stimuli that serve to remind the individual of the traumatic event; (2) avoidance, whereby the sufferer goes to great lengths to distance himself or herself from things that trigger memories and feelings associated with the trauma; and (3) hyper-alertness, where there is a general elevation of vigilance and tension, as if the individual is preparing for a fight-or-flight response.

PTSD is unusual among *DSM* syndromes in that the diagnostic criteria specify an etiologic event: exposure to a traumatic stressor. Whatever the symptoms present, unless a person has been exposed to a qualifying stressor, the diagnosis cannot be made.

The search for a so-called objective category of external stressors was paralleled by the sharp cutoff separating those with the disorder of PTSD from those without it. Not surprisingly, a major concern surfaced related to how to classify and assist individuals who did not meet the full set of diagnostic criteria for PTSD but suffered from clinically significant symptoms. Consequently, the concept of partial PTSD (PPTSD), or subthreshold PTSD, was introduced to describe subsyndromal forms of PTSD. Stein and associates (1997) were among the first to point out the importance of considering the taxonomic standing and clinical import of cases where individuals exhibit only part of the symptoms. Although ineligible for a full PTSD diagnosis, these individuals are essentially suffering from "a partial PTSD."

The prevalence of PPTSD among Vietnam veterans, survivors of sexual abuse, and survivors of other forms of trauma has been deemed quite high (Stein, Walker, Hazen, & Forde, 1997). Stein and associates further noted that unlike PTSD, subthreshold presentations for depression and social phobia have been recognized in the *DSM*. Empirical data showing that the frequency of PPTSD as similar to or even greater than full PTSD suggests that the trauma category, as currently conceptualized, is neither as neatly defined by circumstance nor of response difficulty as might be assumed by a less critical reading of some of the professional literature (Rubin et al., 2008; Weathers & Keane, 2007).

In recent years, a number of researchers have attempted to examine the impact of bereavement and to consider it via the lens of PTSD. For example, Zisook and colleagues (1998) well-known bereavement researchers, examined 350 widows and widowers 2 months post loss and found that approximately 10% had PTSD-like symptoms. At 13 months, some 40% of those identified earlier were still meeting full criteria for PTSD (Zisook, Chentsova-Dutton, & Shuchter, 1998). This held true in cases of chronic illness as well as in cases of relatively unexpected and accidental deaths. The impact of unnatural death, such as suicide, was more highly associated with the PTSD classification. Their research considered many aspects of the response to loss in their sample, but the trauma feature was one that particularly meshes with thinking using that perspective. The significance of violence and its ability to interfere with the processing of interpersonal loss has been documented in recent years in cases of individual violence, such as homicide and suicide, as well as terrorism (Rynearson, 2006). In research with the Two-Track Bereavement Questionnaire, death due to terrorist attacks and suicide was associated with the highest levels of difficulties following loss (Rubin, Bar Nadav, Malkinson, Koren, Gofer-Snarch, & Michaeli, 2009).

Over the years, the conceptual overlap of trauma and bereavement has been considered in alternative ways. Stroebe, Schut, and Finkenauer (2001) have discussed the overlap in symptoms between the two domains. Noy (2000) differentiated between trauma and bereavement where he saw bereavement-related difficulties as difficulty in separating from the deceased and the vacuum created by the death, whereas trauma was seen as related to the suddenness of the event, the fear of its repetition, and the loss of safety in the world. In this conceptualization, the possibility of the two situations overlapping, as when loss is sudden and unexpected, is possible.

Post-traumatic stress disorder (PTSD) is unusual among *DSM* syndromes in that the diagnostic criteria specify an etiologic event: exposure to a traumatic stressor.

The frequency of partial PTSD is similar to full PTSD and suggests that the trauma category is neither neatly defined by circumstance nor by response difficulty.

BEREAVEMENT AND TRAUMA: RESPONDING TO LOSS WHEN EXTERNAL TRAUMA WAS EXPERIENCED BY THE BEREAVED, THE DECEASED, OR BOTH

For purposes of the discussion here, the multidimensional focus of the Two-Track Model of Bereavement on "functioning" (including emotional, interpersonal, cognitive, homeostatic, somatic, psychiatric/PTSD indicators, and meaning structure status) makes Track I suitable for a broad-based evaluation of response to loss as well as to other forms of stressful life events. In that sense, Track I remains a basic framework for a broad-based evaluation of overall biopsychosocial functioning and particularly for such functioning after overwhelming and disruptive major life events. The multiple domains assessed, including the presence of post-traumatic symptomatology make this almost self-evident. Yet these indications of complications following loss under conditions of external life threat to the deceased and/or the self may be associated with the conditions of the deceased's death alone, the exposure of the bereaved to the external life threat to self at the time of death, and/or elements of their interaction. It is important clinically to determine if the bereaved reports traumatic-like imagery surrounding the death event, such as the imagery of the death whether real or imagined. Similarly, understanding the nature of the death and trauma story, the imagery present, and the thoughts involved is important. When the death narrative involves a combination of the risk to the deceased and the bereaved, one may question whether it is at all realistic to separate them out early on in an assessment or early intervention. Teasing these apart may be unnecessary, however, when one can integrate and work with the various aspects of the meaning and experience of the traumatic death. That way, under conditions of external trauma, the narrative of the event and the organization of its meaning are important.

Conditions of external threat or violence that are tied up with loss and death do not only make their impact in the features associated with trauma, such as depression, anxiety, flashbacks, avoidance, and the other expressions of response to loss. A particularly deleterious aspect of death under conditions of violence affecting either the bereaved or the deceased can take its toll on the manner in which the ongoing relationship to the deceased may be experienced. Here, Track II's relational focus considers the state of the nature of the relationship to the deceased to allow for the consideration of how conditions of external trauma may compromise, derail, or complicate the necessary reorganization of the relationship with the deceased and serve as the second leg of the trauma. The organization of the representations of the deceased and the emotions engendered when he or she is remembered is central to the conceptual formulation of cases where grief, trauma, and bereavement are intertwined. Simply put, conditions of external trauma have the ability to affect the bereaved on any number of variables associated with biopsychosocial functioning, and these may complicate and impact the reworking and maintenance of the relational bond to the deceased.

Direct and indirect focus on the life threat aspects of the death and exposure of the bereaved is useful. The critical question, however, is about the implications of those responses for the facilitating, interfering, and complicating the ability of the bereaved to rework the relationship to the deceased. If the death imagery is too overwhelming, tendencies to avoid triggers of the imagery and/or repeated intrusions can be heightened and interfere with the continuing bond. The imagery of the death and events surrounding it can result in heightened avoidance or intrusive imagery. In either case, even in situations of strong and positive attachment, a relatively benign access to the memories and connection with the deceased can be seriously compromised.

With this parallel focus on functioning and relationship at work, the clinician remains open and attentive to both the unique interpersonal nature of the loss event (which may have been objectively stressful to the point of trauma) and to the bereavement experience of losing a loved one. This occurs without neglect of the myriad ways in which response to the disruption and destruction of continuity, safety, and security may occur for an individual exposed to stressors of overwhelming nature. Examining the grief and disruption of the relationship related to the deceased, while remaining open to the characteristics of response to any traumatic event, would seem to be better served by looking at both rather than at either alone.

With such a bifocal approach, it is much easier to revisit the phenomenon of "traumatic bereavement." With the Two-Track Model of Bereavement, both the individual's biopsychosocial response and the complex manner in which the deceased is represented, remembered, and experienced are under consideration (Horowitz, Wilner, Marmar, & Krupnick, 1980). In this way, one takes into account the symptoms of dysfunction classified as acute stress disorder, PTSD, and other symptomatic expressions of difficulty without neglecting the specific relational aspects (Briere, 1997; A. Y. Shalev, 2002).

A question best left for empirical study is the nature of the relation of post-loss functioning and the reworking of the relationship to the deceased. In the early stages of the bereavement response, the changes in functioning and the need to rework the relationship to the deceased may be difficult to untangle. Over time, ways in which the nature of the bereaved's functioning and the manner in which the relationship to the deceased are interrelated can be considered more independently.

Events such as the terror attacks of 9/11 have provided a number of research studies that allow for a look at aspects of the interaction between exposure to traumatic events and the loss of close relatives. An excellent example of the mix of bereavement and trauma examined the responses to the events more than 2.5 years after the event. In this Web-based study, loss of a child was the strongest predictor of complicated grief while watching the attacks live on TV was a predictor of less strength for complicated grief. In this sample of 704 adults located across the United States, 43% were designated as meeting criteria for complicated grief—a screening diagnosis emphasizing difficulties in functioning and strong yearning for the deceased (Neria et al., 2007). Some 65% of parents bereaved of children met these criteria for complicated grief. Of no less interest, however, is the fact that over 50% of those meeting screening criteria for complicated grief met screening criteria for PTSD and major depressive disorder as well. Studies such as this are relevant to our understanding of the impact of loss under conditions of external trauma with the comorbidity associated with these experiences.

In evaluation, is traumatic-like imagery present?

When the death event involves a combination of risk to the deceased and the bereaved, it may not be realistic to separate these out early on.

Conditions of external trauma may affect the bereaved on variables associated with biopsychosocial functioning, and these may complicate and interact the reworking and maintenance of the relational bond to the deceased.

Even when there is strong and positive attachment to the deceased, traumatic events can disrupt and complicate access to the memories and connection with the deceased.

We now return to pick up the case of Sam.

INCLUDING TRACK II IN THE FORMULATION AND INTERVENTION PLAN OF THIS CASE OF TRAUMATIC BEREAVEMENT IN COMBAT

In our discussion at this point, we shall be particularly attentive to these two points: (1) how thinking from a trauma frame can hamper a broader view of the relevant clinical problem, and (2) how bereavement with non-family members may be highly relevant to conceptualizing the experience of loss in general and traumatic loss in particular.

Sam, the Israeli soldier we encountered earlier in the chapter, was involved in a life-threatening combat experience in Lebanon (Witztum, Malkinson, & Rubin, 2001). As a result of his diagnosis of acute stress disorder, the trauma focus was uppermost for the mental health team that diagnosed and planned the intervention (Daie & Witztum, 1991). The picture of the event, the duration of the response, and the presence of symptoms of intrusion, exclusion, and hyper-alertness were addressed in the initial formulation and intervention.

The treatment plan initially used support and cognitive restructuring, with limited results. The treatment supported Sam's strengths and prior competencies and reviewed with him how well he had functioned after the explosion and the lives he had saved by his behavior. This mitigated but did not eliminate the sense of responsibility and survivor guilt that plagued Sam. He reported no change in his condition and expressed frustration at the lack of progress. In the absence of sufficient progress by the symptom management approach, and as a result of attending to the distinct themes of interpersonal guilt and loss that Sam expressed, a shift in the conceptualization of the problem and in the intervention format became necessary.

Intervention Plan Two

The lack of progress stimulated the team to consider an alternative view of what should be the focus of intervention. This conceptualization located the death of Sam's comrades as the nexus of the problem and recast the interpersonal loss and the feelings of guilt as the prime focus of intervention. In this Track II formulation, the trauma experienced involved a relational dimension, the loss of military buddies, and, accordingly, the treatment would require a focus on the relational issues (Mor-Yosef, 2010; Rubin, Malkinson, Koren, Mor-Yosef, & Witztum, 2011).

As is indicated in some cases of complicated grief and problematic bereavement, the advantages of incorporating interventions that assist the progression of grief and mourning were introduced. In this case, leave-taking rituals associated with the cultural traditions of Sam were used as was an exploration of Sam's cognitive reconstruction of what happened that day (Van der Hart, 1983; Witztum & Roman, 2000; Malkinson, 2007).

In one session of the brief treatment, exploration of Sam's guilt feelings was juxtaposed with cognitive restructuring to demonstrate to Sam that his recollections of the unfolding of the bombing event were not logical. In reviewing the sequence of events, Sam was helped to reorder the events into their proper sequence. As a result, Sam understood that his comrades-in-arms were dead before they had fallen on him. This contradicted his earlier conviction that they had chosen to protect him with their bodies in acts of supreme self-sacrifice. Therapist and client agreed that the relational axis remained at the heart of the derailing of function that Sam experienced. Sam's response to the loss of his comrades, in particular his sense of guilt and his conviction that he deserved punishment for having survived, was a significant source of difficulty. In their co-constructed formulation, therapist and client agreed that the paralysis was serving as a severe punishment for Sam, but with the undesirable side effect of severely punishing his family as well. To deal with the need to "punish the guilty," Sam and his therapist agreed to substitute community service as an appropriate "punishment" (and one that did not penalize his family).

Soon thereafter, a crisis erupted in treatment. In the next session, Sam expressed a great deal of anger at his therapist. He was angry that his leg was not better. But there was also a subtext to the anger. Sam explained that he had dreamt that his two friends had chased him and wanted to take him with them. Sam saw the dream message as indicating that he deserved to be with his fallen comrades in death.

The therapist, however, saw this as an opportunity to reformulate the axis of relationship to the fallen comrades. He used his knowledge of Sam's subculture and its meanings to provide a culturally sensitive response with quite a different message. He reinterpreted the dream as a communication that revolved around Sam's abandonment of his friends by not being present at their funeral. Although not religiously mandated or required, Sam's wish to recite the mourner's prayer of Kaddish as if he were a relative was troubling him. By his not being present at the funeral, he had abandoned his buddies and this was something that they wished rectified. Sam was offered the option to attend to the things he had not done at the time of their deaths. He was instructed to go to the cemetery to say the Kaddish memorial prayer for the dead, to ask for forgiveness, to separate from his comrades, and to receive their support.

A visit to the cemetery, in the company of other comrades from the unit, was soon arranged. Sam said the Kaddish prayer, spoke aloud to his fallen comrades, and left feeling better. With this separation done, the symptoms of paralysis and tension lifted and generally normal function was restored. By the eighth and final session, Sam reported the reduction or cessation of the remaining symptoms. He slept well. The dreams appeared with less frequency and were not as frightening as before. Relationships at work had improved and he was becoming calmer at home. In this last session, Sam relayed regards from his wife, who sent her special thanks for conjugal relations being back to normal. A follow-up session 1 year later found Sam feeling good and essentially symptom-free.

What remained was a phobia of entering an armored car of the same type as the one in which he and his friends were sitting when the explosion occurred (Daie & Witztum, 1991).

REFLECTION

The case illustrates the value and clinical utility of addressing the significance of the interpersonal relationships. In retrospect, and given the way in which effective therapy unfolded, it is easier to see this as a case of comrade bereavement intermingled with traumatic exposure to life-threat (Rubin, et al., 2011). In the language of the Two-Track Model of Bereavement, a major feature of the intervention focused on the relationship to the deceased, and intervening there proved to be the key to securing the return to functioning. The combination of interpersonal loss of friends and comrades, the extreme personal life-threat, and the lack of opportunity to engage in mourning for the deceased all served to derail the mourning process and the return to life. The therapy team initially conceptualized its work as trauma intervention around acute stress and PTSD, based on the precipitating event and the symptoms that included paralysis, nightmares, and depression. The deeper focus of the intervention, however, was on the grief and guilt that Sam felt for his buddies. In the dream interpretation, the cemetery visit, and the instructions for including all the elements of a burial and leave-taking ritual with the army "family," this therapy sequence brings home the significance of the focus on relationship, in what we consider a case of traumatic bereavement (where both trauma and traumatic bereavement are operant). The clinician assessment scale for this phase of treatment is presented in the appendix in Table 4.2

The use of metaphor, leave-taking ritual, and directive short-term therapy intervention gave this case an aspect of its particular identity within the bereavement literature (Witztum & Roman, 2000). The combination of factors operant in the traumatic bereavement, however, is consistent with the thesis we are developing here of the significance of relational factors in bereavement—and particularly in a number of forms of traumatic bereavement. Intervention programs aimed at dealing with the experiences of trauma where the loss of a significant affiliation or attachment figure is present need to attend to the loss aspects. This means that relationship to the deceased and the story of the death are significant dimensions deserving assessment, measurement and intervention.

CLINICAL SUMMARY

Traumatic bereavements share with all deaths of significant others the ability to affect the individual in both domains assessed in the Two-Track Model. When the loss of a close relationship occurs under conditions of external life threat and trauma, it is inaccurate to consider the manifestations of acute stress and post-traumatic stress as the preeminent indicators for determining that "traumatic bereavement" has occurred. Similarly, when responses of acute stress or post-traumatic stress are present following bereavement, it is misguided to narrowly focus on their amelioration as benchmarks of successful intervention. Most often, the particulars of the death story are woven into the life story of the bereaved. When those particulars allow for emphasis of the predominant life themes of the deceased and when they include solace creating threads, the effect can be supportive and comforting.

In cases of violence and trauma, however, the details of the death story can overpower the life themes of the individual such that a coherent saga of life and death is not achieved. In place of such a story, there can exist an ongoing engagement with the death event, its horror, and its injustice. Much as the needle stuck in the groove of a phonograph record of old, the death segment can effectively stymie any progress forward or backward in the symphony of a relationship. The predominance of the death theme and its powerful imagery can overpower and effectively disconnect the bereaved from his or her experience of connection to the deceased.

In cases of recognized traumas of bereavement, the clinician's focus on the elements of biopsychosocial functioning contained in Track I responses is important. The outcome desired is not only absence of trauma symptoms, however, but also positive functioning, affect, and engagement with the world. Confused meaning making and jumbled worldview perspectives are important to attend to when trauma is predominant. At the same time, the creation of an appropriate narrative regarding the pre-loss and post-loss engagement with the deceased is central to Track II's formulation. The importance of the successful reprocessing and reorganized content of the ongoing relationship to the memories of the deceased is upset when trauma predominates. Intrusive and avoidant response styles following traumatic bereavement serve to derail, inhibit, and otherwise distort the ability of the "traumatized" bereaved individual to do the work of reorganizing the relationship. Thus trauma symptoms interfere perniciously with the relationship to the deceased and with the reconstruction of a reworked narrative concerning the self and the deceased (see Figure 4.1).

There are a number of well-recognized and documented external traumatic loss events. Many of these, but not all, are related to violent deaths. The horror of death caused by terror attacks, murder, and suicide create a death story that many bereaved have difficulty integrating into a narrative compatible with the reworking of the relationship to the deceased. The particular details of many variations of death can provide the necessary ingredients for traumatic loss. The absence of a body to identify, and conduct final services for, can leave things unfinished and drive repetitive and intrusive thoughts and images that fail to progress toward reorganization. Fatal disappearances that retain the uncertainty that death has unequivocally occurred can inhibit acceptance and acknowledgment of death. In cases where people had responsibility for the death (ranging from murder to medical or vehicular negligence), the search, trial, or living with whatever verdict was

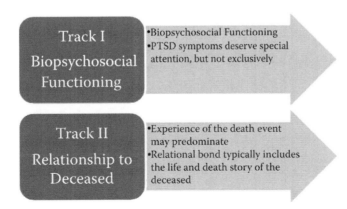

Figure 4.1   The model's two tracks at the interface of trauma and bereavement.

reached can preoccupy or distort the construction of a facilitative relationship vis-à-vis the deceased.

Preoccupation with the loss event and its meanings, rather than with the relationship to the deceased, is a risk factor in traumatic bereavement. The nature of the imagery and content of the thoughts and feelings that preoccupy the deceased have much to tell us about the nature of the bereavement process and the potential need for, and goals of, intervention. We take leave of the focus on traumatic bereavements that are so classified by the objective nature of the "traumatic elements" to continue our discussion with a class of bereavements whose traumatic elements stem more from the subjective experience of the bereaved. After that, we will be able to conclude our introductory discussion to the bereavement and trauma interface for the clinician.

CHAPTER APPENDIX

In the initial clinical formulation and scoring of Sam on the clinician summary for the Two-Track Model of Bereavement, only Track I items were assessed.

In the later clinical formulation and scoring of Sam on the clinician summary for the Two-Track Model of Bereavement, both Track I and Track II items were assessed. The results are presented in Tables 4.1 and 4.2.

TABLE 4.1 Clinician Assessment of Sam, First Formulation

	Track I: Biopsychosocial Functioning
	Difficulties: yes **Strengths: also present**
4	1 Anxious affect
3	2 Depressive
4	3 Somatic
4	4 Traumatic acute stress
2	5 Familial relationships
1	6 Interpersonal relationships
2	7 Self-esteem and self-system
2	8 General meaning structure
3	9 Work or similar roles
3	10 Investment in life tasks

TABLE 4.2   Clinician Assessment of Sam, Second Formulation

Track I: Biopsychosocial Functioning		Track II: Relationship to the Deceased	
1) Difficulties present 2) Strengths present		1) Reconnection wishes – none reported 2) Ongoing relationship – conflict and guilt	
Score range (1–5)		Score range (1–5)	
4	1. Anxious affect	1	1. Strength of reconnection wishes/ longing
3	2. Depressive affects	4	2. Imagery, memory, and physical experience of deceased (*at time of death*)
4	3. Somatic concerns	NS	3. Degree of pre-loss emotional involvement
2	4. Trauma features	4.5	4. Positive perception and affects
2	5. Familial relationships	3	5. Preoccupation with loss and deceased
1	6. Interpersonal relationships	4	6. Negative perception and affects (*dysphoria re: deaths*)
2	7. Self-esteem/ self-system	4.5	7. Conflict re: relationship or loss event
2	8. Meaning structure	4S 3Se 3D 1R	8. The loss trajectory: These are shock, searching (and its opposite, avoidance), disorganization, and reorganization
3	9. Work or similar roles	4	9. Upset of self-system vis-à-vis the deceased
3	10. Investment in life tasks	1	10. Progress in memorialization and relationship transformation

5

The Relational Traumas
of Bereavement

*I*n this chapter, we address the dimension of trauma in bereavement from the relational aspect of the experience. These include a range of features that share one common element: the relationship is the core of the trauma. The traumatic aspects considered here are endemic to the experience and psychological organization of the relationship with the other during life, and the transformation now bound up with them following their death (Rubin et al., 2003). By adopting the bifocal perspective of the Two-Track Model of Bereavement, we are both able and challenged to consider trauma as it relates to each of the tracks. We invite the reader to think more deeply with us about relational aspects of trauma and their significance for our clinical work.

We believe that complications rooted in the relational and interpersonal dimensions of the relationship to the deceased can derail life function. There are complications, in the aftermath of bereavement, that impact the bereaved with much the same disruptive power as exposure to external life threat or harm currently understood as objective or external trauma. Death severs the actual interpersonal contact in the real world, of course, but not every important relationship is characterized by much contact in the "real" world. When death occurs, and when new information that serves as an attack on the way the deceased has been perceived heretofore surfaces, loss can be exceedingly difficult to negotiate. Indeed we can speak of loss experiences of traumatizing proportion in cases of bereavements whose circumstances of the death would not qualify them for the term *traumatic*.

There are implications to unpacking the challenge of grief and mourning as they relate to the trauma occurring regarding the psychological reorganization of the relationship to the deceased. This view will allow us to clarify the traumatic complications of bereavement with particular significance on identifying the difficulty and constructing appropriate intervention for the bereaved.

Complications rooted in the relationship to the loved other can derail life-function similarly to objective or external trauma.

ACCEPTING THE SEPARATION OF BODY AND SPIRIT

People are an amalgam of body and "soul," of concrete physical and the ephemeral, and the combination is what we learn to accept when we think of living persons. That amalgam is highly relevant in the formation of attachment and affiliation bonds, but it is often much less significant in the maintenance of those bonds (Mikulincer & Shaver, 2007). For the adult, physical separation and lack of interaction need not affect the relational bond with parents, children, siblings, or close friends. We are able to go about our lives and are generally able to give little conscious thought to many of the people we are closest to because we remember them within us, and we feel both secure and sufficiently free to distance ourselves. Much as the young child learns to feel secure without needing to concretely experience contact with the caretaker, much of the evolution of security involves not being concerned with physical separation because we reframe the image and memory of the internalized other and the internalized relationship to the other continues. And that works pretty well—until we learn about their death.

In every loss, the process of reorganizing the relationship to the now deceased loved person involves changes in the cognitive emotional schema regarding the deceased. Death forces us to reorganize our mental schema and emotional response to the memories of their presence and their impact, their absence, and the nature of their intertwining with our lives. A major component of the emotional cognitive reorganization required by the death of any significant other proceeds along these lines— which are major as well as ubiquitous challenges following loss. It would be fair to say that this requirement to reorganize from an attachment to one living to one now dead is a challenge present in any loss (Rubin et al., 2003). When this need to reorganize is coupled with an additional major attack on the bereaved's experience of the deceased, however, we are dealing with something of traumatic proportions. Track II—namely, the assessment of the relationship to the deceased and how the loss event is organized together with the relationship to the deceased—may ultimately serve as the indicator of how much traumatic difficulty is present.

The requirement to reorganize attachment from a connection to a living person to one now dead is a challenge present in any loss.

THE TRAUMA STEMMING FROM THE ATTACK ON THE REPRESENTATION OF THE DECEASED

There is a potential source of difficulty relating to the grief, mourning, and reorganization of the relationship to the deceased other that is particularly important to consider. This occurs when, alongside the transition from a bond with a living person to one with someone now dead, something very difficult has been added. Such elements can involve an event of uniquely stressful and traumatic proportions. In such cases of trauma in loss, the circumstances of loss that we need to take into account are not as significant for their external occurrence as for their psychological meaning and impact upon the relationship with the deceased.

Here we are concerned with something that attacks the very coherence and organization of the relationship to the deceased in the mind of the bereaved. It is the psychological association and representation of the deceased that is "blown to smithereens" in this form of trauma in loss. We might say that in these cases, the mental image of the loved one, as alive, whole, and integrated across the life of the relationship, is assaulted by the simultaneous attack on the life, integrity, and integration of the mental representations in unexpected ways.

Let us consider the following example:

> Mrs. Miriam B. is an attractive woman in her late 50s. She suffers from multiple sclerosis and is currently confined to a wheelchair. She has had a relatively severe case characterized by progressive decline, bowel and bladder difficulties, speech problems, chronic pain, and fatigue. Since the worsening of her condition almost 15 years earlier, Miriam has been a courageous figure to those who know her. She has continued to work in her field, although she has had to surrender her managerial and supervisor position that she was unable to maintain. Miriam's understanding of the "secret" of her success in life despite hardship is due to two people in her life: (1) her mother, who raised her and her three brothers after their father's death with strength, love, and integrity and who is no longer alive; and (2) her supportive and caring husband of 36 years. She and John met when they were in university together although he had been a bit older than she. Miriam was thankful that he stood by her throughout her ordeal.
>
> Accordingly, Miriam was devastated to receive a phone call informing her that John had been killed in a car accident. Miriam was scared, bewildered, and hurt. She feared for her personal future and felt her world had collapsed around her. She wondered how she could go on without the support of John and his strength, optimism, and humor. Going through John's computer, she had come upon an encrypted section of the computer that required a password to open, but she was able to circumvent this. To her shock and dismay, she discovered a secret side of her husband's life. John had been romantically involved with another woman for close to 7 years, and their correspondence indicated that he was very much in love with her. She had never suspected it. Closing the computer, Miriam was confused, hurt, and bewildered. As the days went on, however, she found herself unable to think of John without sadness, anger, and confusion. She wondered whether her life was worth living, and indeed, whether their last years together had been only one big lie.

In this vignette, there is new information that serves to attack the fabric of the understanding of who the deceased was and of the nature of the relationship to the bereaved. The inner coherence of Miriam's relationship to John has been upended by the discovery of unexpected, shocking, and unacceptable information about her heretofore beloved. The exposure of John's secret life could have devastating and traumatizing impact upon Miriam. The discovery that her loving spouse John had conducted a parallel life in a relationship with another woman turns Miriam's difficult task of reorganizing the relationship to her deceased spouse into a nightmare more ghastly than she could have imagined. One minute John was one of two loved family members whom she credited with giving her the ability to face her life challenges. The next moment he was also someone who had lied to her and hurt her more deeply than anyone had ever done before. That betrayal, coming on top of his death, makes his loss one of traumatic proportions. The betrayal invests the psychological mourning and reorganization process of self and other with great challenges. The bereavement sets the stage for the need to address and mourn the relationship to John that was part fiction and is now uncovered. At the same time, the perception of him and of the relationship is undergoing the tsunami set in motion by his death. Reorganizing that relationship, reworking the positive and the negative, the real and the fantasized, so that some of the beneficial and valuable aspects of their relationship are not totally lost is now required. The magnitude of this challenge, because of the psychological attack on the image and experience of who John was, is extreme and of traumatic proportion.

There are numerous other instances of new information that was previously unknown and whose revelation has powerful destabilizing consequences in bereavement. Such "secrets" share several common characteristics. In particular, these include a harsh confrontation and intrusion of information that previously had seemed unimaginable to the bereaved. Additionally, they are related to fundamental aspects of the perception of the deceased and the relationship to him or her. The complications in the experience of loss are, in degree and ability to shatter the coherence of one's emotional and psychological world, extremely potent and powerful. In a word, they parallel in magnitude the shock and dislocation experienced in response to external trauma. For example, learning that a respected family member was a war criminal wanted for past deeds is a trauma (Bar-On, 1991), as is learning that a parent or sibling had been sexually abusing individuals (Sirles & Franke, 1989; Tessman, 1996). These are examples of information that make Track II, the relationship to the deceased, the source of the trauma in loss. When such information is combined with the simultaneous challenge of responding to the death of that person, traumatic loss is the best way to describe it. We believe that there is a need to consider how highly troubling information about the person of the deceased that is experienced around the death, or that had surfaced prior to the death can serve as the "trauma" in traumatic bereavement. Under these conditions, the task of working through loss and reorganizing the relationship to the deceased is affected.

Armed with the double understanding that the trauma of bereavement in the relationship track works on two levels, we are better able to consider intervention strategies later on. Knowing that the internal psychological experienced of the bereaved is shaken in death and requires dealing with the transition of connection with a living being to one of connection with someone no longer living is a major challenge. Similarly, reorganizing the relationship to the other when various features of how the deceased was conceived, perceived, and psychologically "constructed" are challenged presents unique obstacles to reorganization. Having presented these points, we can revisit bereavements that are often conceptualized as traumatic because of the circumstances of the loss and consider the "trauma" as belonging to both tracks of the bereavement experience.

Consider the following case:

> Scott was feeling despondent after having lost his managerial position in a large company. He had been transferred laterally with no financial loss, but he felt embarrassed and humiliated. Over the next several months, he succumbed to depressive thinking, lost weight, and repeatedly referred to himself as a failure. He rejected his wife Sharon's suggestion that he see the doctor or a psychologist. Some 4 months after this change in work, things were not improving. One Thursday morning, Sharon got up and, seeing his side of the bed empty, assumed he was making coffee in the kitchen. When she walked out into the hallway and saw what there was to see, she screamed and woke the children. Scott was hanging from the skylight window. He had killed himself.

This case is easily understood as an instance of traumatic bereavement and perhaps too easily and facilely classified as such. The death is sudden, unexpected, and untimely. It is terrifying and horrible and brings with it a painful dislocation of the survivors' lives. The physical confrontation with the body of the deceased alone has the potential to sear itself into the memory of the bereaved. The transformation of one's home, with the safety and security it connotes, to being the location of the shocking death by his own hand further upsets the survivors. Scott's death is shocking and immediate in ways that would overwhelm most persons—at least for a time.

And yet, were the circumstances to change such that an accidental death were the cause rather than suicide, the very fact of the death would remain a traumatic bereavement. An encounter with the body of a loved one in an accident, as well as the suddenness of such a loss, are sufficient to qualify the death as a traumatic loss.

When the psychological association and representation of the deceased explodes, we are talking about relational trauma related to Track II.

Negative information that had seemed unimaginable can become intertwined with the experience of loss to shatter the coherence of the bereaved's base of relationship to the deceased. They can parallel in magnitude and effect the shock and dislocation experienced in response to bereavement occurring under conditions of external trauma.

TRAUMA AS DEFINED BY THE MAGNITUDE OF CHANGE IN THE RELATIONSHIP TO THE DECEASED

Among the more powerful aspects of life change that is perceived as "trauma" stem from the magnitude of its overwhelming and overpowering nature. Adaptation is not automatic in situations where change proceeds rapidly, negatively, and requires major changes in one's life. On the negative side of life change events, small amounts of life threat or pain may be difficult to handle, but we consider them as stressors that fall within the range of stimuli that persons can cope with. Large magnitudes of threat or pain, however, are more likely to be considered stressors of traumatic proportion, because of the larger assault upon one's well-being, homeostasis, and existence. They typically require greater amount of coping resources to handle them, and they have the potential to make a larger confrontation with one's previous worldview (Janoff-Bulman, 1992; Kauffman, 2002).

One would not dispute that the untimely loss of Scott is a sad and shocking event. Had Scott died in an accidental fall in the home, and had Sharon discovered the body, his death would have been untimely, and the confrontation with his body would have been shocking. Here, too, the safety and security of the home would have been damaged. From the perspective of the circumstances of the death, such an accidental death would be highly unsettling and potentially overwhelming to the point of being traumatic.

From the relational aspect, the challenge of relating to Scott and managing the transition of the relationship with him as a living being to one who is no longer alive in the physical world would be a challenge as well. Yet there is another element, Scott's taking of his own life, which introduces an additional level of traumatic upheaval. Scott's strengths and weaknesses, his love for his family, and his status as a fallible human being have been present all along. And yet, by the fact of his suicide, by the trail of pain and anguish that his action will bring to Sharon and his family, grieving his loss will in all likelihood be transformed (Rynearson, 2001, 2006). The nagging questions that may surface in any bereavement may be asked here as well: "Why, why, why?" "How could you do this to me and to us?" "How could you be so selfish?" These are the words of persons who have lost loved ones. But the shock and challenge to the representation of the deceased, the nature of the change in how he or she is now perceived, and potential changes in the meaning of the pre-death relationship are whipsawed in cases of suicide.

Thus the traumas of suicide are many and occur at multiple levels. One set of elements stems from the objective features of the death at one's own hand. They relate to the social and religious taboos as well as the tear in social fabric caused by such deaths. Often experienced as occurring without warning or without clear-cut signals understandable by those closest to the victim, many aspects of suicide are shocking and shatter one's previous worldview. At the same time, however, suicide does not only attack the fabric of the survivor's life and organization of the broader world. Suicide serves to attack the organization of the representations of the person who has died. It destabilizes many aspects of the relationship with him or her.

The components related to the subjective personal organization of the deceased and the relationship to him or her are sorely challenged. Who is and was the deceased? Part of the answer includes the psychological experience of suicide as related to the "choice" of death as it involves the bereaved. In ways that are not mutually exclusive, the bereaved often may face thoughts and feelings connected to the death as an attack upon them, as well as alternative options, the suicide as occurring despite the relationship. Survivors of suicide respond with strong disruptive feelings that empirically meet most people's qualifications for external objective trauma. At the same time, however, the "perpetrator" of the death of the victim may be experienced as the same "perpetrator" who has harmed the survivor. In this way, the psychological organization of the deceased may be drastically challenged. And of course, the relationship to the deceased is also complicated by the deceased's involvement in the death. Ultimately, at the same time that the trauma of a suicide is disruptive to one's sense of the predictability and stability of the external world, it also can be extremely disruptive to the relationship to the deceased (Jordan & McIntosh, 2010). The relationship and the death story, which includes the harm done to the deceased and the harm done to the survivors, ensure that the psychological experience of the loss on Track II is sorely taxed—often to the point of a traumatic experience.

> Suicide attacks the very organization of the representations of the person who has died.

LESSONS FROM TRAUMA FOR INTERPERSONAL LOSS

In the trauma field, following exposure to trauma, it is the combination of appraisal, behavior, cognition, and physiological response that is connected to the external stressor in our diagnosis of post-traumatic distress. Even so, in trauma, we go beyond the stressor event's objective characteristics to explain the contributing factors and the mechanism by which the event and its interpretation, both consciously and unconsciously, serve to produce the response we see. Events by themselves do not serve as the explanation as to why some individuals develop stress responses to the event and some do not. Events by themselves require that the individual classify them, at conscious and unconscious levels, as to their undesirability, their shock value, and the magnitude of the disruption of one's worldview and life course. On top of this, there is an individual or idiopathic contribution to the experience of response to traumatic stress that is ultimately expressed in the individual's response. A variety of mitigating and buffering characteristics and emotional responses interact with coping, the individual's resources, and the degree of social support to contribute to the prediction of the manner in which the individual adapts to the stressor. All these mediate whether the individual will experience the stressful life event as an overwhelming and shattering experience (a) of traumatic proportions and (b) accompanied by behavioral and emotional difficulties that do not resolve.

Life-threatening events and risk to self and other exist on a continuum of exposure. For example, one may be exposed to life threat via a single event (e.g., being shot at by a single bullet) or multiple events, (occurring over weeks or years, e.g., in military combat and civilian experiences in war ravaged areas). Motor vehicle trauma may involve being struck by a car and injured, or it might involve being trapped in a flaming vehicle for some time. The nature of the threat in all these situations is never a uniform event although they are serious and stressful. Logically and psychologically, experiences contain various degrees and various levels of threatening exposure.

If we draw parallels to bereavement, we may arrive at a number of interesting conclusions. If bereavement is a stressful life event triggering a process that may be experienced as being of traumatic proportions, we allow parity in aspects of our thinking about trauma and bereavement. For at the point where we do for bereavement what we have done for trauma (i.e., when we establish an elastic framework to understand that bereavements can be experienced as more or less disruptive, irrespective of the objective characteristics of the loss), we can extend and adapt with flexibility a concept of "traumatic" bereavement that can accommodate the wide range of variations we have been describing. As with any exposure to stress, the response to loss involves conscious and unconscious appraisal and is mediated by coping, resources, social support, and a variety of indicators associated with demographic and other variables. All of these influence both the biopsychosocial responses of Track I functioning and the features connected to the person who lived and has now died. These are associated on Track II with the nature of the ongoing bond and relationship to the deceased.

The general approach to assessment and intervention at the trauma/bereavement interface requires sensitivity to both axes of the experience: (1) attack on the biopsychosocial functioning and life structure (which is often exacerbated under conditions of life threat to self or other), and (2) the attack on the previously constructed relationship and its implications for the ongoing relationship bond with the now deceased significant other.

In the area of integration of self-experience, there is another underlying commonality to trauma and loss, which is only partially reflected in symptom outcome. Decades of research evaluating the impact of loss have found that the loss operates with the potential to change various aspects of an individual's view of things and him- or herself (Lehman, Wortman, & Williams, 1987; Rubin & Malkinson, 2001; R. Shalev, 1999; Tamir, 1987). The experience of change by the bereaved is often quite pronounced, whereas the extent of measurable change by the observer and by the bereaved is often less clear (R. Shalev, 1999). These changes to the integration and organization of self are common to bereavement and nonbereavement trauma. They constitute a response to the crisis that has challenged the individual to reappraise, reorganize, and make new meanings that incorporate the events and their aftermath (Neimeyer et al., 2000; Rando, 1993, 2000). The changes in the self-view and the worldview, reported by many, constitute a fundamental similarity between the fields of trauma and bereavement, in that the underlying awareness of self and world changes (Parkes, 1975; Raphael & Martinek, 1997). For example, there is often a greater sense of vulnerability, a greater feeling of exposure to external events beyond one's control, and many other features that involve recognizing that things can no longer be seen as they once were (Janoff-Bulman, 1992; Kauffman, 2002). These require mourning too.

And yet, the disruptions and attacks on the organization, experience, and accessibility of thoughts and feelings about the now deceased loved one are themselves highly susceptible to qualifying for the name *traumatic bereavement.*

The implications of this may be summarized for the mix of bereavement and trauma in a number of ways:

1. Both trauma as life threat to self and other and as the experience of bereavement exist on a continuum. The extent as well as the nature of the psychological upheaval in one's life in all circumstances are continuous rather than merely present or absent. Phenomenologically and psychologically, there are varying degrees and various levels of perceived life-shaking exposure occurring at behavioral, conscious, physiological, and

unconscious levels for both trauma and bereavement (Bar-On, 1991; D. S. Weiss & Marmar, 1997).

2. It is apparent that in the long run, partial as well as full-blown symptoms of dysfunction characterize only some individuals exposed to trauma, bereavement, or both. Most of those so exposed do not develop extreme, chronic, and dysfunctional reactions. Overall, it can be said that absence of pervasive and persistent dysfunction characterizes the majority of the individuals subjected to these events in their responses over time (Bonanno, 2009; Briere, 2004; Galea et al., 2002) but that some types of trauma exposure and loss are particularly significant risk factors for the development of chronic and problematic responses.

3. In cases of exposure to events classified by objective criteria as "traumatagenic," some individuals will develop persistent symptoms and some of these will meet diagnostic criteria for a variety of disorders (Koren, Arnon, & Klein, 1999; van der Kolk et al., 1996). The same can be said for the experience of exposure to bereavement. In the case of individuals exposed to bereavement under conditions of external life threat, or relational threat, only some will develop symptoms (Rubin et al., 2003; Rubin, Malkinson, & Witztum, 2011).

4. In all these cases, the need to re-create a network of coherence, safety, security, meaning, and continuity is part of the response to these life changes (Herman, 1992; Neimeyer, 2001). There is also a need to integrate, as well as to be able to filter out, elements of these experiences.

5. An individual's world may crash around him or her as a result of a stressor or a bereavement that is subjectively experienced as traumatic or overwhelming but not necessarily perceived to be so from an objective perspective.

6. Ultimately, there exist multiple variations of traumatic events as there are multiple variations of experience of bereavement events. The mix of objective, subjective, and symptomatic criteria for assessing response to bereavement and trauma creates a situation where the distinctions between so-called traumatic and nontraumatic events or bereavements are not justified. We advocate working with an inclusive vision of trauma and an inclusive vision of bereavement—in which both visions take into account the fundamental notion that individual interpretation of life experiences is a feature of the experience.

Life-threatening events and risk to self and other exists on a continuum of exposure.

Symptoms of dysfunction characterize only some individuals exposed to trauma or bereavement.

An individual's world may crash due to a stressor or bereavement subjectively experienced as traumatic or overwhelming.

The need to re-create coherence, safety, security, meaning, and continuity are part of response to life changes encompassing bereavement and trauma.

> The mix of objective, subjective, and symptomatic responses to bereavement and trauma create situations where the distinctions between so-called traumatic and nontraumatic events or bereavements are not justified.

CLINICAL SUMMARY

To understand trauma in bereavement, one is always on more solid ground using both tracks of the Two-Track Model.

For the bereaved, the pain and disruption of loss and the reorganization necessitated by loss are potentially very difficult. When aspects of the relationship to the now deceased other includes what is considered to be "new" information that serves to attack the way the deceased had been understood to date, we can be dealing with a challenge of traumatic proportion on the relational track of bereavement. In such cases, it is not the circumstances of the death but the magnitude of change in relating to the deceased that is of traumatic proportion and elicits the anxiety, intrusive thoughts, and/or avoidant strategies to cope with the loss.

Make no mistake, the discrepancy between the organization of the other as he or she was related to before and after the new information would have been shocking and of traumatic proportions had death *not* occured. But it is the death itself that has the ultimate potential to derail the processes of assimilation and accommodation that accompany such situations. As we mentioned earlier, examples of this include the discovery of facts that are of such magnitude as to damage and possibly shatter the internal image of the deceased. Managing to hold onto both the memories and affects connected to the prior experience with the beloved other, while absorbing the devastating new information about the revolting characteristics of that same person, challenges the bereaved to come to some new organization of the relationship to the deceased. The horrible news can be felt to be so at odds with the prior view that the image of the deceased and the relationship to him or her may remain in a fragmented state and one that is also characterized by anxiety, intrusions, avoidance, and the like. In cases such as these, and in circumstances that are similar but much less dramatic (such as the discovery of financial or sexual betrayals post-loss, the existence of other "secrets," etc.), the bereavement may become traumatic because the relationship has been attacked, and this combines with the attack upon the representations that the fact of death mobilizes as well.

Ultimately, entering into the mourning process and grieving for the deceased will bring with them a diminution of the overwhelming involvement with these same grief and mourning processes. Indeed both overwhelming involvement and the lessening of that involvement are the hallmarks of the typical response to the loss of a meaningful relationship. The vectors of external trauma associated with bereavement can interfere with the entry to and exit from the active bereavement process. The interference can result in heightened difficulties on the biopsychosocial aspects of the response to loss or on the relational aspects of the relationship to the deceased. The reorganization and resumption of connection to the memories, affects, and experience of the relationship to the deceased can be complicated by the traumatic vectors of bereavement.

Bereavement is difficult because it requires a transition from relating to the loved person as a living other and the need to relate to him or her as someone important to us who is no longer living a physical life alongside us. There is always some degree of shock and sense of betrayal in having to integrate the pre-loss experience and memories of the other with the new information that this once living and interacting person is now deceased. In every case of loss, the new information that the loved one is now "a dead person" is sufficiently at odds with the prior view so as to be difficult to process. Yet this is exacerbated when confounded with a major challenge to fundamental aspects of how the deceased was perceived. The need to rework and rebalance the relationship to the narrative, memories, thoughts, feelings, and associations vis-à-vis the relationship to the deceased is the challenge of all bereavement. When it occurs in the context of a major attack on the previous organization and understanding of who the deceased was, however, we are discussing the trauma within the relational track.

Without a doubt, by pushing the boundaries of traumatic bereavement, we risk weakening the desirable attempts to classify, assess, and understand the interaction of trauma and bereavement. Our intent is to assist and challenge those concerned with the study of trauma and bereavement to better classify, assess, and ultimately understand that interface. We hope that researchers, clinicians, theoreticians, and others will look with a sharper eye upon current schemas of trauma in bereavements. The two tracks of bereavement and the multiple dimensions associated with response to loss can assist the attempt to clarify what is traumatic in bereavement.

6

Therapeutic Work With the
Relationship to the Deceased

*I*n this final introductory chapter* on the Two-Track Model of Bereavement, we demonstrate therapeutic focus on the continuing relationship to the deceased. We clarify how the Track II focus in therapy can be used to orient the clinician's work with examples of treatment. Earlier, we discussed how one adaptive task or "goal" of mourning is in the domain of biopsychosocial functioning (Track I). The expectation is for the bereaved to live in as full and rich a manner as possible in a reality from which the deceased is absent. In contrast, the adaptive task or goals of working through loss on Track II is to achieve a way to live on with the memories and feelings associated with the deceased. This translates to achieving a connection and accessibility to the complex of mental events associated with the deceased without being trapped there (Rubin, 2000).

The death of a loved one brings with it a psychological threat to our connection with that significant other. With our connection threatened, we are motivated to seek closeness and rejoin that person at the same time that person is no longer with us in the physical world. This activates the wish to connect and rejoin the person whose connection to us is threatened. At the same time, seeking to be close can be incredibly painful and difficult as the body is responding in the alarm mode of threatened separation. This provokes a sense of desperation rooted in the perceived threat to well-being.

Intense longing, sadness at his or her absence, and heightened involvement with the things that link one to the deceased may become pronounced and salient. These often involve a form of alertness and attention to things that might serve as harbingers of the return of the sought-after loved one. The range of stimuli associated with another is virtually limitless. These can involve the five senses of touch,

---

* Portions of this chapter are adapted from Malkinson, R., Rubin, S. S., & Witztum, E. (2006). "Therapeutic issues and the relationship to the deceased: Working clinically with the Two-Track Model of Bereavement." Death Studies, 30(9), 797–815. Copyright Taylor & Francis Ltd, http://www.informaworld.com. Reprinted by permission of the publisher.

smell, sight, sound, and taste. Anything that is connected to the deceased and was associated with him or her can serve as a trigger for the longing and wish for connection. A reduction in the intensity of such longing and wish to connect generally proceeds with time. And yet, for many persons, the framework of time is not measured in days or weeks or even months, but in the passage of years.

It is useful to think of Bowlby's (1969–1980) portrayal of this form of searching phenomenon and how he linked it to the framework and origins of human development. Such searching served as a means of fostering reconnection with the "lost other." The seeking out of the other along with the distress experienced serve to foster connection with the lost other. Bowlby's inclusion of the many ways in which separation distress serves to communicate the need for renewed connection in mammals and young children assists us in thinking about the "seeking" behavior. It opens up portals to consider how renewed connection with the other may be addressed and modified following death.

The fact that the painful longing and pining for the other are so hard to bear can lead to the idea that successful mourning is the absence of undue longing for the deceased. Indeed, often the "deactivation" of longing and wishing for connection to the deceased is a significant outcome of the grief and mourning process. Measured in terms of the diminution of pain, such a view has deserved credibility. But when also measured in terms of the renegotiation of an ongoing connection to the deceased, the reduction in searching or pining for the deceased does not address the issue of what kind of ongoing and fundamental connection to the deceased remains.

The fact that the wish to be rejoined with the deceased can serve both as a bridge and as a barrier to connecting with the broad conglomerate and inner world of associations, memories, thoughts, and feelings regarding the deceased may seem paradoxical at first. And yet, all of us can recognize times when distress can interfere with the ability to calm down and can derail the ability to connect with both ourselves and others. The more subtle range, depth, and types of links and bonds with the deceased are accessed and experienced differently in stress and non-distress modes.

Thinking of grief and mourning as processes during which the bereaved assimilate and accommodate to their changed circumstances is accurate. At the same time, however, it is important to recognize that grief and mourning also combine emotional, cognitive, and somatic responses that connect the bereaved both to the world and to the deceased and proceed in nonlinear fashion with many ups and downs. When proceeding adaptively, the accommodation and assimilation will allow for the reworking and reintegration of the bonds with the deceased into the bereaved's past, present, and future life narrative (Bowlby, 1980; Klass et al., 1996; Malkinson et al., 2000).

In dealing with bereavement, we believe that there are many reasons to focus intervention following loss on aspects of the relationship to the deceased and its meaning for the bereaved. In this chapter, we consider interventions following loss of a spouse. Our thesis is that reworking relationships serves important functions and can function as an important key to allowing people to live on. This assists them in taking up authorship of their life narratives, living fully in the world with themselves and others, and retaining the connection to the deceased.

It is a psychological truism today that engagement in supportive and positive relationships with significant meaningful figures provides support for the individual (Mikulincer & Shaver, 2003). Emotional flexibility and positive life energy are by-products of this as well. Loss and bereavement have the potential to upset the inner psychological relationship with these persons to whom we have important connections. The significance of the connections to the deceased does not minimize the importance of connections to others. Yet it does point to the importance of reworking and reorganizing the connection to the person who died. Following this reworking, the value of that relationship can continue to serve adaptive, supportive, and interpersonal functions. The connection to the one who was loved and alive and is no longer so is a dyadic story as told, communicated, and experienced by the survivor. It is complicated and can be almost totally derailed because of the disruption of death and what that means. At the same time, acting together with or independently of the disruption that death always brings to a relationship are the traumas associated with the circumstance of the loss (Rynearson, 2001).

The significance of relationships for intervention following bereavement is further developed at this time. We set forth two cases, one associated with a psychodynamic-existential perspective, and the other, with a cognitive behavioral approach. Our concern is not with technique or theoretical orientation but with the phenomena involved and how the therapies played out. The clients involved reviewed the details of the cases below and generously permitted us to share them with you.

> The adaptive task working through loss on Track II is to achieve a way to live on with the memories and feelings associated with the deceased. This translates to achieving a connection and accessibility to the complex of mental events associated with the deceased without being trapped there.
>
> The significance of the connections to the deceased does not minimize the importance of connections to others.

CASE ONE: THE SUDDEN DEATH OF THE HUSBAND WHO WAS ALSO MARRIED TO HIS WORK

Marnie Z. came for a treatment consultation to SSR reluctantly. What was the use of therapy if she believed there was no solution possible for her emotional situation? Aged 60, she was a handsome woman whose sadness and tension were pronounced. Two years after the death of her husband, she was financially secure but far from emotionally so. During the years of marriage, Marnie explained that she and her husband's lives had been closely knit. They had established and run a successful accounting firm together for 3 decades. They had raised two children together. Their son was unmarried while their married daughter had moved away several years earlier.

In our first meeting, Marnie indicated that she had lost interest in her life: "I want to die, not to live." Although the initial remark was not immediately explored so early in the initial encounter, by the end of the first session it was clear that suicidal concerns were not an issue at this time. Marnie was on antidepressant medication prescribed by her physician. He had recommended psychological treatment, and Marnie eventually accepted the recommendation after her children had also strongly suggested it. Nonetheless, she was resigned to a future every bit as bleak as her present circumstances.

In the initial meetings, Marnie was asked to share the circumstances of her husband's death. Zack had died unexpectedly late at night at the office. He was only found when their son went to look for him at the office. Seeing his father's body slumped in his chair, he had called the emergency services, and after they arrived, he went home to tell his mother what had happened. The police initially responded to the death scene as a potential violent death, and this only added to the shock of his loss. Natural causes due to a heart attack were soon confirmed as the cause of death. For Marnie, a more significant complicating factor was the fact that on the day of his death, she and Zack had quarreled and had separated without saying goodbye.

This led to an exploration of their relationship in general. Marnie described her relationship with Zack in very positive terms. "We had friendship and a partnership, and we cared deeply for each other. My husband was a great friend. He loved me. He was quiet, industrious, and warm; a real *mensch*." Among the things she mentioned spontaneously was troublesome imagery. She was bothered by the visual image of the funeral as well as a sense of partial unreality about the death: "I particularly remember their placing him in the ground. That picture comes back. I tell myself this is a dream, a nightmare that will end. And yet, the opposite of this too, I accept the reality."

Since the loss, Marnie also found it hard to look at photographs and videos showing Zack. Whenever she did so, these stimuli brought home to her his loss, and she responded with feelings of agitation and unrest. At the first-anniversary memorial service she had listened to a colleague's speech. He had focused on Zack's work ethic and how extraordinarily devoted to work he had been. Marnie said: "I listened and thought to myself, he essentially killed himself working. I had seen the writing on the wall. Work, always working. In the last weeks I told him I could not bear him working so hard, and that I was going to quit work. He put on a poker face and said, 'So quit.'"

REFLECTION

Marnie presented as a woman whose psychological and behavioral life organizations had been interwoven with her husband, Zack. His death was a major blow to her and required that she reorganize her life and goals to meet the changed circumstances. The death of a spouse is painful and challenging under virtually all circumstances. The fact that this couple also shared a work environment served to limit the ability of work relationships and environment to serve as a buffer and alternative support system.

Viewed from the perspective of the Two-Track Model of Bereavement, Marnie showed herself to be having difficulties on both tracks of her response Track I (biopsychosocial functioning) was plagued by significant dysfunction and a reduction of life energies. Marnie was depressed and anxious, had difficulty sleeping, and her appetite was not good. On the features associated with her personal meaning structures, she questioned God and was angry at him for what he had done to Zack (Neimeyer, 2001). Her social circle was now constricted. She had drastically curtailed her involvement in the world with family friends and associates. By selling the business she had adequate funds to be independent, but in a reclusive rather than an open structure. Despite her discomfort, Marnie's motivation for treatment was limited, but it was possible to engage her. She was involved with her children and grandchildren, and this kept her emotionally and behaviorally connected to life. On Track II (relationship to the deceased), the nature of her current relationship to Zack and his death were also problematic. She found it hard to encounter pictures and images and actively avoided them. Memories of her relationship with Zack were often general, and the details of some of their interactions were not readily available. The chapter appendix contains a schematic rating of her responses according to the clinician rating scale presented in Chapter 3.

The Initial Phase of Treatment

In the first month of treatment, Marnie asked two questions: "What does it mean to love oneself?" and "What does it mean to let go of the deceased?" These questions conveyed her underlying difficulty: How could she take care of herself and be attentive to her needs while still grieving her husband's death? If she did not let go, she remained stuck, but how much did she really wish to transform the relationship? How much of that relationship can be transformed or released from being frozen so as to flow anew?

Three dream fragments illustrate the experiential counterpart of the questions posed by Marnie.

> We were traveling and there was a revolution in South America. They took us to a big room and separated everyone. I needed to go to the bathroom, but they don't let you go without someone. I want a place by myself. Outside in the streets, I recognize nothing. I don't know how to get back. I see my son's therapist, who lives there. She brings me back to the place where we were staying.

Exploration of the dream led to the following threads. Marnie's overall metaphor was being in a foreign country, far away from everything familiar of the life she had lived. She described her sense of what was going on for her now. She used the word "we" but there was no mention of Zack in the dream nor was she reunited with him. Being separated from other people reminded her of the terrorists who seized a foreign airliner and flew the plane to Uganda. A hostage-rescue mission carried out by the Israel Defense Forces commando unit at Entebbe Airport in Uganda on July 4, 1976, saved the passengers. The Jews among the passengers had been separated from the non-Jewish passengers and were in great danger for their lives. Metaphorically, one can see how the death of Zack had affected her. Marnie's life was turned upside down; she was hijacked, and the themes of being separated and sensing danger yet of wanting privacy were intermixed. Hovering throughout are echoes of a rescue when all hope seemed lost. A positive figure, the son's therapist, returns her to safety. She does not take note of the fact that her son's therapist had referred her to her present therapist.

At the same time, Marnie's feelings toward Zack and her tension with him can be seen from another dream that same night.

> We are in the office. I remind Zack that people live there, that we are in someone else's property. We continue to clean, to take/pack things. I throw things out, Zack continues to work. I am separating from the business, but Zack is not.

And soon yet another dream fragment:

> Zack appears and I know he is dead. We all know that he has died and they look at us. Instead of being happy that he is here, [I think] "I don't have the strength to go through this again." [I have] no happiness or joy on seeing him. Only fear, fear that I will have to go through this again.

REFLECTION

The dream material offered spontaneously at this early stage of treatment communicated Marnie's sense of being lost, and her quest to learn how to return to safety. At the same time there was the question of how to deal with Zack, who is a source of tension, at least as long as he remains unchanged. The image of Zack as working no matter what the circumstances was part of the conflict between them. Even when Marnie can accept that he is dead, the question remains of when it is time to make changes and to separate from some things. These three dream vignettes reiterated basic themes of Marnie's experience, with particular emphasis on her sense of tension, the disruption in her life, and the negatively tinged mixed feelings that his memory stirred up for Marnie.

The focus of this phase of treatment was upon restarting the narrative and emotional connection to the generally positive aspects of the relationship to Zack. In this initial treatment phase, themes of anger and longing emerged repeatedly. We explored together Marnie's feelings of anger at many people who had not sufficiently cared for Zack or who had troubled him. Dealing with her anger at family members for their lack of attention to her husband when alive led to her anger also at God for taking Zack. There were also dreams such as the one shared earlier of Zack being in the wrong place and her anger at him. She was ambivalent about her anger, feeling that it trapped her. If she spoke about her feelings and shared what she felt with her family members, she was afraid she would regret the outcome and that they would withdraw from her. But if she kept her feelings bottled inside, she feared the consequences of being in relationships where she felt closed down and inauthentic.

Tolerating the exploration of her feelings, Marnie was encouraged to talk about them first in the therapy. This allowed Marnie to regain a sense of balance and connection with others. As a result of the exploration in treatment, she moved more consistently and openly to express aspects of her anger toward friends and relatives. Soon her anger at Zack for his overworking and his failings in areas of the family came to the fore. Themes of her caring for him and the frustration she felt with him repeatedly alternated in the sessions of the first months of treatment, but they fostered significant changes. Opening up the anger allowed Marnie to feel better about thinking of Zack and led to greater freedom in her interaction with the world. Three months into the treatment Marnie had changed her hairstyle, had become more assertive, and commented that "Zack, after he died, sent me S, my new woman friend and you SSR as my therapist in order to make my life better."

The following exchange reflects the change in her attitude evident at the 6-month evaluation of her treatment:

SSR: If you had seen God 3 years ago, knowing then what you know now, what would you have asked him?
Marnie: To let me and Zack grow old together.
SSR: And if God had refused?
Marnie: A while ago I would have asked him to take me too, but now I have chosen life.

Summary and Commentary

Treatment ended 18 months after it began, and Marnie experienced herself a changed woman. The bereavement focus that had brought her to treatment was important and remained a theme to return to throughout the 18 months of our contact. But the psychotherapy net was cast wider, and the issues that emerged led to a review of many aspects of her life that were significant in helping Marnie understand part of how she had become the girl, wife, mother, and woman she had been—and to open up the possibility of new directions (Golan, 1975). Following the story of her life issues turned the treatment for Marnie into a significant journey on its own. It clearly went beyond what one might call "grief-based therapy," which would be understood as an intervention focused specifically on assisting the bereaved come to grips with the loss and mourning. At the same time that the treatment was casting a wider net, however, the original impetus for treatment and many of the issues explored remained intimately tied up with the bereavement's impact upon Marnie's life. Table 6.1 in the chapter appendix summarizes the clinician rating of Marnie's pre- and post-therapy statuses according to the Two-Track Model of Bereavement.

Where to focus the treatment was an important decision. It was possible to concentrate on improving functioning. Marnie gave numerous indications of her difficulties in experiencing her life, and this might lead one to design an intervention program focused on these difficulties. The depression, the withdrawal from social contacts, and the manifestations of life changes that Marnie had undergone, and had not yet adjusted to, were quite prominent. The pre-loss and ongoing relationship to Zack were of more interest to Marnie, and she was accessible most easily on those areas. Marnie's disinterest in focusing on change, coupled with her willingness to talk about her relationship with Zack, reinforced the value of keeping the relationship to Zack at the forefront of the treatment.

The focus of the bereavement-related aspects of the treatment was to be concerned with many aspects of the pre-loss and post-loss relationship. This tack proved successful in building a therapeutic alliance. The discussion of her relationship and her experiences facilitated changes in biopsychosocial functioning.

The generally positive nature of the pre-loss relationship, the sudden occurrence of the loss in the midst of an interpersonal conflict, and the way Marnie and Zack had lived all pointed to the significance of the relationship for Marnie's psychological and emotional world. So much of their adult lives were shared, and now he was no longer there for her. Zack's death did not sever their connection, of course, but the bereavement process to date had not sufficiently freed Marnie to assimilate and accommodate to a changed internal and external reality. Marnie remained connected to him, and the disagreements at the time of death complicated her ability to grieve as well. Metaphorically, one might say it was as if wife and husband had tied their lives together and were linked by a lifeline on their journey over the years of their marriage. His plunge from life threatened to pull Marnie down with him. Although Marnie had arrested her own fall, she was still unable to proceed on her own journey. There are stories of climbers who were unable to save their partners and chose to cut the rope to prevent themselves from being pulled down too. Yet severing the connection to the deceased spouse is not the only option for allowing partners to continue on. It is possible to maintain an emotionally secure psychological connection and also to move forward. How to help Marnie move forward on her life's journey while transforming her connection to Zack from a physical link to a kind of "wireless" connection became the focus of the first phase of treatment.

This was most pronounced in the initial months of treatment where the focus on the relationship with Zack had been predominant. In those first months, significant changes occurred, which allowed Marnie freedom to explore her world and to return to life that she had not permitted herself earlier. In this treatment, the focus on the relationship to Zack (Track II) resulted in a significant improvement in her functioning and a broader reorientation toward an involvement with life. The depression, anxiety, and constriction in facing life began to change soon after treatment began, and by the conclusion of treatment, many elements of personal change and growth had emerged as well. The early sessions allowed Marnie to explore and discuss what her relationship had been with Zack; they also allowed her to explore and discuss her mixed feelings. Marnie belonged to the group of therapy cases where the focus on the relationship to the deceased, both during life together and after the death, was instrumental and significant for effecting change in many other life areas. This is in contrast to persons entering treatment and where the intervention serves more as a vehicle for resumption of function and less as a nodal point for life exploration. Encouraging her to express and explore her thoughts and feelings was an integral part of treatment. Her husband Zack had been central to her life, serving both as partner and as he whose connection to her was like a part of her very self.

Following Zack's sudden death, a generally positive relationship derailed, and access to the storehouse of positive feelings and memories was essentially blocked. The anger and frustration Marnie felt toward Zack but which she did not follow through and explore resulted in a truncated and incomplete dialogue with herself, her interpersonal environment, and her relationship to her husband. Given the opportunity to open the dialogue, to deal with her anger, and to experience other blocked feelings, she was able her to reconnect to her deceased husband—and to become stronger as a result. Positive changes followed as she continued to explore the meanings of her life and the possibilities that were opening up to her. These included renegotiating her relationship with Zack and its meaning for her, not as the central focus of our work, but as an extension of it. Improperly understood, the case of Marnie risks taking us back to "classical" formulations, which conceptualized the grief process as one of withdrawing energy from the relationship so that one could resume life's functions with renewed energy (Freud, 1917; Rubin, et al., 2000). Today, we speak of the ongoing relationship and continuing bond to the deceased—and consider the accessibility and nature of that bond as a domain within itself. The wish to make contact with the deceased, the physical longing for him or her, is a powerful feature of grief. Yet it is critical to understand the particulars of who is being longed for, and what that person meant to the bereaved. In the case of a close relationship such as a spousal one, much more is needed to understand what is involved. The exploration of a nuanced narrative, complete with general and specific examples of the deceased, and the nature of the relationship are of great importance in understanding who and what has been "lost."

The initial focus on relationship to the deceased and the subsequent exploration of the relationship were the most important feature of this therapy.

CASE TWO: COMPLICATIONS FOLLOWING MORE COMPLICATED AND TRAUMATIC BEREAVEMENT

Fiona came to treatment to RM after losing her husband under very traumatic circumstances 9 months earlier. Her husband went to visit friends and promised to be back home around midnight. Fiona was notified that he had been murdered by terrorists. Fiona's case involved the loss of a spouse under traumatic circumstances without personal exposure to the event and an interpersonal loss.

Fiona, in her early 50s, was left with two sons (ages 22 and 26). The terror-related circumstances of the death entitled Fiona to state assistance (financial as well as psychological). She was referred to psychological treatment, and as a victim of a terror attack. She declined a training course to assist her with returning to work and explained that financially she didn't need to work, and psychologically any type of work would be too stressful for her. Issues related to her marital relationship at the initial phase of therapy were not disclosed.

During the first sessions, Fiona retold in detail the last evening with her husband and her worries over his failure to return home. "I kept awake for his return and sensed that something terrible was going to happen. When there was a knock on the door I feared that I was going to hear bad news. I froze when one of the policemen broke the news. I was speechless." She described how from that moment onward, she was unable to function during the day and couldn't sleep at night. Life had become a horror for her.

In these initial sessions, she described her difficulties in functioning in everyday life. She spoke of her feelings of anxiety, depression, insomnia, and restlessness, as well as loss of interest in life. She talked briefly about her husband and their relationship, hinting that they quarreled on the evening of his leaving home for the last time. He said he wanted her to go with him and she refused. They argued, and he left slamming the door.

FORMULATION AND REFLECTION

From the perspective of the Two-Track Model of Bereavement, Fiona's narrative communicated anxiety, depression, sleep problems, general functioning difficulties, and PTSD-like symptoms. These suggested an initial approach to treatment focused on Track I's attention to symptomatic functioning. Fiona refrained from elaborating on the nature of the marital relationship. The therapist RM hypothesized that a possible conflictual marital relationship (related to the second track) prevented her from connecting to a "painful" and sensitive part of her story. In Fiona's narrative, the elements of the trauma (Track I) were more pronounced and we postulated that these elements should receive priority in the first phase of therapy.

We will briefly describe the initial phase of this treatment, then move to the second phase and describe the treatment with Fiona on the relationship with the deceased (Track II) as the treatment progressed. With regard to the biopsychosocial functioning of Track I, therapy during the first three months was organized based on the assessment of Fiona's traumatic response to the loss of her husband. In the initial phase, two main issues were central: establishing a good rapport with Fiona and creating a safe haven. The latter aimed at helping her regain a sense of inner control over her feelings of anxiety and depression. Restoring even partial functioning as well as attending to her health was assumed to have strengthening potential. Use of cognitive interventions included thought stopping, thought restructuring, breathing exercises, and her choice of physical activity. For Fiona, swimming was a way to encourage her to get out of the house and perhaps meet people. Also, she was encouraged to be more involved with her sons, and, at her request, there were three joint sessions with them.

During these months there was a marked reduction in Fiona's anxiety symptoms, her sleeping improved, and she was more active in taking care of herself, her sons, and the house (cooking and baking, sorting laundry, bills, papers, etc.).

Track II (Relationship): As the first anniversary of her husband's death approached, she became restless and discussed her ambivalence toward her deceased husband. She missed him but felt very angry when she remembered him. She spoke for the first time about their complicated and conflictual relationship, saying this about her immediate response on being told of his death:

> I was furious with him and the way he left the house, he verbally abused me
> for refusing to join him so I wished him dead. Upon getting the horrible news,
> my initial reaction was one of relief. But he had some good things about him
> and I feel terrible for how I felt.

As she unfolded her story, it became clear that conflictual pre-loss relationship combined with the traumatic circumstances of the loss could provide an explanation for her avoidance of discussing their relationship and her difficulties mourning the loss. Anger toward her late husband and guilt feelings for feeling angry with him prevented her from experiencing the pain and the sadness of his loss, an experience which later in the treatment she was able to express. What was to be explored in the treatment was the search for a meaning that would enable Fiona to think of her life without her husband and experience the pain involved without feeling guilty for what she thought were "terrible thoughts." Fiona would be helped to examine the many layers of her ambivalent relationship with her husband—of closeness and distancing, of love and hate, and of dependency—and to find a sense of connection despite past traumatic memories of their relationship. Letter writing to her late husband was the intervention chosen as a way to explore their married life and gain a sense of control over her negative emotions, which would result in a more balanced way of remembering him.

> Letter writing is a strategic cognitive–constructivist intervention to help clients with complicated grief as a way of reorganizing life following the loss, and reconstructing the disrupted life's narrative (Malkinson & Witztum, 2007; see also Chapters 9 and 10 in this volume).

In Fiona's case, applying letter writing required negotiation and a detailed preparing for the possible emotional turmoil she feared it would involve, and we discussed the possible emotional relief as a consequence. Letter writing was used here to assist Fiona to overcome her difficulties (mainly avoidance) and to help her experience negative emotions which she feared would make her "crazy." After a number of sessions Fiona agreed to write to her husband.

In her first letter to her deceased husband, she explained the reason for her writing: "I was asked by Ruth to write to you and tell you what has happened to me after you died." Her writing was a report about life at home with the sons and some thoughts about moving to another house. "Moving to another house would mean leaving some of your belongings, including some of your completed work and equipment, and it makes me feel very upset."

As the letter writing continued, Fiona was able to write about their relationship and how they treated each other. In the session that followed, she talked about a dream she had had about her husband returning home looking at her and smiling; but she felt anxious, fearing that her status as a widow who lost her husband in a terror attack would be rescinded. Her dream seemed to convey the sense of safety she felt with her identity as a widow, who was protected financially and psychologically by the care provided by the state.

In the following letter she wrote to her husband:

> I feared your rage and the way you treated me. You were always very critical of me, saying that I could do more both at home and at work, words that gave rise to many arguments between us. I always worried about our finances and tried to do everything possible to pay our debts. Only towards the end did you express appreciation for my efforts when you said that I was the "minister of finance," and this made me feel better. Now with the financial support I get I worry less, but I realize that you are not here, you are absent, and we miss you a lot.

In this letter, Fiona acknowledges, along with her criticizing her husband, some positive aspects of him and their marriage. There is also a sense of the loss felt by her and her sons. In the following session, she reported she dreamt that her husband was looking for her, and on finding her he looked into her eyes and smiled. She said she was able to look back without being afraid.

After the first anniversary of her husband's death, which Fiona planned carefully, inviting family and friends, she said that she was tense but in a different way, less anxious and less angry. She wrote the following letter:

> My dear, I discussed with Ruth a thought I had about you. I was thinking that although you treated me at times so badly, and I felt so hurt and furious with you, we had some good times, especially during the last period of your life. I thought that during the years when I suffered so much I wanted to leave you and start another life. I had many chances to do so, but I chose to stay with you. Ruth raised the issue of forgiveness. I asked her who should forgive whom? And she asked whom did I think should forgive? This is what I replied: I forgive you my dear for the way you treated me, for the suffering I experienced during so many years, and I cherish the last months of your life when our relationship improved.

Fiona could tolerate the negative memories as she recalled some positive aspects of their married life. Though her journey through letter writing was intense, and at times very difficult, she felt at peace and mainly in more control over her feelings.

Summary and Commentary

Although clinically, both elements of functioning and the relationship with the deceased need to be assessed and addressed, the decision as to what will be the focus of the initial phase of the intervention depends on the narrative told by the bereaved. At times, the traumatic event has an overwhelming effect and holds the bereaved back from approaching the relationship to the deceased. Sometimes talking about the deceased seems to be avoided or blocked and may indicate some difficulties, while at other times the "channel" to this domain is more accessible and can be discussed. Where initial distance from the relationship track may be warranted in early stages of treatment, at some point it is generally included as part of the intervention plan.

Earlier in this book, we discussed how the relationship with the deceased is critical for what the bereavement involves and the centrality of the nature of the relationship with the deceased as the focus of therapy. Not only is a multidimensional perspective essential for assessment, but that assessment should also refer to the magnitude of the elements and their relative primacy in the case presentation. Furthermore, attending to the relative balance allows one to utilize both tracks of the model and to maximize the use of this framework both flexibly and effectively as therapy progresses.

In Fiona's case, the pre-loss conflictual relationship was an important background feature. It was exacerbated when she was notified of the traumatic loss of her husband. Her initial response of relief was mixed with guilt feelings (Track II) which she expressed. She experienced guilt feelings, depression, and anxiety (Track I). Fiona's difficulties in the relationship with her deceased husband (Track II) were initially manifest in symptoms along Track I, biopsychosocial functioning, which were dominant and required initial attention. Therapy commenced with a focus on Track I components but as it progressed the relationship to the deceased became much more the focus of therapy. Table 6.2 in the chapter appendix summarizes the presenting and concluding picture of the therapy.

Understandably, Fiona believed that she should not think nor share her thoughts and feelings with anybody. Given the opportunity to open her "hidden and forbidden" bad thoughts and feelings through letter-writing to her husband allowed her to reconnect to them and overcome her avoidance. The result was that she could experience the range of these shameful feelings and cognitions. Fiona's reworking of the relationship with her husband followed the initial stage of therapeutic rapport building and focusing on relieving the symptomatic difficulties manifest in her functioning. The treatment plan made effective use of both the focus on function and on relationship to the deceased.

CONCLUDING REMARKS ON THERAPY, RELATIONSHIP, AND THE BEREAVEMENT PROCESS

Individuals enter therapy following loss because of discomfort and difficulty. Their difficulties may be manifest in one or both of the domains outlined in the Two-

Track Model of Bereavement. Clinically, one may plan an intervention focused on restoring the bereaved to coping adequately, or better, with the demands of living following loss; such a course includes biopsychosocial features (Track I). Any number of psychological, medical, and community-based interventions may help with such a focus, which is aimed at improving the life functioning of the bereaved. Conversely, one may design an intervention focused on how the bereaved manages the relationship to the complex representations and memories of the person who has died. That focus-on-the-other maintains more of a *relational perspective* specific to the deceased (Track II).

Designing a dual focus is logical, and often the interventions are specifically targeted to address both aspects of the response to loss. Simultaneously and in waves, the bereaved tack between addressing aspects of coping with life's tasks and with issues related to connecting and reworking the relationship to the deceased (Rubin, 1984b, 1985, 1999, 2000; Stroebe, Hansson, Stroebe, & Schut, 2001). Specifying the separate tracks of the Two-Track Model of Bereavement provides a useful perspective on the nature of the response to the death of a significant other. Such a view goes beyond the question of how one greets the world. That question is always relevant in any investigation of how people function adaptively and productively in their lives and considers the extent of distress and dysfunction present. Yet in following loss, the new and highly relevant domain for questioning becomes how one manages the memory of the relationship to the deceased, the loss event, and the degree of preoccupation, longing, and conflict.

The relationship to the deceased, and the manner of reworking the bonds to a person who has died, is an exceedingly important focus for therapy. While we all exist in social matrixes that affect our lives, the relationship to the deceased should be at the forefront of our thinking about what makes bereavement the painful and upsetting experience it is. Many therapists view it this way. They see the significance of response to bereavement as rooted in the fact that it is a response to the death (or loss) of a significant individual. Intervention and formulation are often intertwined, and the manner in which individuals practice psychotherapy has implications for the manner in which they conceptualize and plan their interventions. The nature of the relationship to the deceased, and how it affects the bereaved, is at the heart of the mourning experience (Goss & Klass, 2005; Kasher, 2004). From a linear perspective, it is possible to attempt to describe the majority of the responses to the loss of someone in the following way: "Reality testing has shown that the loved object no longer exists, and it proceeds to demand that all libido shall be withdrawn from its attachment to that object" (Freud, 1917/1957, p. 244).

In line with a less linear perspective and the adoption of a more multivariate model of complexity, it is useful to understand that interpersonal loss can continue to operate throughout one's life. Often, it sets in motion a number of unhooking features. The person bereaved of a significant other can be cast adrift from the social, economic, psychological, and physical anchors of stability and identity. The length of time in which this experience is paramount, and the degree of disruption in life experience, varies significantly. At the center of this process is the loss, through death, of a significant figure, important to the bereaved.

The amount, complexity, and richness of how the deceased is recollected are related, but not identical, to how well the bereaved functions after loss (Adres, 2011; Bar Nadav, 2007; Rubin, 1992). In advocating the Two-Track Model of Bereavement, we emphasize that the dimensions of a person's functioning are but one province or domain reflecting how an individual's personality, life situation, and grieving processes (among other things) influence coping and living following interpersonal loss. How one manages one's life following the loss of a loved one is intimately associated with how the ongoing relationship is with the complex of memories, thoughts, emotions, and needs associated with the person who has died (Silverman, Sherman, Baker, Cait, & Boerner, 2003). These domains of general functioning and relationship to the deceased are related, as both characterize the bereaved individual. What is important to remember, however, is that they are far from identical (Prigerson & Jacobs, 2001).

When it comes to assessing the relationship to the deceased, the fluidity, richness, and depth of the descriptions and memories shared are important. The narrative thrust in therapy has sharpened our awareness of the nature of the stories about our significant others that emerge (Neimeyer et al., 2000). While numerous features are associated with resilience as categorizing those who are able to integrate the experience of loss, the manner in which the memories of the deceased are integrated is particularly significant. This is a different interpretation and conceptualization of the meaning of "resilience" from that which is sometimes asserted in the literature (Bonanno, 2004, 2009). The suggestion that resilience is a kind of invulnerability to disruption of function following significant interpersonal loss deserves further examination, but many in the field will find it difficult to be convinced by data that do not reflect the nature of the ongoing relationship to the complex of memory and emotion associated with the deceased. This is true also for the psychiatric point of view that may overemphasize disruption of functioning as the hallmark of post-loss difficulty.

> Ultimately, how and when the deceased is recollected (consciously and unconsciously) can be a source of strength, and can contribute to the psychological strengths of the bereaved. Attending to the appearance or avoidance of the memories and emotions bound up with the deceased as therapy progresses is important. It continues to demand our sustained attention as therapists no less than it can preoccupy the attention of the deceased's loved ones to more and less adaptive ends.

CHAPTER APPENDIX

In the appendix are the clinician evaluations of Marnie (Table 6.1) and Fiona (Table 6.2) at the beginning and end of treatment.

TABLE 6.1   Marnie: Clinician Rating at Initial Presentation and at End of Treatment

Track I: Biopsychosocial Functioning Difficulties			Track II: Relationship to the Deceased		
1) Difficulties were manifest in virtually all of the 10 vectors of biopsychosocial functioning. 2) Strengths: Her history suggested that she had many with good prognostic.			1) Strong desire to reconnect with the deceased and concern and avoidance noticeable. 2) Ongoing relationship to the deceased: Positive relationship to the deceased, conflict in the relationship, sense of trauma in the experience of death.		
Scoring (1–5)			Scoring (1–5)		
Before	After		Before	After	
2	1	1) Anxious affect	3	1	1) Strength of reconnection wishes/ longing
2	1	2) Depressive affects	3	2	2) Imagery, memory, and physical experience of deceased
3	1	3) Somatic concerns	4	4	3) Degree of pre-loss emotional involvement
2	1	4) Trauma features	4	4	4) Positive perception and affects
2	1	5) Familial relationships	4	2	5) Preoccupation with loss and deceased
3	1	6) Interpersonal relationships	2	1	6) Negative perceptions and affects
2	1	7) Self-esteem/ self-system	3	2	7) Conflict in relationship and the loss event
3	1	8) Meaning structure	1S 2Se 4D 1R	1S 2Se 1D 2R	8) The loss trajectory: Shock, searching (avoidance), disorganization, and reorganization
3	1	9) Work or similar roles	1	1	9) Problem in self-system vis-à-vis the deceased
3	1	10) Investment in life tasks	1	4	10) Progress in memorialization and relationship transformation

TABLE 6.2   Fiona: Clinician Rating at Initial Presentation and at End of Treatment

Track I: Biopsychosocial Functioning Difficulties			Track II: Relationship to the Deceased		
1) Difficulties were manifest in virtually all of the 10 vectors of biopsychosocial functioning. 2) Strengths: Her history suggested that she had many with good prognostic.			1) Strong desire to reconnect with the deceased and concern and avoidance noticeable. 2) Ongoing relationship to the deceased: Positive relationship to the deceased, conflict in the relationship, sense of trauma in the experience of death.		
Scoring (1–5)			Scoring (1–5)		
Before	After		Before	After	
4	3	1) Anxious affect	4	2	1) Strength of reconnection wishes/avoidance
3	2	2) Depressive affects	4	2	2) Imagery, memory, and physical experience of deceased
3	2	3) Somatic concerns	4	4	3) Degree of pre-loss emotional involvement/avoidance
5	3	4) Trauma features	4	4	4) Positive perception and affects
3	2	5) Familial relationships	3	2	5) Preoccupation with loss and deceased
3	2	6) Interpersonal relationships	4	2	6) Negative perceptions and affects
4	2	7) Self-esteem/self-system	1	2	7) Conflict in relationship and the loss event
4	2	8) Meaning structure	4S 4Se 4D 2R	3S 2Se 2D 3R	8) The loss trajectory: shock, searching (& its opposite—avoidance), disorganization, and reorganization
4	3	9) Work or similar roles	5	3	9) Problem in self-system vis-à-vis the deceased
4	3	10) Investment in life tasks	2	4	10) Progress in memorialization and relationship transformation
Note: Initial high scores on items 1 and 2 on Track II were due to heightened avoidance.					

Section *III*

Integrating Various Therapeutic Approaches With Insights From the Two-Track Model of Bereavement

Figure S3.1   Yafa Sonia Witztum, "Many Faces of the Persona." Thanks to the Eliezer and Menachem Witztum families for permission to reproduce this image.

Section III is devoted to developing the ramifications of what we have presented in the previous two sections for a variety of models of psychotherapy. The five chapters in this section make liberal use of clinical material to illustrate the concepts and how they are applied in practice. The presentation of different models conveys our belief that there is no right model to use in working with the bereaved, but rather the richness of each enables therapists to tailor the most suited one for each client. Chapter 7 presents a psychodynamic perspective whose concepts and therapeutic applications are relevant to almost all clinicians. Past and present, conscious and unconscious, then and there and here and now are considered in the case presented. The cognitive behavioral approach, emphasizing the centrality of cognitions, is addressed in Chapters 8 and 9. These incorporate the insights and practice of the Rational Emotive Behavior approach, as well as imagery and mindfulness. Chapter 10 discusses the strategic integrative approach, which combines concepts, tools, and structural analyses of clients' needs to demonstrate its contributions to the therapies in grief and bereavement demonstrating its application in letter writing as a ritual leave-taking. Finally, in Chapter 11, the family perspective is considered from the systemic approach. Interpersonal loss is about relationships, and the family's interactions are often best understood in that context. What the family therapies do, of course, is to work directly with that system. Including a systemic perspective can broaden and deepen what is seen through the therapist's lenses working with the individual bereaved. The insights of the Two-Track Model of Bereavement contribute to the therapeutic models presented. The chapters inform each other. Individually and jointly, they are written to be relevant for *all practitioners*, irrespective of the models of therapeutic practice they may identify with.

7

Psychodynamic Psychotherapy
Traditional and Relational
Aspects of the Encounter

*T*his chapter considers features of dynamic therapy that are relevant and effective in treatment with the bereaved. The most sweeping contribution of psychoanalysis is its focus on the complexity of forces that influence and drive human experience and behavior from an intrapsychic perspective. The psychoanalytic tradition emphasizes that our conscious understanding of ourselves and our lives is an important but incomplete organizer of our lived experience. From the time of Freud's early writings until today, as a culture, we in the West have come to accept that we are subject to psychological forces beyond our control.

The psychodynamic corpus approach to interpersonal relationships includes a well-developed worldview that sees these relationships, historically termed *object relations*, as the very core of human development and organization (Bowlby, 1969, 1973, 1980; Frankiel, 1994; Mitchell, 1988; Sandler & Sandler, 1978). The significance of interpersonal relationships for individual development and lifelong well-being is central to bereavement because of the interpersonal nature of loss. The conscious and unconscious aspects of our relationships with others reflect both their ongoing influence in our mental lives and the opportunities to rework them so as to change their effects on our current thoughts, feelings, and behaviors (Bollas, 1987).

Many of the elements of psychodynamic psychotherapy have found their way into other systems of treatment, often under different names and with differing emphases (Weston, 1998). Not surprisingly, the influences of other theories and approaches, coupled with the spirit of the changing times, have found their way into the range of dynamic therapies as well. The result is that psychoanalytic and psychodynamic thinking and therapies refer to an entire range of theory and technique that defy easy classification, but whose applicability extends to practitioners with alternative conceptual frameworks.

It makes more sense today to speak of soft psychodynamic approaches to psychotherapy and psychoanalysis rather than hard and narrow psychoanalytic approaches to change. In contemporary psychodynamic treatment of bereavement, we choose to highlight elements of treatment that are relevant for the therapist meeting bereavement. These include the appreciation that conscious and unconscious features of the response to loss are operant; that past and present features of the relationship to the deceased are significant; and that the relationship between therapist and client is always relevant. Finally, in evaluating the response to loss, we may paraphrase Freud's reputed designation of mental health as "to love and to work" and observe that bereaved individuals need to evolve a balance between the intensity of the ongoing relationship with the deceased and their openness to living in the world. The layers, themes, and dimensions that run through psychodynamic therapy with the bereaved are many (Mitchell & Black, 1995). Among the most relevant themes in bereavement are those related to the apportionment of emotional involvement post-loss, the experience of the self, how the bereaved's psychological and actual interactions with others are conducted, and finally and most importantly, the pre- and post-loss relationship and organization of the memories of the deceased.

EXPLORING GRIEF

In addressing emotional well-being, there is much for the therapist to learn. To what extent does the bereaved experience grief? Does this grief interfere with the responsiveness to other aspects of life demands and invitations? What does the grief entail from the emotional, cognitive, somatic, and behavioral perspective? What does this grief and mourning remind the bereaved of and have these been encountered in the past? What previous losses were experienced and what were their trajectories?

Exploration of the experience of the self is very important. How is the post-loss self experienced? Harry Stack Sullivan spoke of the personified self to convey what it was that people meant when they describe the "I" (Sullivan, 1970). To help us understand, we seek answers to questions such as: How empty does the bereaved feel? How guilty? How despondent? How relieved? How angry? How bereft? How abandoned? How empowered? How emancipated? How scared? These are a number of emotions and their accompanying cognitions that clarify the experience of self following significant interpersonal loss.

Next, the management of interpersonal relationships with others who are not the deceased nor necessarily associated with him or her considers the realm of the social fabric of the bereaved. Whom is the bereaved close to? What is the history and the change in those relationships? Irrespective of one's theoretical orientation, these questions help orient us to understanding what the bereaved is going through.

BEREAVEMENT AND RELATIONSHIP

The most central theme, however, in grief and mourning revolves around the pre- and post-loss experience of the deceased, the relationship to him or her, and the nature of the function, quality, and primacy of the bond. A helpful way of thinking about the functions of psychological relationships may be found in a short story. Primo Levi (1989) makes one of the clearest statements about the nature of self and other representations in a story titled "The Mirror Maker." As is often the case with others of Levi's fictional characters, the hero is a technical expert who is unsuccessful in making a success of his expertise. Timoteo has invented a mirror that is placed on the forehead of another person. This special mirror, called the Metamir, is a metaphysical mirror that allows the gazer to see him- or herself reflected in the mirror exactly as the other sees him or her. On the hero's mother, the Metamir reflects Timoteo as an angelic pink-cheeked young boy. On his current female companion in a relationship that appears to be doomed, the Metamir shows a balding unattractive and overweight man. On the forehead of the woman who seeks his affection, however, he sees himself reflected as a handsome, gallant, and dashing figure.

The idea here is that the way in which we believe we are seen and appreciated by others has meaning and influences our sense of well-being (Kohut, 1971, 1977; Rogers, 1951, 1957). When bereavement occurs, the communications from the internal psychological organization of the relationship may be distorted. For example, if we think of the bereaved "as if" communicating with a Metamir following bereavement, it is possible to experience the loss as acting to have smashed the mirror so that no further communication has any chance of being received. Death has effectively stopped all communication. Alternatively, the Metamir may have survived, but the ability to transmit communication has been disrupted following the death and can be restored. This would be the equivalent of disruption following bereavement, resulting in avoidance of memories or any number of intrusive thoughts and feelings that allow for partial, albeit incomplete, connection to (and communication from) the deceased. A third possibility is that the Metamir continues to send the messages of positive regard and support despite the death of the person who had initially transmitted them. This basic communication continuing to be sent out from the Metamir of those who love us has powerful and continuing effects. Having been loved as children by our parents, our continued sense of well-being need not be affected by the death of the parents of our childhood—and so the experience can feel as if the Metamir has continued to send forth its positive message. The fourth possibility is that the Metamir continues to send mixed or predominantly negative messages that require a reworking of elements of the relationship itself.

Looking to the nature of the ongoing relationship to the deceased carries with it implications both for the experience of the self as well as the experience and recollected relationship to the deceased. The openness of psychodynamic thinking to the illogical, conflictual, and irrational aspects of one's inner psychological world gives them a place in the therapeutic space. In bereavement, this allows these contradictory and confused emotions, thoughts, and memories to enter into the therapy and permits modifications in these aspects of his or her inner psychological world. The modern attachment literature, based on Bowlby, has focused on the nature of the attachment bond and the readiness to form attachment bonds particularly in the developmental and pair bonding contexts. Bowlby himself, however, skillfully blended his attention to real-life interaction and to the nature of the psychological and intrapsychic construction of self and other. He linked up "internal working models" of self and other that characterize persons to bridge internal and behavioral dimensions.

A second critical aspect of psychodynamic thinking relates to the value of not drawing a sharp distinction between "alive" and "dead and gone" in some areas of the emotional life of the bereaved. This understanding of bereavement directly relates to the transitional space and play phenomena so wonderfully described by Winnicott (1971). What makes Winnicott so compelling for the work of bereavement is his concentration on the space of play and the construction of things that allow persons to transition from where they are to where they need to be. For the child, holding a "security blanket" or engaging in security behaviors in the absence of parent figures can allow adaptive functioning. Allowing the bereaved space to think, feel, and have reveries not entirely in the realm of "reality" or of "fantasy" is extremely important in both spontaneous and psychotherapeutic adaptation to loss. We return to Winnicott in the context of linking objects in Chapter 10.

In contrast to a perspective that defines successful bereavement as acknowledging the reality of the loss, the implication for Winnicott's attitudes to the creation of a space of possibility are many. These allow for playful and creative engagement with possibilities and wishes outside of the limits and demands of harsh reality. This space is essential for healthy development of children and also for adults. In bereavement, such transitional spaces span a wide range. They may include belief in the afterlife and the continuation of the spirit or soul which may flourish totally out of context and inconsistent with the logical and organized belief system of the bereaved. Even deeply spiritual persons who profess belief in the continuation of the spirit also have a side that may doubt the veracity of these same beliefs. The transitional space of the bereaved allows for detection of the "presence" of the deceased in signs, sensations, and feelings experienced by the bereaved. Using this transitional space for activities such as talking to the deceased, "being" with the deceased, writing to him or her, and other ways of blurring the distinction between living and dead can be very helpful for adapting to change. Dreaming, chair work, letter writing, and visiting places where the spirit of the deceased has had some association all operate, at least partially, within the space that in the psychodynamic corpus is associated with Winnicott.

For the bereaved, being open to the inner reality of continuing existence of the representations and impact of the person who has died can be highly adaptive. This works so long as that blurring is not confused with external reality. In other words, so long as the cognitive ability to recognize the reality of death is present, there are adaptive aspects of allowing a transitional space where the real world and its constraints are not the dominant aspect of one's emotional life (Winnicott, 1971). The mental processes often referred to as the "unconscious" in shorthand does not distinguish between inner and external reality. There are many "ego" functions that attend to the demands of external reality. If they extinguish the connection to the space where reverie and transitional phenomena are allowed, the bereaved can lose important sources of emotional support and potential for growth.

ON THE MEETING OF THERAPIST AND CLIENT

In recent decades, developments within psychodynamic thinking have focused on the interaction between therapist and client from perspectives that extend far beyond the conceptions of transference and countertransference in their myriad variations. The intersubjective and postmodern influences upon the therapeutic frame have sharpened greatly current sensitivity to the therapist's personal history and ongoing experience of the human encounter with the bereaved (Berman, 2004; Davies, 2004). Most simply put, the therapist's own attitudes and history to the gamut of loss and bereavement are major players in creating the conditions for successful bereavement work. Who the therapist is, both generally and moment to moment, sets the stage for the therapeutic encounter. At times, the therapist may work within a more classical view of the therapist–client interaction, which addresses the therapy focus through the lens of a one-person psychology (Kirman, 1998). There what the client brings with him or her to the bereavement experience is relevant, and the therapist works with the processes in treatment with relatively little formal attention to his or her own contributions to the process. The notion that the primary transference relationship is not with the therapist but with the deceased functioning as a variant of selfobject has been addressed in earlier work and will not be developed here (Hagman, 1995; Rubin, 2000). This is not to say that the relationship between therapist and client is not important, but rather to emphasize that much of the work relates to the interconnectedness of the deceased and the bereaved. At other times, the theoretical perspective may emphasize a two-person view of the therapy and ultimately adopt a relational view of the interaction. This will consider the intrasubjective experience of the two protagonists in the room and what each is experiencing. Two individuals, meeting uniquely, cannot help but influence and impact each other (Ogden, 1994; Sullivan, 1970). In therapy with the bereaved, the relationship with therapist may be important to address very directly. At other times, it may remain "background" for much of the therapy work.

Whatever therapeutic frameworks one is comfortable using, the task awaiting the bereaved in dealing with loss is its own theme and follows its own pathway. How to enter, traverse, and transform the experience of loss concerns us as therapists. When clients are unable to continue on with their lives as a result of the experience of loss, the salience of bereavement is more apparent. When clients live their lives without clear evidence of bereavement-related dysfunction, and when the bereavement has occurred many years in the past, linking loss to current difficulties can neither be assumed nor ruled out without careful listening over an extended period of time. In a case such as the one we consider now, the opposite situation occurs. There, the immediacy of the turn to therapy raises questions about why therapy is being asked for so early into the mourning response.

The bulk of the material and the intervention reflect a way of listening to the client, thinking with her, and sharing her journey into herself and her response to loss. Following presentation of the case and the discussion of it, we shall conclude the chapter by considering a few of the relevant insights of this therapeutic theoretical framework.

CASE ANALYSIS: LOVE, AMBIVALENCE, AND DEATH*

Laura, age 55, called SSR for an appointment saying that her husband Terrence had died 2 weeks earlier and that she needed to talk to a professional. Laura was a well-dressed professional woman who looked somewhat younger than her age. Her handshake was firm, but her eyes looked red and tired. In the first minutes of the session, she presented as an intelligent woman who was feeling overwhelmed by what life had thrown at her.

After the preliminaries had been addressed, Laura began by explaining the circumstances of her husband's death. She and her husband had been married for 25 years and had one daughter, aged 23. Two weeks before, she had gone to sleep by herself in their bedroom. Upon awakening in the morning, she had gone down the hall and suddenly saw her husband lying on the floor next to the bed in the guest bedroom. The door had been left open. At that moment she realized he was dead and she almost fainted.

When Laura recovered from the initial shock, she phoned the emergency medical services and then her daughter. The ambulance arrived almost immediately, and the staff pronounced her husband dead. Her daughter Amy arrived some 2 hours later, having driven as quickly as she could to arrive. Terrence's body was taken for autopsy and was released for burial the next day. The time of death was fixed at around 2 a.m.

Although a secular individual, Terrence was buried in Jerusalem at the Mount of Olives cemetery because his own parents had been interred there. At the funeral, Amy spoke movingly, and Laura found herself overwhelmed by the rush of memories of Terrence and herself as parents. Terrence's older brother spoke as well, but he said nothing of a personal or emotional nature. He spoke of Terrence's achievements in business and his reputation for honesty. Laura ruefully remembered how her brother-in-law had been investigated along with Terrence for questionable tax practices. The investigation had been inconclusive, and the brothers celebrated the closing of the investigation with a festive meal along with their wives. At the meal, they confided as to just how close they had come to indictment and probable conviction. Bringing up the "honesty" theme at the funeral struck Laura as hypocritical. "Once he said that, I tuned him out. There were plenty of good things to say about Terrence that were true; why bring up that old stuff and then lie about it?"

The eulogies completed, Laura was surprised to be dismissed from the remainder of the funeral. The burial society representative told Laura that neither she nor her daughter would be "invited" to accompany the body to the burial. Attendance of women at the burial was against the traditions of this particular burial society's custom. Instead, she would remain behind and receive condolences while

---

* Some features of this case have been modified to protect the client's privacy.

Terrence's brother would accompany the body and those going to the burial site would leave with him. Although Laura felt estranged from the ultra-Orthodox persons conducting the funeral and was pleased to be done with them and the ceremony as soon as possible, she had wanted to be present when her husband was laid to final rest. Too exhausted to protest, she and Amy went home with her sister-in-law for the *Shiva* (7-day mourning period in Jewish tradition). Laura mentioned that she was surprised at how insensitive some of the people who came forward could be. Nonetheless, she appreciated the visits from her close friends and coworkers and found time to talk to Amy when no visitors were present.

When speaking of Amy, Laura mentioned that several months earlier, Amy had told her parents that she was gay. "While not something that I would choose for either myself or her, they say this is usually not a choice anyway. Both Terry and I believed that her happiness was what was important, not the shape of her partner's privates."

Laura said that Terrence's brother and wife stayed with her for 3 days before they flew back home. She said that she kept her reactions to his eulogy to herself, and although she resented their intrusion, she could not object to their staying with her. At the end of the *Shiva*, Amy went back to school and Laura went back to work. Even before the *Shiva* was complete, Laura decided she needed to see a therapist with expertise in bereavement and was recommended by a friend who had been a patient in the past. Laura said she either felt wound up and angry—at herself and at everyone else—or depressed, guilty, and weepy.

The session was almost over and Laura still had more to say and a need to talk. We agreed to another meeting later in the week. At the second meeting, Laura was less tense and elaborated on her responses and gave more background. Much of the material described next emerged during the second session.

Physically, Laura suffered from high blood pressure and sleep difficulties that preceded the loss. The night of Terrence's death, she had slept fitfully. Since her husband's death, however, her sleeping difficulties had exacerbated, and she took medication to help her sleep. Her blood pressure was not under control, and her physician was adjusting her medications for this. Laura's sleep difficulties were not confined to insomnia. Since Terrence's death, she avoided the master bedroom and was sleeping in the other guest room downstairs. Laura had little appetite and ate at the canteen at work or prepared foods at home. She spoke to Amy daily with either she or her daughter telephoning. On weekends, Amy was coming home now and they spent some time together. Laura's friends stayed in contact and they "check up on me." Laura was continuing her work and put in the requisite hours, but she found herself inefficient and questioning the value of her contributions. "What is it all for? I have no one to share it with, and there are plenty of people who would love to take my job and who would do it better too."

I asked Laura what her marital relationship had been like in the period prior to Terrence's death. Married couples evolve ways of being together as the ebb and flow of the relationship changes over time. What had it been like for them? In response to this question, Laura shared that the day before his death, she and Terrence had quarreled sharply. She had been "incensed" at Terrence for his lack of cooperation in keeping the house clean and for his "tightwad ways" in giving her monies to run the household. The couple saved her salary and invested it for the future. Part of Terrence's income was placed in the household account from which Laura ran the home. The night before Terrence's death, the couple had quarreled. She had shouted at Terrence about how he liked to dole out the money in dribs and drabs in order to belittle her and her independence. This arrangement was unfair and it was time for Terrence to accept that she deserved greater control over her own money and to use it for things without consulting him. Once the fight began, Laura said other things that were "hurtful" and "cutting." Laura attacked Terrence for being overweight, for his lack of initiative at work, and she told him that his daughter had become gay because of how little value he added to his wife or the family. That night they slept in separate bedrooms. Terrence had taken the guest room and she had slept in the master bedroom. When she awoke, Laura was still smoldering with anger when she discovered Terrence's body. Confronted with his death, she wondered how she would live on and said, "I wish it had been me that died." After this, both Laura and I sat silently for several minutes.

When she next spoke, Laura asked if therapy could help her. Asked what it was she wished for in treatment, Laura replied that she felt guilty and responsible for her husband's death. The coroner had determined that Terrence's heart attack was due to unknown causes; Laura was convinced that she'd contributed significantly to his emotional turmoil and so she had served as the trigger for his death. If she had not been so angry and if Terrence had been sleeping in bed next to her, Laura believed she could have heard something and would have been able to call an ambulance that could have saved her husband. "I may not deserve to live," she said, "but Amy needs at least one of her parents. Can therapy help me with that?" To dispense reassurance quickly would have belittled her concern. At this early stage in treatment, it seemed wisest to proceed with an eye to seeing how things developed. Let us give the process some time, I suggested, and offered an initial period of twice-weekly sessions for the coming month, and at that time, we might determine our course from there.

REFLECTION

From the perspective of the Two-Track Model of Bereavement, on Track I's biopsychosocial functioning, Laura was experiencing somatic difficulties in sleep and appetite. She had lost the belief that life was worth living. The sense of turmoil and distress, occurring so soon after the loss, would not by itself make her a candidate for psychotherapy per se, but would bear watching in the coming weeks. From the perspective of Track II, however, the matter was more sharply drawn. On the relationship to the deceased, there were numerous indicators of potential difficulty. For one, the manner of their parting the night before the death was problematic. In addition, the ongoing relationship between Terrence and Laura contained chronic and pronounced areas of conflict. Her persistent anger vis-à-vis Terrence was entangled in elements of remorse and guilt, and those alone could well predict that she would benefit from attention to that amalgam. The manifestation of the acute anger and guilt rooted in the last hours of their interaction and the words exchanged

between the couple also negatively colored things. Similarly, her belief that if they had shared the bed that last night, she might have been able to save her husband was the kind of belief that can often prove to be insidious and resistant to confrontation and logical dispute either from within her or from the outside. All of these features increase the likelihood
of interference with the ability to retrieve and rework the relationship from a position of psychological freedom and openness. Given this picture, an ongoing therapeutic connection was adopted.

A supportive relationship with Laura that allowed both for a focus on the immediate response to Terrence's death as well as trying to understand a bit more of her history in their history seemed appropriate. This could be a short-term therapy relationship or it might evolve into a longer term relationship. Keeping an eye out for the availability of the natural network of her interpersonal support, Laura's familial and interpersonal world as well as her internal psychological journey would provide important clues as to what she would need. The twice-weekly sessions for the immediate timeframe would allow us to jump start our own relationship and also allow her to benefit from the emotional support of therapy as well as a place for her to explore her response to loss without concern for external censure.

THE THERAPY

Beginning the Work

Therapy attended to Laura's state of mind and to her feelings and associations surrounding Terrence. At times it was necessary to defuse the more extreme manifestations of her feelings of guilt and responsibility. We also explored this couple's history and Laura's response to the death. In addition to the blame she attached to herself for her harshness and anger at her husband, which may have subtly affected his emotional state and his willingness to live, there were other aspects of interest as well. She believed she should have insisted that Terrence go regularly for his health checkups rather than be satisfied by his simple statement of how well he felt. Terrence was a smoker, drank moderately, and did not exercise. He loved to watch sports on television and he had a weekly poker game that he attended religiously. When younger, the couple enjoyed weekend hikes with friends who had children the same age as Amy. In adolescence, Amy began to spend more time with her friends, and family trips tapered off while Terrence had continued to gain weight and become more sedentary.

Responsibility was not the only issue. The sense of pleasure was there as well, although it did not often emerge. There had been positive features of their interaction. Laura described the couple's weekly dinner date at a restaurant either with other couples or by themselves as good times. Terrence was supportive. As an individual, Laura enjoyed her competence at work and the many opportunities for personal expression and development. Her job brought her in contact with a variety of people and she enjoyed this aspect of her work as well. While Terrence was sometimes a source of tension and somewhat pedantic, he was also her coach, audience, and support group. They often quarreled, with Laura doing most of the shouting and the dramatics. Of all their disagreements, the most emotional of their fights were related to questions about fidelity. Laura reported two periods of prolonged tension when she suspected that Terrence was conducting an affair around the time that Amy entered adolescence and again, 2 years ago. The matter was never resolved as Terrence had denied all and had called her "paranoid." The couple's sexual relationship had been adequate although Laura felt that Terrence had been insufficiently attentive to her needs and satisfaction. Laura typically waited for Terrence to initiate intimacy and sometimes, when he did not, she felt frustrated and angry. She believed that initiating sexual contact was something that men did and women did not do.

As she described these things, Laura paused and indicated she had a confession to make. Talking about sexuality was not easy, she said, but what she had to say was particularly difficult. With a mixture of pain, embarrassment, and guilt, Laura admitted to having been involved in an affair with a younger colleague for "purely sexual satisfaction." In that relationship, she behaved quite differently and felt both sexually satisfied and validated as desirable. Immediately after Terrence's death, Laura had made it clear to her lover that their relationship was over and could never be resumed. "I cheated on him, and he never knew. He deserved better. Maybe it is a double standard, but what I did was unforgivable." The next several sessions focused on the issues of their relationship and the ways in which her anger and disappointment found expression in behavior and action outside the marriage, as the partners found ways to get back at each other rather than explore and work through some of the tension in their relationship.

Therapist: It seems to me that Terry was sensitive and supportive of you, and yet he also did things that hurt you. When it came to matters of sexuality, both when you felt that he was having an affair, and when he was not taking responsibility for some of your own sexuality, you felt particularly hurt and angry. Perhaps underneath that rage, or alongside it, you might have also felt that you were not desired and validated. Sometimes, a relationship outside marriage can serve to get back at a spouse, as well as to express aspects of one's sexuality and feelings of worth that have other meanings and significance.

Laura: I didn't want to be so dependent on him, I didn't want to be that dependent on anyone, but a part of me was that way. And when I found out he was having an affair, I was so hurt and scared, and I did what I do sometimes, and try to hurt back. I shut him out and barely spoke to him. I went out of my way to hurt him and I didn't care. I was not going to be helpless— and he did not fight or hurt back. I know he broke off the affair right away, but I continued to call him a liar and a hypocrite, cheating the tax man and cheating on his wife and being a fake. I was so mean to him. He deserved better, and I know I hurt him deeply. I shortened his life.

Attempts at this stage in treatment to also connect her to Terrence's caring for her and his wishes for her that could be experienced as positive and supportive were unsuccessful. She remained focused on her failings toward Terrence, occasionally dealt with some of her anger at him, but had not yet reconnected to the source of positive feelings that were also a mainstay of their relationship. At the same time, Laura was continuing to have great difficulty resuming her life after the death of Terrence. Her appetite remained poor and she was losing weight. She left Terrence's disheveled half of the bedroom exactly as it had been when she discovered him that morning. Her performance at work had deteriorated, and her subordinates had covered up for her several times at presentations to clients when she had not been sufficiently prepared. Laura said that she cared little whether or not her performance was adequate. She felt life was not worth living, and only her concern for Amy kept her from acting more rashly and harming herself. Laura's friends continued to support her at this time and invited her to spend time with them, which she did. Her friends were supportive of her feelings and listened to her describe her guilt and responsibility for Terrence's death. Friends recommended a number of alternative therapies, including telepathic communication with the dead, psychiatric antidepressant medication, support group for bereaved widows, but Laura rejected them all. She felt that her depression was the least that she could do to identify with Terrence and his death. The fact of Terrence's death was one thing, but removing his books from the nightstand of his side of the bed, taking his toothbrush out of the bathroom, moving his robe from its hook in the bathroom were things that Laura could not bear, as they added layers of finality and reality to the already too large and painful core awareness of Terrence's death and unavailability.

The mixture of positive and negative aspects of the relationship between Laura and Terrence was confusing for Laura. She felt guilty for the negative side of things and benefited from the opportunity to explore and share her confused feelings in the therapy sessions. It was also striking that although she described many features that involved caring aspects of Terrence and his concern for her, the guilt she felt and her feeling that she had failed Terrence by her thoughts, feelings, and behaviors prevailed. Her conception of what Terrence might say, think, and feel about her response became the focus of therapy. Laura was unwilling to consider chair work and bringing Terrence into the sessions. Of more import was the fact that she was unable to construct a coherent picture of Terrence and what he might have wished for her following his death. She did not think of him as angry, vindictive, or punishing toward her. At the same time, she was unable to translate the many positive interactions and mini-stories of their lives together into what he might have wished for her. The result was a kind of ruminative preoccupation with her "failings" toward him, and a notable limitation in her ability to experience her anger at him. Laura's sharing of her own affair was important both for the expansion of her own dialogue with herself in the therapy as well as for its significance in the trust vis-à-vis the therapist. The intent to do more in the reworking of the relationship to her deceased spouse, and to reconnect her to the positive and supportive aspects of her relationship with Terrence, was still stymied.

Deepening the Therapy and Going Back to the Past

By the third month of our work together, Laura was feeling more comfortable in the sessions and more trusting of her therapist. She was sharing more of her life and was less focused on the ruminative aspects of responsibility for Terrence's death. She reported some pockets of more optimistic thoughts and feelings, but for the most part, she felt that she was in much the same place she had been when she entered treatment. At this point in therapy, she was also more amenable to exploring her earlier history and was less focused on her relationship and interactions with her husband.

In previous sessions and our early work, Laura had shared the barest outlines of her earlier history. She was the only surviving child born to her parents. There had been a series of miscarriages prior to and after her birth. Her parents only agreed on the importance of scholastic and professional success in life. She remembered growing up feeling embarrassed and self-conscious at her circumstances. Laura's mother ran a small grocery store in a poor neighborhood and worked long hours while her father worked as a bus driver. Her classmates thought her childish, and she had few friends. Laura excelled at elementary school and won a scholarship to study at a private high school. Despite the requirements of school uniform at her new school, Laura recalled having had to endure comments about her mode of dress, hairstyle, and shoes that she found humiliating. She was neither particularly attractive nor athletic in an environment that valued both, and she remembered how isolated she had felt during her adolescence.

Things had changed when she met Terrence in her second year of college. He was 3 years older than she and was popular and had a reputation as a ladies' man. Initially she had been flattered by his attention and went out with him even though she thought he was not as smart as she was. As they dated, however, she found herself looking forward to their meetings. Laura's sexual encounters prior to Terrence had been partial and furtive, and Terrence had been her first full partner. He had been loving, and she found herself drawn to him. They married when she was aged 23. Although she had wanted a bigger wedding, they did not have the money. Two days after their wedding, they were both at work with Laura assuming the burden of housework as well. On top of her displeasure with this aspect of the "traditional wife role," she felt that her husband's disregard of her expectations for a clean house and his refusal to help her out by at least not seeking to limit his contributions to the mess were maddening. Happy to be married, at the same time, she felt that she was the poor relation that was ignored and required to serve "the country squire."

Terrence and Laura's interactional pattern balanced love and aggression in varying degrees. There was no physical violence, but Terrence would passively resist many of Laura's suggestions and initiatives. This often led to violent outbursts during which Laura would berate Terrence and criticize him for his failings. Terrence would rarely answer back but would either ignore Laura or get up and leave the room. The frequency of these disagreements varied. Laura was often quick to criticize, but most of her criticisms did not escalate into her more tense and violent outbursts or elicit the withdrawal and avoidant responses of Terrence.

As she explored these issues, Laura moved beyond the description of the interactions between Terrence and her. Laura was able to talk with insight about the sense of security and value she felt in the relationship with Terence and how that had been a constant for her across the years of their marriage. When they were not quarreling, he was a fun companion and listened to her about work and her ups and downs with her girlfriends. Her sense of shock and betrayal when she discovered his affair had served to "break something fragile and trusting in me," and despite the passage of time, Laura said she never lost the fear and anger that he might leave her for someone else.

As therapy progressed, additional layers of meaning associated with the conscious and unconscious experience of her relationship with her parents and their relationship to each other began to emerge. She described her relationship with her mother as difficult. In an embarrassed tone, she reported that she had received "more than the normal" share of physical discipline from her mother. Yet these had been less difficult to bear than the emotional distance that her mother generally displayed toward her. Typically, despite her pain and anxiety, Laura experienced the verbal and physical attacks as times when she felt connected and closest to her mother. When things were quiescent, she experienced her mother as withdrawn from her and indifferent to her life.

Laura's father had been a hard-working company man, and he was basically supportive of her although he rarely stood up to his wife. When it came to discipline or other active interactions, Laura was either on her own or at the mercy of mother. Father was "away at work" returning only late at night. When she was in her early teen years, Laura heard her parents arguing. Her mother had been cursing her father (a relatively common occurrence), but two things struck her as different. One, her father had answered back and accused her mother of pushing him away, shouting "that the only reason he had not left the home was to provide for his daughter Laura whom he loved" and not for his wife whom he "barely could stand." The second was her father saying "and if I choose to have relationship with other women, that is none of your business, God knows I barely have one with you."

This set of sessions signaled a loosening in the repetitive ways that Laura had related to the death of Terrence. She relaxed visibly in the sessions as she acknowledged that the issue of fidelity and infidelity had roots that extended beyond their appearance in her relationship with Terrence. She spoke again of her own extramarital affair and how it had allowed her to claim an independence that she had needed so as not to be as dependent on her husband as her mother had been on her father.

Having opened up aspects of her earlier history, it was now easier for her to reconnect with the picture of Terrence that included his caring for her and his interest. She could be open to the loss without being devastated by it or to overly punish herself for it. The opening up of her developmental history and the story of her life with her parents took some of the pressure off of her considering her relationship with Terrence. By separating out her relationships with father and mother from her relationship with Terrence, she was able to reconnect to Terrence's contribution to her "rescue" and to revitalize the positive interest and concern that Terrence always had for her.

This was manifest in her now being able to hear his voice telling her "things would be OK" and that he cared about her and her well-being. Laura's imagination and her sense that Terrence's positive presence could be felt returned their relationship to its positive aspects. Terrence was once again accessible, supportive, and meaningful for her. The kind of positive emotional material that began to emerge here resembled what had been attempted and suggested earlier in therapy. The difference was that that it could now emerge.

Bringing the Therapy to a Close

The approaching end of the therapy began to receive attention in month six. Laura was becoming increasingly aware of how her relationship with Terrence could have benefited from couples therapy while they were both alive. That opportunity had been lost, but something of the perspective remained useful as Laura considered how she and Terrence had managed to lose track of how important their relationship was to both of them. Therapy began to move more in the direction of a place for remorse and grief regarding the missed opportunities and the myopia that characterized their relationship in the last years. The preoccupation with the mode of Terrence's death and her unavailability receded palpably.

The movement in the way Laura thought of Terrence and his attitudes toward her also led her to allow a greater degree of separation from some of Terrence's things. His books were placed in his nightstand's lower shelf, his toothbrush and toothpaste were put away in a drawer in the bathroom, and many other small but significant changes occurred that placed Laura more securely on the path to living following loss. Along with the strengthening of the connection to the positive and supportive aspects of the relationship with her husband, Laura reported an easing of her somatic symptoms and an improvement in her work and emotional functioning.

The final piece that entered into the relationship focused squarely on how important the therapist SSR had been to Laura. "You were there for me in a way that communicated to me that I was a good human being, and that nothing you learned about me would shake that. I had feared that your being a religious person would mean that you could not accept me as someone who had relationship outside the marriage. I learned that your acceptance was there all the time, and it was my own that I needed to work on. Thank you for giving me back myself, my relationship with Terrence, and a better way to support myself in life." Eight months after it had begun, Laura felt she had achieved what she needed in treatment and was ready to continue the process of grieving as well as living on her own. Her appreciation of the relationship with the therapist was an important part of the saying goodbye but retaining the connection to the other that is so important in separation and loss.

CASE COMMENTARY

Beginning the Work

In the initial consultation coming so soon after a sudden death, it can be quite difficult to determine how much of the response is related to the dislocation of loss. The various strands of Laura's narrative conveyed anger (e.g., at Terrence, her brother-in-law, and the burial society, among others) and helplessness (in response to the same three sources), which coexisted with the ability to receive support (her friends, daughter, and coworkers) as well as indications that Laura had many strengths (intelligence, candor, and competence). She seemed to sense that she needed therapy, and it was not yet clear on what she based this idea. Certainly her sense of being over-whelmed was present. Did it reflect the initial shock stemming from the discovery of her husband's body? Was it also related to her realization of the impact of his death upon her life? Her wish for help might also reflect a deeper resonance of something that was not yet apparent. How did Laura balance her strands of dependence and her independence? Did she know something about her previous history that would be important for the therapist to learn as well? Were thoughts and feelings of depression (or unvoiced ideas of suicide) contributing to her wish for therapy? To what extent was her apparent wish to enter therapy a way of her regaining control over her life while at the same time serving as a declaration of the loss of that control?

The description of the religious funeral is noteworthy for a number of reasons. The importance of spirituality, religion, and the belief narratives of the individual and his or her subculture regarding what happens to the deceased are all relevant for understanding the meaning of loss. For Laura, there is sufficient invocation of traditional rituals and belief narratives regarding the survival of the soul that go along with the choice of a ritual funeral that is in keeping with such beliefs (Lamm, 1969; Spitz, 2000). As we noted in the introduction, however, the importance of leaving transitional space allows the mind the freedom to go off in different directions regarding the question of the accessibility of the deceased. Leaving that space intact can be helpful, as it was, with regard to religion for Laura. In general, even among persons who profess not to believe in any notions of the supernatural, god, or survival of the soul, the therapist should be willing to acknowledge and work with a totally different set of assumptions that reflect the magical and primary process aspects of our makeup. Irrational thoughts and beliefs are powerful organizers of our beings, and the psychodynamic therapies are particularly sensitive to their importance. Whether or not the bereaved openly acknowledges the possibility of survival of the soul and the possibility of continued interest by the deceased in the life of the living is not the issue and may actually be irrelevant. We should assume that within the unconscious, there exist beliefs, associations, fears, and irrational thoughts intimately connected to the primary process mode. These are not based on logic or conforming to reality but reflect the thought processes of dreams, young children, etc, and are representative of thought that characterizes this layer of our mental life. Much of the work of metaphor and the deep levels of communication that transcend rational discourse and logical thinking work at the deeper levels of unconscious processes.

The early sessions were exploratory. In those initial weeks following the sudden death of her husband, it was not clear if Laura was a candidate for anything beyond a supportive relationship. Given that she had discovered Terrence's body, and given the traumatic nature of such a death, how was she managing the imagery of the loss? Was the manner of death and its discovery interfering with the painful process of coming to grips with the loss? Of course, the manner of recollecting the deceased, the relationship to him, and the ways in which that relationship had played out needed to be understood. The theme of questionable honesty had been raised both at the funeral and with regard to Terrence's marital fidelity—surely it was more than a coincidence. But what that honesty and dishonesty might mean needed more clarification. The relationship was in its earliest stages, and prior to any decision about a therapy contract, more information about the couple's relationship was needed.

Similarly, early on it is too early to construct more that a tentative psychodynamic formulation of the treatment. These centered on a number of goals and foci. First, the pre-loss relationship and way the couple interacted needed to be better understood. At least some of the anger that Laura had directed at her husband was now turned upon herself for how she had separated and treated Terrence. Working with her distress at the manner of his death and the imagery of discovering his body would require work as well. Intervention with people who have had a conflictual pre-loss relationship can assist in their negotiation of the bereavement process (Freud, 1917/1957; Raphael, 1978; Rubin, 1984b, 1990). Second, a fuller and more nuanced understanding of the developmental relationship between Laura and Terrence would be particularly helpful in considering intervention along the relational track. What was their early relationship like? How had it changed and evolved over the years? What was the pair bond relationship they had evolved and how had it worked for each of them? Third, exploring Laura's own developmental history and what her individual life trajectory had been as a girl and as a woman prior to her involvement with Terrence would be useful. Understanding the role played by earlier losses and getting a picture of how she responded to other losses and what they might have been would make sense as well. On the basis of this information, it would be possible to understand more of Laura's experience of self and some of the ways and meanings that had become intertwined in the relationship with Terrence when he was alive and how that might now change.

Once Laura had agreed to therapy, the sessions also allowed for a more complete exploration of the extent to which she felt guilty and depressed. As a matter of course and clinical responsibility, suicidal thinking and potential were addressed directly and ruled out as a concern for this stage of treatment (Elitzur & Omer, 2001; Orbach, 2001). The absence of suicidal ideation was not equivalent, however, to the absence of a wish to punish and harm herself. She fantasized of publicly acknowledging her mistreatment of Terrence, so that she might expose her faults to others since Terence was not alive to hear it from her.

Deepening the Therapy and Going Back to the Past

Laura's unwillingness to change many of the physical things related to the reminders of Terrence's physical existence in her life could be seen to reflect an attempt to delay the process of living without Terrence himself. The unwillingness to separate from Terrence's things and her concern that all be left present and unchanged communicated a sense of the fragility of the connection to Terrence. As long as the positive and negative sides of their relationship were confused and threatening in some way, the freedom to dispose of even some of the physical features associated with him threatened to overwhelm the connection to him. This too would be consistent with the multiple layers of logical and illogical thinking characteristic of the human mind.

When the more open discussion of her family life entered treatment, the impact was strongly felt and it related to the evolution of Laura's experience of herself, her gender role, and the role of sexuality in her life. The new material allowed us to consider these implications both for her own sense of herself and for her relationship with Terrence. The emergence of this material had not been immediate, and using it to interpret or explain Laura's behavior opened up possibilities for alternative ways of understanding her experience. What she shared allowed us to address three major areas with links to her earlier history and to open up access to all.

First, it connected the nature of her fights with Terrence to the conflicts she had experienced with her mother, the way her mother had experienced her relationship with her own spouse which served as a model for her, and it opened up her own needs for validation and support. She had received some of this support from her father, but his distance from the home had been experienced as abandonment and had left her quite vulnerable. At the same time, the closeness she felt to her mother was something she experienced only when her mother was attacking her. The shifting closeness and aggression she experienced with Terrence reflected both these relationships—and connected her very deeply to Terry.

Second, at a more experience-near position, it opened up the ways in which Laura identified with her mother, and also with her father, in the experience of the sexual affairs that she had described. On the one hand, she was identified with her mother and upset that her husband was having a relationship with someone else instead of her. On the other hand, she was identified with her father, having the affair and thus getting back at the spouse who was so difficult to be with. She was in the role of victim and of aggressor, and part of working through the implications of the sexual affairs in her own marriage went through this channel.

Third, it allowed Laura to think of her relationship with Terry as one that was very important to her and impressed upon her how couples therapy and/or individual therapy could have assisted them in their relationship. More importantly, it also set the stage for direct work on the relationship with Terrence. In particular, this was related to the supportive and basically positive relationship they had and of his wish for her that she live on and live well rather than remain trapped in remorse.

Ultimately, the relational bond between Terrence and Laura was very strong and served many functions for Laura. On the positive side, they had a long-standing relationship that had served as a secure base and place of value for both of them. On the negative side, there were elements of tension that had become entrenched in their interactions. The more active aggressive side of Laura's personality met with a more passive and self-involved side of Terrence.

Nonetheless, they both had developed additional spheres of influence and work that made their outside lives interesting to them. At the same time, the marital dyad maintained an attachment bond with dependent overtones as well as elements of mutuality and affection. Their sexual relationship was imbalanced, with Laura's transfer of control to Terrence on this matter as well. Not feeling truly in control, but rather dependent on her partner for her money and parts of her independence, cleanliness at home, parts of their intimacy and connection had cooled. Laura's affair had addressed an area outside the marriage that might well have been amenable to treatment had the couple chosen such an approach. From Laura's perspective prior to Terrence's death, a significant part of her life was based in the home, but a far larger segment of the interesting parts of her life revolved around her work, her interaction with friends, and the physical experience of having a lover.

The couple's interpersonal conflict, her anger, and aspects of her identification with her mother as the "wronged" woman had blocked aspects of the connection to Terrence who loved her and cared about her. This Terrence would not want her to suffer and be consumed by guilt or by a need for punishment. The result of the exploration of both her experiences with her family of origin and how her relationship with Terrence were associated with more positive phase of her life made a difference. With these insights and with the expansion of the view of therapy, Laura's sense that Terrence would not want her to feel guilty was something she could imagine and give voice to. Her sense of guilt diminished significantly, although she still regretted the harsh words said their last night together and still believed she might have prevented his death had they been in their bedroom together. As in Primo Levi's use of the Metamir, the importance of reconnecting to experience a positive communication and feelings from the significant other are important both for the individual's sense of self and for the relationship. The intervention that had allowed her the freedom to reconfigure Track II of her response to loss was critical. The freedom to rework her relationship to the deceased was achieved via the exploration of her relationships with her father and mother and the distinguishing of those from the relationship to her husband. She could then begin to reorganize and re-experience her relationship to Terrence in ways that freed up some of the more positive features of their relationship.

Bringing Therapy to a Close

The ending of therapy with the bereaved is usually, but not always, linked to the separation from the person of, and relationship with, the therapist (Rubin, 2000). It is highly important to remain open to both positive and negative parts of the relationship, and to address those prior to closing the work. Often, a follow-up session may be indicated as a way of both supporting the strengths of the client, as well as allowing for the continuation of the relationship. The "termination" of psychotherapy differs from loss by death as the therapist and former client can renew, if the client chooses, their contacts. This message is supported by a follow-up meeting at some not too distant time after the end of therapy.

CONCLUSION AND SUMMARY FOR CLINICIAN

The case presented is representative of a case of early response to loss, where the intervention used psychodynamic principles (Shedler, 2010). The response of the bereaved spouse was manifest in difficulties in biopsychosocial functioning as well as the relationship to the deceased. The understanding that the relationship to the deceased was conflictual emerged early in the contact with the client. The quarrel and tension that accompanied the parting interaction were identified as well. Nonetheless, the actual reworking of the relationship to the deceased was, in this case, linked to additional aspects of the history and life experience of the client. The initial attempt to reconnect to the positive aspects of the relationship to the deceased did not succeed. Following a period of exploration of other aspects of the history and relationships to significant figures in the client's earlier life, the ability to move forward and rework the relationship to the deceased was possible.

One of the more interesting elements of this case presentation is the fact that direct interventions focused on either improving the biopsychosocial function of the bereaved or reworking aspects of the relationship were not initially successful. The exploration of the guilt that the client felt, and its origins, was likewise helpful only to a point. For this particular client, going back to earlier history, not only of the relationship to the deceased but also of the connection to the family of origin, proved significant in the unlocking of positive aspects of the relationship. The conflict and ambivalence in the relationship remained, and these aspects were only partially addressed in the later sessions. The amalgam of difficulties on Track I and Track II is familiar in the initial months of the response to loss. In the present case, the predominant focus of the transformative intervention was on the relationship to the deceased. It encompassed the pre-loss relationship across a long span of time. The loss event and the manner of death and the death narrative were part of the intervention. A number of changes in the easing of the painful response to loss on the functioning occurred after the relationship to the deceased was freed up for exploration. In interventions early in the response to loss, the connections of Tracks I and II are striking. Years later, the connection is not as direct nor as linked as what was described here.

Direct interventions focused on either improving the biopsychosocial function of the bereaved or upon reworking aspects of the relationship may not achieve their ends. Sometimes, by going back to the client's earlier life history, both with regard to the relationship to the deceased, and also to the family of origin, can prove to be a combination significant in unlocking important aspects of the relationship to the deceased.

An amalgam of difficulties on Track I and Track II is often familiar in the initial months of the response to loss. In cases such as the one in this chapter, however, the predominant focus of the transformative intervention was on the relationship to the deceased and its meaning, over time, for the bereaved.

8

A Cognitive Behavior Approach
Rational Emotive Behavior Therapy

INTRODUCTION

What upsets people are not things in themselves but rather their judgment about things. For example, death is nothing dreadful (or else it would have appeared so to Socrates), but instead the judgment about death is dreadful—that is what is dreadful.

Epictetus
(1890, p. 326)

In general, the goal of grief therapy, regardless of its theoretical adherence, is to assist the bereaved to assimilate and accommodate to life that has changed forever. Furthermore, its aim is to facilitate an adaptive, healthy though painful experience that involves cognitive, emotional, and behavioral processes of reworking the relationship with a significant person who is now deceased but whose memory remains "alive."

In the present chapter, a cognitive perspective is presented. This views loss through death as an external and often uncontrolled event followed by a process of accommodation to its consequences, known as grief or bereavement. A characteristic of cognitive therapy is its focus on the individual's cognitions and organization of meaning, and related emotions in response to life events. Similarly, cognitive grief therapy approaches loss through death and dying as a type of adverse event. These affect one's way of thinking about oneself, others, and the world. The process of grief is one of gradual discovery of a new meaning to life without the deceased.

As the name implies, cognitive grief therapy focuses on the centrality of the cognitions in understanding emotional distress. In general it is a short-term, phase-related mode of intervention. In most cases, the focus is on the here-and-now. The client's past history serves as a background to understand the way cognitions have been formed and are presently maintained. Also central is the establishment of a therapeutic alliance. This facilitates a collaborative relationship and a mutual understanding of the process of therapy, its expectations, and mutually agreed upon goals. The aim of this chapter is to outline the cognitive approach, focusing on the ABC model of CBT–REBT (Cognitive Behavior Therapy–Rational Emotive Behavior Therapy), originally developed by Ellis (1962, 1994), as applied to loss through death and the ensuing grief reactions, processes, and outcomes. The application of cognitive assessment and interventions in cases of traumatic bereavement and complicated grief with a case illustration will be presented to acquaint the reader with the CBT-REBT model.

COGNITIVE GRIEF THERAPY AND THE CONCEPT OF CONTINUING BONDS

The relatively recent shift away from Freud's (1917/1957) conceptualization of grief as a normal process leading to breaking the bond with the deceased (i.e., *decathexis*) had major implications for both research and clinical work. By viewing grief as a process of reorganizing one's life and worldview without the deceased, where bonds will remain intact and unbroken—the concept of continuing bonds (Klass et al., 1996)—new possibilities emerged. From the continuing bonds perspective there is no final point to grieving; rather it views grief as a continuous process of accommodating to the loss, which continues to preoccupy the bereaved in his or her search for the meaning to life without the deceased (Niemeyer, 1999). It is a process where the relationships with the inner representations of the deceased continue long after loss has occurred (Malkinson & Bar-Tur, 2004–2005; Rubin & Malkinson, 2001). As such, bereavement is viewed as a cognitive, emotional, and behavioral process of continually adapting to the new reality.

Thus an adaptive outcome of the grief process is a balanced reorganization of life in which there is neither denial nor avoidance of the memories nor emotional flooding of the bereaved (Horowitz, 2001). The majority of individuals who experience a loss find ways to reorganize their lives. Others, however, encounter difficulties in accepting the loss and experience a sense of loss of interest in life, with intrusive thoughts and memories about the deceased. It is therefore not surprising that clinicians and researchers alike expressed their interest in in-depth studying of these difficulties as distinct from depression. A number of researchers have proposed that these difficulties be viewed as indications of complication in grief or complicated grief (Horowitz, 2006; Prigerson & Maciejewski, 2006; Rubin et al., 2008). From a CBT-REBT framework, prominent complications in grief include difficulties in organizing the interpersonal relationship with the deceased, characterized by an avoidance response or flooding, and a continuous sense of loss of control over life.

As a consequence of these conceptual changes in the field of bereavement, there are also advances in CBT in understanding the purpose of grief and bereavement, responses, their outcomes, and possible complications in the process. As a result, the reformulation of cognitive interventions and strategies now aims to facilitate an adaptive process to life without the physical presence of the deceased in accordance with the continuing bonds and the bifocal framework of the Two-Track Model of Bereavement (TTMoB) discussed in this book.

UNCOMPLICATED AND COMPLICATED GRIEF FROM THE COGNITIVE PERSPECTIVE

Let us consider the two vignettes:

> Life has changed forever. A year after my daughter was killed in a road accident, I woke up one morning and made a decision to continue with life and think of the family that needs me. When I see her friends growing up and getting married, I cry and miss her tremendously. I remind myself that she had a wonderful life and will always be remembered and loved by us. Her memories are with me and I cherish them in spite of the pain. (Ann, a bereaved mother who lost her daughter 5 years earlier.)

> Life has lost its meaning. I can't stop thinking that I never had a chance to tell her how much I love her. I think she felt I was nudging her … I wake up in the morning and go to bed at night thinking of her and the life that was lost. I sometimes wish that my life would be over. (Betty, a bereaved mother who lost her daughter 5 years earlier.)

Both women are mothers who lost their daughters in a road accident 5 years earlier. The circumstances and time of loss are similar, and yet there are differences in how each of them has constructed the meaning of life following the loss: Ann has accepted the reality of the loss of her daughter and she has made a decision to move on with life; she has memories of her daughter blended with pain and yearning. Betty's life has lost its meaning; she has intrusive thoughts related to the lost relationship and wishes her life would be over.

A wealth of studies on bereavement, including both clinical and nonclinical populations, has contributed significantly to understanding the phenomena of both uncomplicated (normal) and complicated (pathological) grief. A number of trends have been identified: (1) The experience of grief involves a painful process of adaptation to one's changes (psychological, social, financial, etc.) in life as a result of the loss. Grief is seen as a normative personal and social experience that takes place within a specific cultural context. (2) Whereas death is permanent and unchanging, the process of grief does change, affecting the mourner differently at different times over the rest of his or her life. (3) Complications in grief are observed among individuals who, as time passes, continue to experience (without decrease in intensity) cognitive and emotional difficulties in reorganizing their inner relationship with the deceased and difficulties in accommodating to changes in their lives following the loss. Their life disruption is one that cannot be amended (Bonanno, 2009; Parkes & Prigerson, 2010; Rubin et al., 2008).

Table 8.1 presents a summary of cognitive emotional and behavioral elements characteristic to adaptive and complicated outcomes of grief.

TABLE 8.1   Adaptive Grief and Complicated Grief and Mourning

Adaptive Grief and Mourning	Complicated/Prolonged Grief and Mourning
Loss and grief are interwoven with life, a sense of acceptance of life.	Life is overwhelmed by grief, value of life is questioned.
Pain, sadness, and yearning are balanced part of life.	Experiencing separation anxiety, distress, and intense yearning without change. Avoidance of pain.
Finding meaning to life and to loss.	Unable to find meaning in life and/or to the loss.
Positive attitude, self-efficacy, and trust in others.	A sense of emptiness and lack of purpose in life, a continuous search.
Investing in life roles and old and new relationships.	Detachment from others. Distant involvement in relationships.

COMMENTARY

From Table 8.1, we can notice the differences in the mothers' narratives. Whereas Ann's narrative communicates acceptance of life blended with pain and yearning for her daughter, it is life-focused. Betty's narrative is a deceased focused, her life is overwhelmed by grief, and she questions the value of life.

CBT-REBT IN GRIEF

From the cognitive perspective, a loss through death is an adverse external event over which the person has no control but which nevertheless changes one's belief system and its related emotions and behaviors. Grief is a normal and human response to loss and is a process that is experienced cognitively, emotionally, behaviorally, and physically.

Due to emotions' flooding effect, especially during the acute phase and/or due to the traumatic circumstances of the loss, it may seem that emotions dominate cognitions. Yet the role of cognitions is viewed as central, emphasizing the element of self-control and that of choice that the bereaved person has over a choice-less event (Ellis, 1962; Malkinson, 1996, 2001, 2007). The cognitive perspective, in Rational Emotive Behavior Therapy (REBT) in particular, focuses on the circular relationship between one's emotions and behaviors and one's cognitive evaluations about oneself, the world, and the future (Belief-Consequence, referred to as the B-C connection). In grief, the process of cognitively reorganizing what has been shattered following the external event, of modifying one's knowledge, thoughts, and feelings, of giving up old meanings to life, and of forming new ones is a painful internal process. Cognitively, the loss event is new information that has to be processed and then assimilated (revising and processing new information into preexisting cognitive structures) or accommodated (adapting preexisting knowledge to the new reality; Piaget, 1950). Whether primarily cognitively processed or emotionally experienced, the cognitive perspective asserts that the more traumatic the event is, the greater its impact will be on one's belief system and other cognitions. Thus the cognitive approach upholds that, for the grieving process to take an adequate course toward functional and satisfying outcomes, grief-related cognitions should be identified, included, and treated as an equal part of intrapsychic processes.

According to the cognitive approach, maladaptive grief takes the form of distorted thinking related to the deceased (Track II in the TTMoB) and/or to life without him or her, which can involve one or both tracks. The salient feature in complicated grief is preoccupation and emotions directed toward the deceased characteristic to Track II (Kelly, 1955; Malkinson, 2007; Niemeyer, 1999, 2005; Rando, 1988).

We will examine the treatment of complicated grief based on the CBT-REBT model for treating grief.

THE ABC MODEL OF CBT-REBT

The ABC model of CBT-REBT was developed by Albert Ellis (1962) in the 1950s and emphasized, in common with Beck (1976) and Lazarus and Folkman (1984), the cognitive centrality in understanding emotional distress, and in the case of post-death, complications of bereavement. Several tenets underlie the ABC model of CBT-REBT (Ellis, 1991): The origins of emotional disturbance are cognitive, emotive, and behavioral; cognition is a mediator between an event and its emotional consequences; dysfunctional emotions largely stem from irrational thinking (demandingness); human beings are born with a biological predisposition to think irrationally, and some are born with a greater tendency and therefore exhibit more irrational thinking; the biological tendency to think irrationally coexists with the healthy human tendency to think rationally and actualize oneself (David, Freeman, & DiGiuseppe, 2010; Ellis, 1991; Malkinson, 2001, 2007).

According to the CBT-REBT model, people's emotional consequences (C) are not solely determined by the activating event (A) but largely by the beliefs (B) they have about the event. Death (especially sudden and unexpected death) may be regarded as an adverse external event (A) that affects one's belief system (B) and, consequently, one's emotions and behaviors (C). A cyclical interaction occurs between the event (A), beliefs about the event (B), and the emotional and behavioral consequences (C; Ellis, 1962, 1994). In CBT-REBT, rational thinking denotes a logical, flexible, and reality-focused attitude leading to adaptive emotional, cognitive, and behavioral consequences (philosophy of preference); whereas irrational thinking is an illogical, rigid, inflexible, and absolutistic evaluation of events leading to maladaptive consequences (philosophy of demandingness); (David, Lynn, & Ellis, 2010). The most central theme is the assumption that the grief process following a death event is a painful psychological process, which is very intense in the acute phase (which subsides as time passes) and involves negative emotions. In this model there is a distinction between negative, emotional adaptive responses and maladaptive ones; in other words, between moderate negative feelings (sadness, yearning, moderate pain, anger etc.) and extreme intense negative ones (depressive response, anxiety, overwhelming pain, uncontrollable anger, etc.). The assumption in this model concerns the evaluation or meaning that we make regarding adverse events: Is the evaluation of the event a negative rational one leading to adaptive consequences, or is the evaluation an irrational one with maladaptive consequences?

We mentioned earlier that an important basic assumption of CBT-REBT relates to people's innate tendency to think irrationally during crises such as a loss through death. Research studies support the notion that human tendency to think irrationally is likely to increase after stressful life events (Boelen, Kip, Voorsluijs, & van den Bout, 2004; David, Freeman, & DiGuiseppe, 2010) and that cognitive changes occur following such a loss (Fleming & Robinson, 2001). The process of adaptive grief from the cognitive perspective is the ability to adapt (change) the thoughts to the new life situation; difficulty in doing so signals fixation of irrational thoughts that enhances the risk of complication in grief.

Such findings support the proposition that there is a relationship between the adaptation to loss and the ability, even partially, to change the beliefs and adapt them to the new situation following the loss. It means that treatment interventions should focus on identifying the patterns of irrational thinking and the emotional, nonadaptive consequences and adopting patterns of rational thinking, whose consequences are healthy negatives. The notion emphasized the idea that people can transcend their irrationality by employing cognitive emotional and behavioral methods and can choose to adapt more healthily to an unwanted situation (Dryden, 2009). In the case of the death of a significant person, an adaptive and healthy response during the mourning process includes, among other things, feelings of sadness, yearning for the deceased, pining, and pain related to the changed situation and its recognition. Table 8.2 summarizes the interaction between the adverse event and the Belief-Consequence connection, distinguishing between healthy and unhealthy evaluation of the loss.

THE APPRAISAL OF PAIN: A SECONDARY SYMPTOM

Grief is a process of experiencing the pain of the loss, yearning, searching, and re-searching for a new meaning to life without the dead person, and reconstructing and restructuring one's "irrational" (dysfunctional) thinking to a more rational (functional), realistic mode. Unlike depression, grief is a deceased-focused process of searching for alternatives to life without the loved one who is the center of the pain and the yearning. Grief is a two-track process (Rubin, 1981, 1999), which Stroebe and Schut (1999) emphasize as an oscillation between grieving loss and restoration of life. Having to make choices regarding a relationship with the deceased and the reality of the loss is painful.

Pain in grief is undesirable but also unavoidable. The thought of experiencing pain is often stressful, and frequently bereaved persons will tend to find ways to avoid or bypass it only to realize that this is almost impossible. In CBT-REBT terms, the loss (A) is followed by an emotional consequence (C) related to the belief (B) that "I will never see her again." According to Ellis (1976, 1994), humans have a pronounced biosocial tendency, particularly following adverse events like death, to evaluate emotions in a dysfunctional way that often creates a disturbance about disturbance. In the case of pain following a loss through death, the appraisal of the primary emotion (i.e., pain) as too painful is dysfunctional because it creates a secondary symptom of pain (or anxiety) about pain. *Meta-cognition* and *cognitive*

TABLE 8.2   Healthy and Unhealthy Beliefs and Emotional Consequences

A	Adaptive Evaluation: Flexible, moderate, "fluent" narrative		Maladaptive Evaluation: Rigid, extreme, "frozen" narrative	
	B Belief	C Consequence	B Belief	C Consequence
Activating Event	I miss her but life goes on.	Yearning	I will never get over the loss.	Depressive response
	My life has changed forever.	Sadness	Since her death, my life is worthless.	Depressive response
	I know that pain is part of my life.	Frustration tolerance	When I think about his death, I can't stand the pain.	Frustration intolerance
	I did all I could to prevent him from going, I realize it was his decision.	Moderated anger	I should have insisted on him staying at home. I will never forgive myself. It's my fault.	Intensified anger and guilt

attentional syndrome are terms used to describe dysfunctional evaluation related to human nature of thinking about thinking (Kassinove & Tafrate, 2002; Wells, 2005). It is a cyclical dysfunctional evaluation about the harmful consequences (cognitive, emotional, physical, or behavioral) that frequently results in efforts to avoid the undesired or feared consequence. Helping bereaved clients therapeutically not to fear pain but rather accept it as a normal part of grieving as well as teaching them functional ways to handle or manage the pain will facilitate a more adaptive process.

This is one client's evaluation of his ability or inability to cope with the intensity of the emotions experienced after a traumatic event: "When they told me that my son was dead, I experienced an overwhelming pain, and I started crying. I was alarmed at my distress because I think it is awful to cry" (a father whose son was killed in a military training accident).

Another example is of a bereaved mother who lost her teenage son in a road accident (Adverse event), who feels angry with herself (emotional Consequence), and is telling herself (B) that she should have functioned better following the loss; she then tells herself (a meta-cognition) that she shouldn't condemn herself and is angry at herself as she fails to do so. The mother's anger directed toward herself over feeling anger at herself is a secondary symptom.

COMMENTARY

We can see how the cognitive element of evaluating the emotional consequence forms a cyclical dysfunctional pattern which increases the distress.
In the case of the father, it is the evaluation concerning crying which results
in self-depreciation and anger. The mother is grieving and is self-devaluing
because she is not functioning, an evaluation that increases anger toward
herself. The meta-cognition increases the distress, forming a secondary
symptom.

THE THERAPEUTIC FRAMEWORK OF CBT-REBT IN GRIEF AND COMPLICATED GRIEF

Within the CBT-REBT conceptual framework, the grief process is an adaptive form
of thinking and emoting that helps bereaved persons construct their disrupted and, at
times, shattered belief system into a more meaningful one. Thoughts about death are
neither avoided nor constantly remembered but are rearranged into a balanced system of sadly deploring but successfully living with the great loss and reorganizing the
relationship with the deceased. Grief that has a healing effect and that adapts to the
sad reality, which no longer includes the deceased, involves pronounced negative emotions, such as sadness, frustration, and pain. Yet it minimizes unhealthy, self-defeating
feelings of depressive response, despair, anxiety, and self- and other-deprecation.

THE THERAPEUTIC ALLIANCE

In cognitive grief therapy, a therapeutic alliance is a tool to encourage the clients
to reevaluate and change their distorted thinking. Moreover, in addition to cultural
sensitivity, cognitive therapy approaches the therapeutic alliance as a vehicle that
needs to be tailored to each client's idiosyncratic needs. Some clients will benefit from a more formal type of therapeutic relationship, whereas others will be
more comfortable with an informal one (Dryden, 1991). Establishing an effective
therapeutic alliance in working with the bereaved is particularly critical as clients
are vulnerable and susceptible to the way the therapist responds to their distress.
Also, the alliance is viewed as a dynamic process so that its reevaluation along
the course of therapy is recommended. Similarly, in cognitive therapy the choice
and application of intervention is in accordance with each client's idiosyncratic
needs. Some clients benefit from a more cognitive type of intervention (an inner
dialogue), whereas others do better with behavioral ones (Malkinson, 2007, 2011).
These interventions will be discussed in detail after the following case example.

COGNITIVE ASSESSMENT AND ESTABLISHING B-C CONNECTION

Cognitive perspective denotes the centrality of cognitions in the grief process in
making sense of the loss and constructing a meaning to life without the loved
one who died and in rearranging inner relationships with the deceased and then

integrating them into one's beliefs that were shattered. It involves a painful search of what was lost, never to be regained, and what could be remembered in spite of the pain these memories elicit. In this sense the grief process is similar to weaving, where each thread is a significant element in the fabric. For this reason the importance of a detailed assessment of the belief (B) and how it influences the emotional, behavioral, and sensational consequences (C) is essential.

Thus, a triple assessment is carried out: (1) a general demographic assessment (details about the loss, the circumstances of its occurrence, relationship to the deceased, etc.); (2) a Two-Track Model assessment addressing the needs of each axis, and (3) a cognitive assessment. An accurate and comprehensive assessment of the bereaved person's appraisal of his or her loss will disclose the nature of the "story," the narrative, with focus on the way in which the event is described. In addition to assessing both functional and dysfunctional cognitions about the adverse event and the consequences, an initial assessment of the "hot" cognition is made. A "hot" cognition is the one most connected to the emotional experience (Ellis, 2002). Ellis (2002) maintained that evaluations of the event "as 'good' or 'bad' … on some level or other, are emotional assessments, they include feelings" (p. 22).

FORMULATING A HYPOTHESIS

A hypothesis is a tentative formulation of the therapist's understanding of the client's belief system and the related emotional and behavioral consequences that maintain the distress. A hypothesis represents the therapist's own view of how the client's beliefs, emotions, and behaviors form the B-C connection, and it is based on feedback the therapist receives from the client (Selvini-Palazzoli, Boscolo, Chechin, & Pratta, 1980). To formulate a hypothesis regarding the client's thinking, and its interaction with emotions and behaviors (DiGiuseppe, 1991; Malkinson, 2007) and meaning construction, the therapist should first seek to explore details concerning the activating event (Adverse event). The way the story is told, language used by the client, nonverbal cues, body gestures, breathing, tone of voice, pauses, and so forth, are part of what is being observed by the therapist as important sources for formulating the hypothesis that will assist in planning the intervention.

In CBT, between-session assignments are an integral part of therapy and have several functions:

1. A tool to evaluate the client's difficulties during the process
2. A way to practice cognitive, emotional, and behavioral changes
3. A way to strengthen therapeutic alliance and assess its process

A CASE ILLUSTRATION APPLYING CBT-REBT WITH COMPLICATION IN GRIEF

Helen, a woman in her 50s, requested therapy following the sudden death of her husband from a brain hemorrhage 10 months earlier. The family was on holiday and the husband collapsed suddenly. The medical team that was called immediately pronounced his death. She is the mother of three children: two sons aged 18 and 13 and a daughter aged 8. She works as a secretary. She described her husband as a healthy, energetic person, a loving husband, and a devoted father to the children. She describes their loving relationship this way: "[He was] a friend and a lover, [and] life without him lost its meaning. I don't know how I can continue life without him." He was under stress during a transition period in his life. Since the sudden death of her husband, she has had difficulties in functioning. She cries a lot and worries that if "she doesn't pull herself together," it will be terrible, and the children will suffer. She feels angry with herself for not being able to return to her previous level of functioning (a secondary symptom). Following the death, she told the children that life will go on, and she made efforts to return to the usual routine but alas without success: "I can't take it any longer." She has difficulties in sleeping, has lost her appetite, and has lost interest in her work. She is repeatedly asking, "Why, why did it happen to me? I lost my best friend and life lost its meaning; why did it happen to me?"

FORMULATION

From the perspective of the TTMoB, we can make an initial assessment and identify components from both Track I (biopsychological functioning) and Track II (relationship with the deceased). From the perspective of Track I, Helen describes experiencing a noticeable sense of turmoil—that of a shattered world. There is a marked sense of shock, disbelief, and difficulties in functioning at work, somatic difficulties in sleeping and appetite, crying and distress and loss of control, indications characteristic of traumatic loss—that of witnessing the sudden loss of her husband while on vacation. Helen expressed anger toward herself for being unable to function. From the perspective of Track II, the information provided by Helen is an indication of positive effects regarding her deceased husband, with some elements of difficulty of coming to terms with the loss and acceptance of the finality of the loss. There will be a need to assess whether difficulties are related to the sudden and traumatic circumstances of the loss.

Identifying Irrational Beliefs and Formulating a Hypothesis

In Helen's narrative we can identify a number of irrational beliefs: "I must pull myself together." "I must return to routine and must not cry." "I must find the answer to why it happened to me."

Helen's irrational beliefs were self-directed and included self-devaluation resulting in emotional consequences of anger, depressive mood, and difficulties in functioning. We can hypothesize that these increase her distress over the tragic loss of her husband and affect her grief, as she repetitively demands from herself to find an answer to why it had happened to her, to pull herself together, and not to cry. From a cognitive perspective, these irrational beliefs and asking herself over and over again "why?" questions may complicate a healthier experience of grief.

The Therapeutic Alliance, Cognitive Assessment, and Agreement on the Goal of Therapy

The therapeutic alliance with Helen was carried along with assessment and by the provision of information about the grief process, normalizing her overwhelming experience and legitimizing the temporality of her emotional state and feeling of the shattered world: "You lost your husband so suddenly, and it's normal to feel that your world has been shattered. This is grief that people experience after such a loss, and many times it feels as if you are going crazy." It was hypothesized that the shock and trauma of the sudden death of Helen's husband threatened her role as a mother and was mixed with pain of loss of her best friend and lover. Helen's concern oscillates between the two tracks of functioning and of the relationship with the deceased.

To the question what she would expect from therapy, Helen replied: "I don't really know what to expect." Helen accepted the therapist's suggestion to meet two or three more times to explore what she could and would like to gain from therapy.

During the next two sessions, the ABC model of emotional distress was explained, and details about rational and irrational thinking and the emotional consequences were provided. Also, information was given to Helen about what is distinctive about an adaptive course of grief (sadness, pain, yearning, moderate anger, moderate feelings of guilt). The introduction of the ABC components of the model brought Helen to comment on the way she was obsessively asking "why?" questions, which increased her distress but did not help her in finding an answer. Helen wanted therapy to focus on assisting her to adopt a healthier way of grieving, to function better as a mother, to learn a more rational way of thinking about the loss and life that followed it, and to search for ways to function and continue with life and the pain and sadness that are part of it (primarily Track I). In addition, the overarching goal was to assist Helen in her search for ways to reorganize life without her deceased husband while continuing an inner bond with him.

Because of the flooding effect of her rumination over the death of her husband, an intervention into a dialogue with repetitive thoughts that are expressed as questions is applied with Helen. This was followed by planning a visit to her husband's grave. This is demonstrated in the next section.

A Dialogue With Repetitive Thoughts

The flooding effect following a loss event, especially a sudden unexpected loss under traumatic circumstances, is frequently expressed in a repetitive manner, often in the form of questions such as "why" or "how" could it happen to me. Often, intrusive thoughts appear as repetitive questions, also known as rumination, that are defined as "engaging in thoughts and behaviors that maintain one's focus on one's negative emotions and on the possible causes and consequences of those emotions" (Nolen-Hoeksema, 2001, p. 546). Paradoxically, the bereaved is engaged in a search for an answer, but the repetitiveness forms a continuous cognitive loop that blocks the solution and increases the distress. The bereaved person's thinking is irrational: "I must find the answer" (a demand), "I must function, and I must not cry" (thinking about thinking that creates a secondary symptom) that increases emotional and behavioral distress.

To help Helen experience an adaptive grief process in addition to thought stopping and distraction, a dialogue with repetitive thoughts was applied. Creating a dialogue with the "why" question is a way of increasing cognitive control over an inner sense of not having one. If distraction and thought stopping aim at distancing oneself, at least momentarily from the disturbing emotion, a dialogue with a repetitive "irrational" thought involves attending to repetitive thinking and its emotional and physical consequences, and in searching for a more "rational" reply.

Applying a Dialogue With Helen's Repetitive Thought

Following normalizing the sense of flooding of the question "why," the therapist distinguishes between the loss as an external uncontrollable event and its internal way of cognitive processing as a way to increase the feeling of control. This is followed by an explanation about the idea of the dialogue in which there is an answer to each question that pops into the head. Thus, the question "why" is not left unanswered but instead is being answered. The question–answer form increases a sense of inner control and, as a consequence, minimizes its flooding effect.

In Helen's case it was a way of introducing an alternative way of thinking about her anger at herself for not being able to overcome her crying.

Here is an excerpt of applying this intervention with Helen.

Helen: I can't stop thinking why, why did he die? How could he have left me? Why, why did it happen to me? Why did my best friend and lover die?

Therapist: This is a justified question, but you also say, "I must have an answer," followed by additional questions. What could you possibly tell yourself as an answer?

Helen: That's the problem—that the question keeps popping up over and over again.

Therapist: Let's think of an answer because without an answer to the question, as you described, it will keep popping up.

Helen: I have no answer to that question. I can't think of an answer, only of the question.

Therapist explains the nature of rumination in terms of a thought that repeats itself but can be identified.

Therapist: In a way this is an answer—can you tell yourself, when the question "why" pops again, "I have no answer to that question"?

Helen: (Listens and pauses for a minute, takes a deep breath, and then says loudly) Why, why? (Then hesitantly): I have no answer to that question. Rationally, I know that it is irrational. I realize that I need not insist on finding an answer.

Therapist encourages Helen in her effort and comments on the deep breath she took.

Therapist: Did you notice what you did? You took a deep breath, that's good. And, you are right in realizing that as of now there is no point in insisting "I must have an answer" on finding an answer. How do you feel now with the answer of "I don't have an answer and I need not insist on finding one"? Do you feel more, less, or the same level of flooding?

Helen: Less.

Therapist: Good. That helps you take better care of yourself in moments of great pain and sadness. Paradoxically, not answering the question increases your sense of helplessness. So, I suggest you practice and apply it when you feel distressed as well as in between these feelings so that you master it.

In the next session Helen reported the following:

Helen: I cried and couldn't stop thinking that he left me never to return. The thought that my life is worthless was running in my head and I couldn't stop thinking "Why? Why?" And then I remembered what you told me about "why" questions. I reminded myself that it is better to find an answer rather than repeating "why" questions. It helped because then I could think about other things. It helped to make me feel less overwhelmed. In a sort of a way it eased the pain which was mixed with yearning for my husband. The yearning was most intense and at times unbearable.

The therapist's next comment referred to both efforts to apply the dialogue and the experience of pain and yearning:

Therapist: So you felt more in control over your questions and that's good, but you also experienced intense yearning for your husband. Can you recall what you told yourself over the feeling of yearning?

Helen: I was thinking that I don't know whether I am strong enough to withstand the pain of yearning.

Therapist: This is how you feel as of now. Would like to explore it?

Gaining control over the "why" question was made possible by giving up the "must," the insistence of finding an answer. However, at this point in therapy, it was perceived by Helen as partial and specific and not yet generalized. In a way the therapy will proceed by further exploring the meaning of inner control and the issue of the choice one has over feelings of pain (a secondary symptom) that come with the yearning and searching for ways to deal with the pain involved in thinking about her husband. Helen was asked to continue practicing in between sessions the dialogue with the "why" question, identify irrational beliefs, and change them into rational ones. She was also instructed to be attentive to her breathing as a way of reducing physical tension.

Homework assignments given between therapy sessions are composed of two tracks: the functional life–focused track whose aim is to assist the client to take responsibility for various activities, reduce anxiety, and increase his or her motivation for renewing interpersonal relations; and a relationship loss–focused track, in which the focus is to help the client reduce emotional distress, and facilitate a balanced relation with the deceased's representations. It includes such activities as writing, visiting the grave, practicing Rational Emotive Imagery (REI), or a combination of these.

Planning a Visit to the Grave

Helen was telling the therapist that since the death of her husband, she has avoided visiting his grave. It is part of Jewish tradition to visit the grave and put a gravestone and pray for the soul of the dead, and as the first anniversary was approaching, Helen talked about her fears as the day was approaching, mostly the thought of seeing the grave. The therapist normalized these thoughts and the related fears, commenting that this is a common reaction among bereaved persons and asked if, for Helen, visiting the cemetery and the grave signals the finality of the loss which she tried to avoid. Helen confirmed it. Helen's belief "If I go there then he is really dead, and I don't want to think of him in this way" is followed by the behavioral consequence of avoidance. It was important to normalize and legitimize her fears and explore her thoughts and the emotional and behavioral consequences that block her from visiting the grave and consequently delaying coming to terms with the loss. Helping Helen to get over her fears and overcome her avoidance will enable her to explore alternatives of reorganizing her relationship with the deceased husband.

This is an excerpt from the discussion with Helen about visiting the grave:

Helen: If I visit his grave then I must really believe he is dead, and I am not ready yet to tell it to myself. Rationally, I know he is dead but emotionally I don't believe it.

Due to its flooding effect, it is common to experience emotion as a belief, as Helen indicated, implying difficulties in controlling emotions. She distinguishes between knowing "rationally" but not believing it emotionally. As a way to assist Helen to regain control over her reactions, the therapist makes a distinction between a cognition and an emotion and also explains the difference between rational and irrational beliefs and their related emotional consequences (healthy and unhealthy).

Therapist: Indeed, this is painful and perhaps your way of evaluating it is what makes it more painful. Let's try to distinguish between a thought and an emotion: When you tell yourself "Rationally, I know he is dead but emotionally I don't believe it," you really mean that the emotion is very intense and we want to find out what the irrational belief is "behind" the emotion. When emotion is so intense, we tend to confuse between a belief and emotional or behavioral consequence. And when you say,

"I am not yet ready to tell myself he is dead," this is a belief (probably an irrational one), and what do you feel (an emotional or behavioral consequence)?

Helen: It's too painful to tell myself that he is dead.

Therapist: Yes, it is painful. So maybe you are cognitively telling yourself that it will be too painful and you will not be able to stand it, and the behavioral consequence is avoidance (explaining secondary symptom)?

Helen: (Tears in her eyes, quiet for a moment) Yes, I will not be able to stand it, it's awful, I don't even want to think about it.

Therapist explains the difference between the pain that is a normative emotional consequence in a healthy grief experience and the evaluation (meta-cognition) that it is too painful and awful which increases the distress (Malkinson, 2007).

In understanding REI (we will elaborate on REI in the next case example) and applying it, Helen imagined herself going to the cemetery and visiting her husband's grave. She was instructed to focus on her emotions (fear) and measure it on the Subjective Units of Distress (SUDS) (9), and, at her own pace, do something to reduce its intensity. Helen's face looked very tense at first and gradually she looked less distressed and said she reduced the intensity of the pain to 7.

Therapist: Good, what did you do?

Helen: I told myself that it's painful, and pain is part of my life nowadays.

Therapist: That's a good way of self-talk. What is the difference between pain intensity of 9 and 7?

Helen: There is a sense of a little relief.

Therapist: That is the idea: to be aware of the pain but to relieve its intensity.

The purpose of the REI is to assist Helen through self-search for a way (cognitive, behavioral, or somatic) to reduce her emotional stress and find how this leads to a change of her evaluation about the pain that cannot be avoided but can be accepted. Helen's thinking about the loss of her beloved husband is painful, but avoiding it increases her suffering.

Helen's homework assignment was to practice REI daily, which she did, and as the day of the first anniversary approached, she reported in the following session how difficult and painful it was to visit the grave. She said that what had helped was reminding herself that she was able to experience the pain and overcome its avoidance.

Preparing for Termination and Follow-up

Therapy terminated a number of sessions after the first anniversary of the death. Helen said that she felt stronger and wished to end therapy. At follow-up 3 months later, Helen summed up her experience during therapy: "This was very hard; I was very skeptical that anything could help me after my life shattered. I miss my husband a lot and feel very sad when I think that he will not be with us to see that the children he loved so much are growing, but we talk about him and laugh when we remember his playfulness. It will always be sad."

REFLECTION

Helen requested therapy to help put some order in her shattered life following the sudden loss of her husband. She was overwhelmed by the difficulties she was experiencing and was specifically anxious about her inability to function as a mother. Regaining her ability to function was her major concern. She was not yet ready to delve in Track II—relationship with the deceased issues. Thus, from the TTMoB perspective, the focus of therapy was primarily Track I, and Track II was indirectly introduced and discussed. From a cognitive therapy perspective, the goal was to reduce Helen's distress, facilitate a healthier way of mourning, and teach her an alternative way of thinking (less rumination) so she can function better as a mother. For her, at the time she entered therapy, the most important issue was to regain control over her life. Helping her to overcome her fear and avoidance of visiting the grave as the first anniversary of her husband's death was approaching opened up some of the relationship to the deceased and worked on her accepting pain and yearning for her husband as part of her life.

CLINICAL CONCLUDING REMARKS

In the case example, we introduced the reader to the ABC model of CBT-REBT. CBT-REBT in grief stresses the centrality of cognitions and the idea that they are changeable even though the loss of the beloved person is not; it emphasizes that in spite of the unchangeable circumstances of the loss, the choices people have over its interpretation remain. Central to this model is establishing the Belief-Consequence connection as a way to teach the bereaved client that appraisal of the event can be changed. We described the framework of this model and ways to formulate therapeutic interventions that are appropriate to idiosyncratic needs of the bereaved individual. Therapeutic alliance, assessment, and hypothesis formulation are carried out collaboratively with the client toward determining the goal of therapy so that grief can take its adaptive course. Strengthening the therapeutic alliance, applying between-session assignments, and assessing the process continue throughout therapy.

Cognitive therapy, similar to other therapeutic models, approaches grief as a human and natural response to loss, applying interventions that are aimed at facilitating a healthy process of functioning in life (Track I) and continuing relationship with the deceased (Track II) and of which painful emotions such as yearning and sadness are part. Often, bereaved people have an evaluation about their grief, and pain and yearning, an evaluation of the emotional consequence (a meta-cognition) that increases their distress and disrupts the normal course of their grief. The CBT-REBT model highlighted the distinction between adaptive (rational) and maladaptive (irrational) grief. The interventions used in the case to facilitate a healthy though painful grief process included cognitive strategies (a dialogue with repetitive thoughts) and behavioral ones (a visit to the grave) as ways to restore what was shattered with the death of the loved one.

9

Cognitive Therapy
Applying Imagery and Mindfulness

*I*n this chapter we describe a CBT-REBT intervention in complicated grief using Rational Emotive Imagery incorporating elements of mindfulness (Segal, Williams, & Teasdale, 2002). Works by Linehan (1993), Kabat-Zinn (1990), and Fletcher and Hays (1995) introduced new strategies in applying CBT that emphasize awareness and paying attention to the moment along with the development of interventions that focus on positive alternatives in positive psychology (Lyubomirsky, 2008).

A central feature in these models is nonjudgmental acceptance of symptoms and self-acceptance. Mindfulness-based cognitive therapy of depression is widely applied today (Segal et al., 2002; Wells, 2005). The idea of nonjudgmental self-acceptance was postulated by Ellis (1962) as distinguished from self-esteem when he stressed that we are fallible human beings, and our tendency to judge and devaluate our worth increases emotional distress. In line with his model of rationality Ellis advocated that self-acceptance of ourselves nonjudgmentally is possible with a forceful challenging (disputation) of irrational beliefs. According to him, changing irrational (dysfunctional) beliefs to rational (functional) ones is mainly a philosophical change that decreases emotional disturbance. Rational Emotive Imagery (REI) was first developed by Maultsby (1971) as a technique to help the clients feel less emotionally disturbed. By imagining the stressful event (A) and the emotional consequence, the client was instructed to force him- or herself to change belief (B), which consequently led the client to change the disturbing emotion into a moderate one (C).

Changes were made in the belief system (B-C connection). Ellis (1993) modified REI to be applied "in a more emotive-evocative and less disputational way" (pp. II.8–II.10). In the revised version the client is instructed to imagine the worst thing that might happen (Activating event) and feel the emotional consequence (C) as intensely and as vividly as possible. Similar to awareness in mindfulness, concentrating on the image and experiencing emotions eventually lead to a decrease in the intensity of the negative feeling. Ellis postulated that the change in the intensity of emotions enables a self-prescribing of a rational belief or a coping statement. In mindfulness, the focused attention on thoughts, feelings, and body sensation is applied as a way to increase awareness of the present moment and toward gaining a greater sense of self-acceptance and minimizing the evaluative judgmental elements. Ellis's concept of nonjudgmental self-acceptance denotes a nonberating evaluation of oneself for one's weakness (Ellis, 2006).

In this chapter we will incorporate elements of mindfulness in REI, with a special focus on paying attention to body sensation in a case of complicated grief. We will refer to it as REBI (Rational Emotive Body Imagery).

The emotional consequences in grief, such as pain, anger, shame, and depression, are frequently very intense and overwhelming. The flooding effect of emotions can lead to an evaluation (a meta-cognition) by the bereaved person as too painful and therefore be avoided. Acknowledging the emotions, gaining awareness of them, being attentive to them nonjudgmentally, and accepting them as part of grief can help in experiencing an adaptive process.

APPLYING RATIONAL EMOTIVE BODY IMAGERY

The interventions of imagery and exposure have been part of cognitive therapy repertoire for a long time and are known as effective interventions applied in treatment for a variety of emotional disturbances (PTSD, depression, anxiety, etc.). Prolonged Exposure (PE) is a well-known evidenced-based protocol developed by Foa and Rothbaum (1998) for treatment of PTSD and, since its first application, it has been adapted to treatment in a variety of problems.

The basic assumption underlying REBI is that the client links his or her emotional distress (including a body sensation) to the event (Activating event–Consequence connection), and not to its interpretation or evaluation (Belief-Consequence connection; Humphrey, 2009; Malkinson, 2007, 2010). It is thus important to carefully construct a safe setting to guide the client for the imagery. The focus is on the imagined framework, not the content of the imagery.

THE FRAMEWORK OF APPLYING REBI

1. The therapist creates the setting and guides the client in the imagined framework (not the content of the imagery).
2. The client chooses the event and relives it.
3. The focus of the REBI is the consequence aiming at reducing the emotional distress by establishing a new B-C connection.
4. Once the client reexperiences A-C connection, he or she is instructed to do something to reduce the intensity of the emotion or physical body sensations (C). This can be done by changing the imagined scene or by focusing on physical senses or changing the cognition.

5. The intensity of the emotion or body sensation is measured, and the client is asked what he or she did to decrease it.
6. A new B-C connection is formed.
7. The difference between rational (adaptive) and irrational (nonadaptive) beliefs and the emotional/sensational consequences is introduced.

By using an imagined recollection of the client's choice of the event (A) and its accompanying distress (C), the client is instructed to measure the degree of distress by using the subjective units of distress (SUDS), the therapist guides the client toward doing something of his or her choice that will lessen the distress. This instruction introduces the cognitive element that will guide the client in choosing the way: cognitive (I said to myself …), emotional (I felt less angry), behavioral (I did something else), or body sensation (there was a sense of relief in my chest) to reduce the distress. It is the beginning of the introduction of the cognitive element as an intermediary between the event and the accompanying emotional and physical outcome (B-C connection). It allows the client to recapture the event that he or she considers is the origin of the distress and, as this is experienced at the moment, to either alter its intensity or reduce it. REBI emphasizes the client's choice (and control) of the distress level even when he or she has no control over the event. Finally, the therapist introduces the difference between rational (adaptive) and irrational (nonadaptive) beliefs and the emotional/sensational consequences.

The treatment described below with Neli, who was referred to therapy because of what she presented as depression, consists of 10 sessions and a follow-up session 3 months later.

FROM DEPRESSIVE RESPONSE TO ADAPTIVE GRIEF: THE CASE OF NELI

The framework of treatment with Neli included establishing a therapeutic alliance, an evaluation of the problem, availability of social support, and cognitive assessment of the B-C belief-emotional framework, assessing potential to change and possible difficulty. Demographic evaluation and loss-focused exploration (circumstances of the loss, connection with the deceased, details of the family history, etc.) were also done, and a third type of assessment according to the Two-Track Model of Bereavement (TTMoB) was used to determine the nature and relative significance of the tracks. On the basis of these assessments, the choice of intervention strategies was made. The course of therapy also included legitimizing, normalizing, and providing information on the grief process as well as teaching the difference between adaptive and nonadaptive bereavement, and agreeing on the aim of treatment. Between-session assignments are given to maintain a therapeutic continuity and strengthen cognitive, emotional, and behavioral changes.

PHASES OF TREATMENT

1. Establishing a therapeutic alliance and a triple evaluation of the problem (demographic evaluation, TTMoB, and cognitive)
2. Legitimizing, normalizing, and providing information on the grief process, the difference between adaptive and nonadaptive bereavement, and selection of the interventional strategy
3. Agreement on the aim of treatment and between-session assignments to maintain a therapeutic continuity and strengthen cognitive and behavioral changes

Establishing a Therapeutic Alliance, Assessment, and Agreeing on a Goal

Neli, unmarried, aged 29, requested treatment for what she describes as acute depression, profuse crying, difficulties in sleeping, and general unease.

Neli had previously received CBT for social anxiety and was helped considerably. This familiarity with CBT made it easier for Neli to establish therapeutic alliance and focus on her depression within the framework of this model. When asked about her reasons for the present request for treatment, Neli responded that she had been depressed since her brother committed suicide, and as the first anniversary of his death approached, she was increasingly depressed. When she awakes, she immediately thinks of him and is angry at him and at herself, has trouble getting up in the morning and concentrating at work, takes time off, and has no interest in her surroundings. This description resembles one of complicated grief, and the therapist's hypothesis is that Neli's intrusive thoughts regarding her brother's death have increased her distress.

Neli talks about herself, her family and brother, and the circumstances surrounding his suicide. Neli works as a secretary in a law firm. Her parents, an older brother, and younger sister are still alive. The brother who committed suicide was younger than she and was closest to her. When asked about her family relationships, Neli answered that they were normal—neither too close nor too distant.

Concerning her suicidal brother, Neli relates that he suffered from acute mental problems, was hospitalized for several months and then released. He took drugs for some months. She said that they were close and had a mutual understanding. In the days preceding his death, he was severely depressed, seemingly asking to be helped. Neli bursts into tears as she describes how she sat beside him, telling him how much she was concerned and how much she loved him. The crying intensifies when she goes into detail of how, because of her own problems, she was unable to continue sitting by him and got up and moved to another room. While she was sitting in the other room, she heard a thud that puzzled her. A little later, they told her that her brother had fallen off the fifth floor balcony. Neli knows that her brother ended his life and that it was no accident. He had told her in one of their earlier conversations that he had no strength to carry on with his life, and she had begged him not to hurt himself. She felt guilty that she hadn't looked after him properly, and she felt she deserved to be punished. Also, she was angry with him for ending his life by suicide.

FORMULATION

From the perspective of the TTMoB, we can see that components from both tracks are apparent. Feeling depressed, crying, somatic difficulties in sleeping and functioning at work, and questions relating to self-worth represent elements of biopsychological functioning of Track I. There are marked features of Track II, relationship to the deceased, mainly concerning the relationship prior to the loss as well as the circumstances of the death: To what extent does thinking about her brother lead Neli to a negative self-view and negative feelings toward her brother? Recalling the circumstances of her brother's death is accompanied by feelings of anger toward herself and her brother, and guilt for not being sensitive to his distress and preventing him from committing suicide, which causes her difficulties with coming to terms with the loss and accepting the finality of the loss. In therapy these areas of conflict will be explored along with inner reorganization of the relationship with her brother and a search for an alternative, healthier cognitive appraisal of his death.

As mentioned before, Neli had been in CBT and there was no need to introduce her to it but reinforce it instead and give her information about the grief process, legitimization for experiencing it, and normalization for strengthening her responses.

Evaluation of Neli's Cognitive Process Regarding the Loss

As part of involving the client in the therapeutic process, a self-report is used to assess changes. At the beginning and end of therapy, Neli is asked to fill out the list of statements that dealt with irrational thoughts about bereavement, for evaluating her thinking as therapy progresses. The questionnaire is solely used for clinical evaluation and includes 10 sentences in which the client answers and evaluates the statements reflecting his or her thoughts (1 = disagrees; 5 = agrees completely). The maximum score is 50. Neli's score was 46. Table 9.1 shows the list of statements.

TABLE 9.1   Neli's List of Grief-Related Statements

Below is a list of statements that are frequently expressed by bereaved persons. Read the list and indicate on scale from 1 to 5 the level of your agreement with each one. Please note that 1 represents no agreement at all, and 5 is a high level of agreement.

Do not agree 1____2____3____4____5 Fully agree

I must get over the loss. 4

Just thinking about life without … is awful. 5

The pain of the loss is too much for me. 5

Life without … is unbearable. 5

I should have done more; I will never forgive myself. 5

Why did … do it to me? 5

It's terrible to think that I continue to live. 4

Nobody understands me. 3

I will never get over the loss. 5

Total 46

Assessment of Neli's Belief-Consequence (B-C) Connection

The self-report provides information regarding Neli's evaluation of the strength of her cognitions, which will be assessed by her again at the end of therapy. The next step is to assess Neli's "hot" cognitions, the thoughts that are most connected to her emotional experience.

Client: I am angry, but I miss him and still love him.

Therapist: What are you thinking about when you are angry?

Client: I remember how it was just before it happened: He looked as though he was giving in or was angry, he looked tense … and then he is leaving the room (she passes into the present tense), going in and out, and I am thinking about what is happening to him … (still in present tense) and then I hear a terrible thud and I enter his room—he flies out of the window, and I feel as though I could have saved him and I ask myself: Does he want me to save him? (Cries) And perhaps he is angry with me that I didn't save him.

Therapist: This is indeed very traumatic. What are you feeling?

Client: Terribly angry with him for doing this and with myself for not saving him.

Therapist: It seems that anger is very dominant and intense. You describe what happened and express anger with yourself and your brother's anger with you; could you please tell me which anger is more difficult for you?

Client: I am thinking all the time that he wants me to save him or do something.

Therapist: And when you feel so, which anger is greater for you?

Client: (Ponders and appears stressed) … my brother's anger with me.

Therapist: And what do you say to yourself about that?

Client: I feel responsible.

Therapist hypothesizes that Neli is thinking about her brother's anger with her, which makes her feel guilty as she blames herself for not saving his life as she must have done, which is a thought about her thought, a meta-cognition.

Therapist: Responsible for what?

Client: For his death.

Therapist: Let us try to understand what goes on in your mind that makes you see yourself responsible for his death. What are you telling yourself?

Client: I guess … for not going into his room and not paying attention … I was angry with him, that he was sick, I didn't want him to be sick.

Therapist: And as this is what you are thinking, what do you feel when you …?

Client: (Hesitates and has a painful look on her face)

Therapist: I can see how difficult it is for you, but perhaps we can try to see what happened and distinguish between the facts and the thoughts and your emotions about what happened. You were sitting with your brother in the room, you got up, left, and went into the other room, and then you heard a sudden thud. What are you telling yourself?

Client: (Is silent and then speaks) Something like "You were depressed and not aware," or something similar, "and he tried to tell you something."

Therapist: That is an important part you are mentioning. You are aware of your distress. How did you feel when you thought you were depressed and nonresponsive when he tried to tell you something?

Client: Not sincere, inconsiderate, awful ...

At this stage the therapist becomes aware of Neli's hesitations and of her inability to express her thoughts aloud ("I was selfish and insincere") and her emotions (guilt that she feels but cannot terminate), a difficulty that leads the therapist to hypothesize that this is Neli's "hot" cognition, one that is associated with self-criticism, and her diffidence in saying this aloud stems from her (incorrect) evaluation that making a verbal statement would be too painful and commit herself in both her and the therapist's eyes, as being "bad and unworthy." The therapist provides information about the B-C connection, about thinking about thinking, and differentiates between thoughts that she has about her brother, her anger with him that he chose suicide as a means of solving his problems, her fear that she will never be able to forgive him, her thoughts about herself for not saving her brother because she was immersed in her own problems, and the accompanying feeling of guilt that he will never forgive her (the link between thoughts and emotional outcome, B-C connection).

The therapist provides information on bereavement (personal, individual): about normative grief (pining, sadness, moderate anger, and pain) and how, especially under very traumatic circumstances like suicide, there are feelings of depression, anxiety, guilt, and anger. The therapist suggests that therapy will concentrate on trying to help Neli experience adaptive grief, and Neli agrees to this. Together, the therapist and Neli examine Neli's list of grief-related statements (Table 9.1) and the table of thought-induced responses and the accompanying emotional sequelae (see Table 8.2 in previous chapter). Neli gets a copy for exercises. At the end of the session, Neli agrees to do homework and write down all her thoughts in connection with her brother's death.

At the next session, Neli presents her lists containing details of her irrational beliefs about herself and her brother: "I am insincere, bad, and irresponsible, I was involved with myself, and I didn't hear his cry for help." "It was wrong for him to commit suicide—he was wrong." Neli's most prominent irrational beliefs are self-condemnation and self-devaluation for being insensitive to her brother's distress and for taking responsibility for his death.

Neli describes her difficulties in writing down her thoughts and her inability to concentrate. She is encouraged to write through the pain, but at the same time, her pain is recognized as valid and hard to bear. Neli learns to identify and differentiate between the various responses and the relationship to thoughts about grief, while emphasizing the difference between rational and irrational beliefs and the accompanying emotional feelings. The traumatic circumstances of her brother's death are repeatedly reexperienced by Neli. She seems to be preoccupied with her brother's final hours before his death, and images of the last moments keep popping up. The evaluation of the repetitive nature of Neli's experience following the traumatic event and its flooding effect on her life led to applying REBI.

The Intervention: Rational Emotive Body Imagery With Neli

There are several steps in applying this strategy: (a) preparation, that is, explaining to the client what REBI is and how it will be applied and introducing the use of the SUDS (Subjective Units of Distress Scale); (b) reliving of the event while the therapist guides the client's efforts and directs him or her, especially regarding nonverbal expressions; and (c) follow up after completing the imagery. In cases of clients choosing to shut their eyes, the therapist asks them to nod with their head as a way of signaling.

We will detail REBI as it pertains to Neli, as detailed in the moments when she heard the thud of her brother's fall and felt the intense anger at not saving him. Neli is prepared to reconstruct the event after getting explanations on imagery, the SUDS, and their application. The therapist emphasizes that Neli is the one who does the reconstructing of the event and tries to recall her experience, and if she feels distress at any stage, she can signal to the therapist and be helped.

1. **Construction of the imagery**: "Neli, please try to recreate a sort of image or picture of the event of your brother's death. You may shut your eyes and tell me when you are ready."
   Neli closes her eyes and after a while nods her head.
   Therapist: "Recall as close as possible the feeling you experienced when it happened, and make a sign when you are ready." Neli nods her head, and a tense look appears on her face.
2. **Identifying the emotion and body sensation**: "What do you feel?" "Anger" is Neli's response. Neli's body looks very tense. Therapist notices and asks, "How do you experience the anger?" Neli points to her chest. Therapist tells Neli to attend to the body sensation and be aware of it. Neli puts her hand on the chest and seems to be attentive to her experience.
3. **Measuring the intensity of the response**: "Imagine the scale of response and measure its degree: 1 is low intensity, 10 is high intensity." Neli concentrates and answers, "8."
4. **Reducing the intensity of the response**: "Now, as you concentrate on the intensity of the response, try to do something in any way you think will help to reduce the intensity of your emotion. Take your time and as you concentrate, think to yourself that you want to be less distressed. Make a sign when you are done."
   Neli continues to hold her hand on the chest. Therapist encourages her "to listen" to her body and at the same time leads her to do something to reduce the intensity of her distress as a way of empowering her sense of control over her distress. Neli concentrates, takes her time, and at a certain moment, a look of relief appears on her face and her body looks less tense.
5. **Measuring the intensity of the emotional and/or body (physical) response**: The therapist tells Neli that she can open her eyes and asks whether there is a change in the intensity of her anger: "Can you tell me what is the level of the intensity that you feel now?" Neli answers, "6" and opens her eyes.

6. **Evaluating the cognitive change**: Praising Neli for her efforts to do the imagery and change the intensity went together with the assessing the cognitive component. "What did you do? What did you say to yourself to change the intensity from 8 to 6, and what is their difference?"

   Neli answers that she feels a relief in her body in the intensity of the anger after she said to herself: "Don't be so angry with yourself; you know that he was sick." The therapist encourages and reinforces the cognitive and emotional change. She encourages Neli to repeat the statement and to experience the difference in emotional intensity and body sensation and to give it validity. The experience will be reinforced by homework assignments.

7. **Introducing the differences between adaptive (rational) and distressing (irrational) belief and the differences in emotional and body consequences**: Neli's irrational belief "I am insincere, bad, and irresponsible, I was involved with myself, and I didn't hear his cry for help" increased her anger and she kept on condemning herself for not saving him, which further increased her anger. Changing her belief and telling herself, "Don't be so angry with yourself; you know he was sick" decreased the intensity of her anger. She describes how being aware of the tension in her chest and "listening to it" made her feel somewhat relieved. She experienced the difference between healthy and unhealthy anger, and by telling herself not to be so angry with herself she becomes less judgmental of herself.

Practicing the REBI between sessions strengthens Neli's belief in her ability to regulate and control the level of her distress. Neli is asked to repeat the imagery exercise and write her thoughts and accompanying emotions. In the following sessions, Neli reports practicing the imagery, which she says helped her to differentiate between the various responses (pain, fear, guilt, and sadness, mild versus intense anger) and discern again the "bad" thoughts: "If I hadn't left the room … if I hadn't been preoccupied with myself …" Neli's cognitive change with its emotional (and physical) consequences lead the way to experiencing an adaptive grief process.

RATIONAL EMOTIVE BODY IMAGERY

1. Constructing the imagery (A)
2. Identifying the emotion and/or body sensation (Consequence: emotional and body sensation)
3. Measuring the intensity of the response (SUDS)
4. Reducing the intensity of the response (the client is experiencing the moment at his or her own pace)
5. Measuring the intensity of the emotional and/or body (physical) response (SUDS)
6. Evaluating the cognitive change (B)
7. Discussing the cognitive change and its emotional and body consequences (B-C connection)

Preparation for the Gravesite Visit

The therapist emphasizes the hardship in changing thoughts but points out the emotional and physical relief Neli reported when she did the imagery. This relief also indicated a change of irrational into rational beliefs. Therapist suggests that she write a letter to her brother, with the approach of the first anniversary of his death. Neli agreed to write the letter which she planned to read on the anniversary day at the gravesite. We address letter writing to the deceased as a therapeutic technique with a proven therapeutic potential in the next chapter (Malkinson, 2007; Pennebaker, 1993, 1997). From a cognitive perspective, writing down thoughts and emotions while describing the significant living events gives a chance to "release locked in" thoughts. Many of these are irrational cognitions (and their accompanying distressing emotions) and are generally not spoken aloud but rather repeated in the client's mind. Writing and reading the thoughts aloud as an observer allows distancing from the circulating thoughts and effects a change. Also, writing a letter "as if" to the deceased provides an opportunity not only to identify and express these irrational beliefs and to change them into more rational ones but also to explore ways of forgiving oneself and the deceased; it also affords a way of reorganizing the relationship with the deceased. In Neli's treatment, a one-time use of letter writing was indicated to be read at her brother's gravesite as a tool to express her distressing thoughts and feelings so that her appraisal of the tragic loss of her brother will be more adaptive.

The preparation for writing the letter to her brother included the following outline: the choice of time, place, and duration of composition; the choice of details that Neli considered as painful and hard to write; and the choice to express the fear that she will be prevented from writing them down. Simultaneous with the preparation of writing, the visit to her brother's gravesite is planned, and Neli asks her sister to accompany her to ensure that she is not alone as she reads the letter. As with the letter writing, the practicalities of the gravesite visit are chosen, and she imagines the scenario and what will happen to her—a kind of pre-preparation for the day. Neli is requested to keep a log of her thoughts as she prepares for the day.

The following session took place after Neli's visit to the gravesite, where she read the letter. This is Neli's letter that she read at her brother's gravesite, with her sister at her side:

> I am very excited. I want to tell you what is happening to me when I think about you, no day passes without me thinking about you, I understand how you suffered and how hard it was for you, I forgive you … I love you, and I don't want to be angry with you, I don't want to be angry at all. I want you to know that that I wasn't sensitive enough to your state, I hope you understand and forgive me, I know you understand me. I am really sorry that we can't talk, laugh, and cry together. I miss you very, very much.

In the following session, Neli reads the letter to the therapist and describes the pain she experienced while writing the letter and during the visit to the grave the day of the first anniversary. As she reads it aloud, she breaks into tears over the letter to her brother and how much her sister supported her while reading it. She talks about the relief she felt afterward. Neli looks sad and pained but calm and not distressed, and says afterward that she can now, for the first time, recall her brother in better days. During the session, Neli accepted the therapist's remarking that it was tough writing the letter, visiting the grave, and reading it, but it was a necessary path she had to experience in order to reconstruct an inner relationship with her deceased brother.

PREPARING THE TERMINATION OF TREATMENT, AND FOLLOW-UP

In the final session, Neli recalls the difference between the feelings of sadness and those of depression and obligates herself to continue identifying the "mad" thoughts, as she calls them, and change them to healthy ones. The therapist legitimizes her longing, sadness, and pain that surround her brother's death as part of life without her beloved dead brother.

In the follow-up session 3 months later, Neli reports an improvement, that is, reduced depression and anger with her brother. She says she is very sad, disagrees with the path her brother chose, "but I can't change anything, and basically I know that my brother cared and was concerned about me, and I think he forgives me." At the end of the session, Neli's changes in irrational beliefs are assessed, especially those related to her reduced self-appraisal, with a more realistic insight of herself and her life. During the follow-up session, Neli filled out the list of statements for a second time; now her score was 31, as opposed to the previous one of 46. Together, the therapist and Neli completed a comparison of the scoring of the level of her irrational thoughts that indicates a change from irrational to rational and reflects an adaptive process to the traumatic loss event.

> **REFLECTIONS**
>
> Neli's loss of her brother illustrates the complications that can arise in a loss under traumatic circumstances such as suicide. Although there are indications of both functional and relationship to the deceased components (based on the TTMoB) in assessing her bereavement, the latter was the focus of the intervention to assist Neli through changing her beliefs in order to experience a healthier grief process, one which is not without sadness, pain, and yearning; on the contrary, they become part of her way to remember her brother and to continue inner bonds with him.

CLINICAL CONCLUDING REMARKS

In this chapter we elaborated on the application of REBI in grief therapy as an intervention to facilitate an adaptive process of a client who lost a brother to suicide. In grief, emotions such as pain, anger, and shame are overwhelming. The intensity is evaluated by the bereaved as too painful and consequently avoided. With the case example presented, we introduced the reader to the application of REI incorporating mindfulness elements, namely, awareness to body sensation in complicated grief. It was assessed that within the safe framework of therapy, the use of imagery will provide an opportunity for the client to reexperience the traumatic loss and its consequences. By becoming more attentive and aware, the experience will be evaluated more rationally and enable the bereaved to regain inner control over emotions and body sensation. The centrality of cognitions as mediators between the loss event and the consequences (emotional, behavioral, and physical), as well as the distinction between adaptive and maladaptive consequences that preceded the imagery, was described. The imagery with the mindfulness elements led the client to be less critical, less angry, more accepting of herself, and better able to forgive her brother as part of her grief. A one-time letter writing and a visit to the grave on the first anniversary of the brother's death were planned as ways to reorganize her inner relationship with the deceased brother and feel less angry with him and herself over the traumatic circumstances of the loss. The view taken was that adapting to loss is a dynamic and continuous process of searching for meaning of what was changed forever.

At a time when a traumatic life experience such as the sudden death of a loved one has created total chaos, cognitive grief therapy, with its focus on one's beliefs makes it possible for the bereaved to create a sense of coherence between what was lost and the new meaning that has yet to be found.

10

Strategic Integrative Interventions
Applying Letter Writing, Leave-Taking Rituals, and Metaphor

INTRODUCTION

S trategic intervention is a meta-therapeutic approach by which the therapist draws on today's broad knowledge base of psychotherapy to intervene following bereavement. Leave-taking ritual is an approach that is based on the significance of ritual as a means of transitioning to and reordering a life shattered by loss. As practiced, leave-taking rituals create a structured framework for the adaptive progress of the natural mourning process. The rituals make use of letter writing to the deceased and finding place for "linking objects" to facilitate mourning. In this chapter, we present three cases to illustrate the principles and provide the reader with additional material for the therapist arsenal.

INTERVENTION IN COMPLICATED GRIEF

Complicated grief is one of the conditions for which grief intervention was found to be efficacious (Schut et al., 2001). Grief and mourning can be facilitated by a variety of therapeutic methods that can ease suffering and assist the bereaved who is experiencing complicated grief and interconnected depressive syndromes (Witztum & Roman, 2000). In such situations, follow-up and continued preventative treatment for identified high-risk groups is vital.

The therapeutic implications of these considerations underscore why cognitive and cognitive-constructivist therapies are efficient modes for grief intervention. Cognitions are significant in understanding human emotional disturbances of all kinds. When a loss through death occurs, the need to renarrate and reconstruct a shattered story necessarily involves modifications of cognitive paradigms (Malkinson, 2007; Neimeyer, 1996, Neimeyer et al., 2000).

GRIEF THERAPY THROUGH LEAVE-TAKING RITUALS

The idea of using rituals and symbols as a way of reordering what was shattered stems from religious traditions. Most religions emphasize the importance of using ritual as a means to harness cognitive, social, emotional, and behavioral experiences at different points in the life cycle. Nowhere is this more apparent than in matters relating to death.

In line with the idea of a ritual as a way of reordering life that was shattered, a therapeutic approach was developed in the 1980s that emphasized the symbolic ritual components of the treatment of grief and highlighted the therapeutic effect of leave-taking rituals (Van der Hart, 1983, 1986; Witztum & Roman, 2000). In the original formulation of this ritual-based approach, the bereaved individuals, aided by the therapist, perform a series of symbolic acts in which they separate (break the bonds) emotionally from people or situations in their past. By distancing themselves from the people or objects, a resumption of functioning and rebuilding relationship with other people is expected (Van der Hart, 1983, 1987). Van der Hart pointed out that the common denominator of the various forms of this therapy is that they return to the two periods of traditional mourning ceremonies, described by Janet in the early 20th century (for a detailed description, see Van der Hart, 1987). At first, the clients are encouraged to speak about or to the deceased and to act as though she or he is still alive; afterward they are helped to change their position, vis-à-vis the deceased, free themselves, and take their leave (Van der Hart, 1983). First, there is a separation from, or a change in, old behavioral habits connected to the deceased; afterward, there is a separation from the deceased. The differences between the various therapeutic approaches are expressed in the different formulations of stages, in the coping with grief, and in the types of help offered to develop new behavioral patterns.

Originally the model constructed a structured framework for the mourning process using a variety of cognitive and behavioral strategies. Those included continued letter writing to the deceased, accepting a linking object from the client, and planning a leave-taking ritual. The term *linking objects* describes mementos and symbolic objects which are precious to the client and whose symbolic meaning serves to link the client to the lost other. The significance of these phenomena were originally described by Volkan (1972). The client was expected to bury or separate from their precious linking object, as a completion phase of relinquishing the bonds with the deceased. While burial of the deceased is a feature of many cultures and religions, burial of objects or placing them in sacred spaces which have symbolic and ritual functions may be less familiar. In the Jewish tradition, placement of objects that have some degree of holiness in a sacred space termed a *Geniza* is practiced. In therapy, giving the object that links the bereaved to the deceased to the therapist for temporary or permanent storage can be a powerful transition. In its initial formulation, one of main purposes was to help mourners to express their feelings, resolve the inhibiting emotional block, and facilitate alternative ways of expressing the whole range of feelings so that the process of separation from the deceased could be completed.

With the growing empirical support for continuing a relationship with the deceased, this therapeutic approach underwent changes in defining complicated grief and in how it conceptualized the aim of the employment of these strategies.

The main purpose of utilizing a leave taking through the use of letter writing is to facilitate an adaptive process of meaning making (Niemeyer, 1996, 2000). One of the main purposes of this approach as applied within the continuing bonds framework is to help the bereaved to express thoughts and feelings through writing. By means of opening up, the bereaved construct alternative cognitive and emotional responses that facilitate the creation of new meanings so that life after the loss may take an adaptive course. Moreover, grief therapy, and especially cognitive and constructivist approaches, views interventions as a means to reconstruct the disrupted life narrative. Therapy can facilitate an adaptive process within which a meaning construction to life without the deceased is seen as a central theme in a reworked life narrative. Leave-taking rituals and continuous letter writing are applied within this framework. Another important therapeutic tool is using metaphor. Metaphors are seen as ideal meaning-making symbols that are isomorphic with the content of the narrative. The objective, therefore, is to help clients in developing structural, orientation, and physical metaphors that ideally symbolize the meaning construction process in any narrative (Gonçalves & Machado, 1999). An example of a metaphoric statement and its use is found in Rothenberg (1984). He used a metaphoric statement to link his client's symptomatic skin condition to her problematic relationship with her mother; the results were striking. He used the metaphoric statement "She really gets under your skin, doesn't she?" (in the context of an ongoing therapeutic relationship) to make what was a transformative intervention for the client.

The therapeutic impact of metaphors lies at the general strategic level where employing a single metaphor is a central issue of the therapy. At the same time, metaphors can constitute tactical interventions as ways to address specific aspects or issues within treatment. The value of metaphor can be seen in treatment where trauma and grief have occurred. In such cases, working through the problem directly can be too anxiety provoking or complex. Metaphor frequently deactivates the defenses without heightening the anxiety by allowing clients to defocus on the issue itself and focus in the metaphoric domain. They may then refocus on the problem with new information or a new way of framing the situation gained from the interchange in the metaphoric field (Witztum, Van der Hart, & Friedman, 1988). A fuller exposition of the details of applying metaphor in therapy will be considered in the first case example in this chapter.

There are therapeutic effects to leave-taking rituals that hark back to religious rituals.

Therapy can facilitate an adaptive process within which a meaningful construction to life without the deceased is seen as a central theme in a reworked life narrative.

Leave-taking rituals and continuous letter writing are applied within this framework. Metaphor frequently deactivates or circumvents client defenses without heightening the anxiety by allowing clients to defocus on the issue itself and focus in the metaphoric domain.

LETTER WRITING IN THERAPY

Letter writing can be applied in cases of complicated grief at any phase. Letter writing during both the acute phase and the chronic phase of the mourning process may be appropriate for years following death. In the "post-mourning" that continues without a clearly defined time demarcation, it is equally appropriate.

The healing potential of writing is well established (O'Connor et al., 2003; Pennebaker, 1993, 1997; Smyth, Stone, Hureaitz, & Kael, 1999). Writing is putting into words thoughts and feelings about the writer's past, the present, and the future life. Dreams, hopes, traumas, and losses are issues and raw materials that can be expressed through writing. Writing involves cognitions and emotions and has psychological as well as physical health benefits (Smyth et al., 1999). The incorporation of writing in general (which is also referred to as expressive writing) in therapy, and in grief therapy in particular, has become widespread and is applied in a number of ways (Malkinson, 2007). In some cases writing is done over a limited number of consecutive days, whereas others prescribe this technique to be carried out daily for a period of time (O'Conner et al., 2003; Pennebaker & Beall, 1986) or in a daily diary or journal (L. Miller, 2002). In addition to considering its use in therapy, we shall consider the value of writing as a supplement to the therapeutic process in Chapter 14 on facilitating growth.

CONTINUOUS LETTER WRITING IN GRIEF

Whatever the chosen structure or setting, writing is believed to help the individual express the pain in a "private" way with the "writer" choosing the words, the pace and emotions, and a reconstruction of the narrative.

Structured treatment in continuous letter writing as a "leave-taking ritual" in grief therapy greatly resembles traditional mourning rituals. Van der Hart (1983, 1987), following Pierre Janet's ideas, has outlined four steps of "leave-taking" ritual that address preparation, reorganization, finalization, and follow-up.

Preparation

This first step is sometimes called the cognitive building phase. In it the client is not yet ready to talk about the deceased. The therapist explains the different options for therapy and what will be asked of the client. The therapist also points out that therapy can be difficult, painful, and very emotional. As part of this approach, a family evaluation is also recommended and may result in the family being included in the therapy.

Reorganization

Most of the working through of grief is done in this phase. The mourner usually acts as though the deceased is still alive. Continuing letter writing at this point is one of the most important techniques that can be used (Van der Hart, 1983, 1986). The bereaved is asked to write to the deceased every day, about feelings or anything else they want to share. Writing and reading the letter is an important tool for expressing the ambivalence vis-à-vis the deceased. The writing has its own dynamics, and some clients may also choose to write to additional people from their past.

The client brings the letter and sometimes reads it in therapy. The client enlists the therapist's aid in dealing with traumatic or difficult experiences. Through the letter-writing process, an increasing awareness of the reality of the death of the loved person occurs. The cognitive and emotional ways of relating to the deceased become less intense and more balanced. The intensive letter writing tapers off, as do the heightened emotions, and the client begins to reorganize both the inner relationship with the deceased (Track II of the Two-Track Model of Bereavement) as well as a functioning relationship with others (Track I).

The model includes an additional focus connected to linking objects. These physical objects, which are precious to the client, are to be deposited with the therapist during therapy. Handing over a symbolic object gives the client the feeling that he or she can cope and separate from these connections, which operate also to increase the ability to separate from the deceased (Van der Hart, 1983, 1987).

In the original conceptualizations of this treatment, at the end of this phase, the client was expected "truly" to be able to separate from the deceased with the help of the leave-taking ritual. At present, the strategic approach of using linking objects emphasizes the continuing bonds perspective of adaptive bereavement. Linking objects are explored for the meanings attached to them, with consideration of the possibilities to reevaluate and explore how they can be integrated into the life of the bereaved in a more balanced way.

Finalization

In the initial model, the important component was the leave-taking ritual. The purpose of the ritual was to validate the change that had occurred in the relationship to the deceased. Although the deceased was to be remembered and respected, there was also the expectation that the bereaved resume life. In the leave-taking ritual, the symbolic objects, which might have been the notebooks or letters, were released. They were buried, burned, or strewn in a canal or lake. The idea underlying the intervention was that through this ritual, the client acknowledged that life with the deceased belonged to the past. Other forms of the finalization phase contained a leave-taking ritual, a purifying ritual, and a unification ritual. Van der Hart (1987) describes a ritual that includes a ceremonial meal after the leave-taking ritual.

In continuous letter writing from the perspective of continuing bonds, the client is not requested to discard or bury the letters. The shifts in the relationship are assumed to cumulate with the completion of writing. This in itself represents a coming to terms with the idea that the deceased is part of the bereaved's inner world and that memories and commemorations are an integral part of life that are now internalized.

Follow-up

After the completion of the letter-writing phase, staying in touch is important. During follow-up sessions, a memorial ceremony or a memorial corner can be discussed as part of the reorganization and memorialization following loss. At the same time, addressing emotional themes, such as how the client might cope with future negative emotions such as pain and sadness, is important.

APPLYING LETTER WRITING IN THE PROCESS OF GRIEF

The phases of continuous letter writing therapy correspond in many ways to the process of grief. In the first phases of assessment and preparing the client and the initiation of the writing, the client is still unable to speak about the deceased, and intervention is within the framework of the client's difficulties. The client writes to the deceased and talks to him or her as though the person is still alive. Most of the working through of grief is done during this phase. In cases of avoidance of reminders of the deceased or conversely "clinging" to such reminders, the use of a linking object where the client is asked to choose an object and bring it to the session can become an apogee, as this symbolic object gives the client the choice of rearranging and rewriting the way these objects can represent the deceased. Only then are the thoughts and feelings that follow experienced in a more adaptive way to life without the deceased. In the finalization phase, the mourner reorders not only the inner memories of the deceased but also the transformed identity.

The healing potential of writing is well established.

Structured treatment in continuous letter writing as a "leave-taking ritual" in grief therapy greatly resembles traditional mourning rituals.

The bereaved may be asked to write to the deceased about feelings or anything else they want to share.

Writing and reading the letter is an important tool for expressing feelings and ambivalence toward the deceased.

The writing has its own dynamics and some clients may also choose to write to additional people from their past.

The therapeutic process and the application of continuous letter writing as a leave-taking ritual in a search of meaning will be illustrated initially with the case vignette of the loss of a parent in midlife. The following case illustrates the transformation of grief such that the client can experience pain and yearning as part of an adaptive grief process rather than being overwhelmed by guilt, dysfunction, and depression.

CASE ONE: A VERY NARROW BRIDGE

(Witztum & Roman, 2000)

Maria, 53 years old, a dentist by profession, married and the mother of four, came to therapy with a clinical depression that developed after the death of her father. Maria's 85-year-old father had immigrated to Israel after she convinced him to come and live with her. Shortly after his immigration, he became ill and was hospitalized by his devoted daughter. He died suddenly after 3 days' hospitalization. Maria, who was not at all involved with her father's medical care, felt great hostility toward the medical staff in attendance. She also developed strong guilt feelings about her father's death. Within a short time she sank into depression, stopped working, neglected herself and her home, stopped eating, and lost weight. She spent most of her time in bed with obsessive thoughts connected to her father's death.

Past History

Maria, middle daughter to a family with three children, was born in South America and emigrated to Israel at the age of 24, together with her boyfriend, whom she married shortly after emigrating. She stayed in close contact with her family in South America via weekly letters. She studied dentistry, worked successfully in her field for over 20 years, and was considered a devoted and excellent worker. Maria has four children; the oldest is a soldier serving in the Israel Defense Forces. In all her years in Israel she had never complained of problems and had not been in therapy. Her mother had died a year before her father, but the event passed without any unusual reaction.

Maria's depression fits the criteria of a major depressive episode. It included loss of appetite and weight, severe sleep disturbances, and severe deterioration in functioning. Treatment with medication (high dosages of Elavil—250 mg) was tried together with supportive therapy, but with no response. At this stage Maria transferred to our clinic. On her first visit we observed a very sad woman dressed sloppily in overly large clothes (which we later discovered had belonged, in part, to her deceased father). Because there had been absolutely no response to the medication, an additional attempt was made with a different antidepressant. After 6 weeks with no response to imipramine, all medications were stopped.

From the perspective of the Two-Track Model of Bereavement (TTMoB), we can make an initial assessment and identify components from both Track I (bio-psychological functioning), and Track II (relationship with the deceased). From the perspective of Track I, Maria describes experiencing a noticeable sense of turmoil—that of a shattered world. There is a marked sense of severe depression with somatic symptoms like difficulties in sleeping and reduced appetite and difficulties in functioning at home; she also stopped working. These are all indications characteristic of traumatic loss following the sudden loss of her beloved father. From the perspective of Track II, Maria expressed anger toward herself for convincing her old father to emigrate to Israel to live with her. She felt guilty and blamed herself for her father's death. She was completely disorganized and spent most of her time in bed with obsessive thoughts connected to her father's death.

The Intervention

Attempt at Therapy With the Family   In the beginning of therapy, the therapists (EW and OVDH) asked to meet the whole family and had two sessions with them. Maria was clearly not functioning as a wife or mother. Emphasis was placed on the need for the whole family to help Maria separate from her father. Family members told the therapist about Maria's strange habits, such as wearing her father's clothes, (including socks, underwear, shirts, and sweaters) and keeping all of her father's old clothes and possessions in the children's closets, which she had emptied of their clothes. Maria protested that she would resist any attempt to separate her from these "precious" objects.

The family sessions were very difficult. The children only came to the first session and the husband stopped coming after the second session. The therapists understood this to mean that the problem was Maria's, and Maria and the therapists decided that from the third week, therapy would be individual. Although the family did not participate actively in therapy, the family's brief meeting with the therapists gave them essential information and explanations as to what was happening to Maria and the therapeutic plan. The family members continued to participate indirectly in therapy, and this became part of the family experience.

Letter Writing as Part of the Therapeutic Process

Maria repeated that she could not accept her father's death. She felt as though he was still with her and even had sensations and special signs as proof of his presence. She hung her father's scarf from a high spot in the living room and maintained eye contact with it from every place in the house; this helped her feel constantly connected to him. The therapists recommended that she write to her father and tell him about herself. Maria accepted the suggestion and requested to write to her mother as well.

Organizational Stage and the Beginning of the Letter-Writing Process

The therapists suggested that Maria purchase two special notebooks and write in them at a set time every day. They also suggested that a picture of her father or an object characteristic of him might help her. She chose the magnifying glass her father had used to read the newspaper. In the next session, Maria said that she had bought the notebooks but had been unable to write. She said that she had previously written to her parents twice a week. The therapists encouraged her to continue trying. Sure enough, she soon reported excitedly that she had succeeded in writing seven pages! Maria emotionally read her letter in its original Spanish and then translated it into Hebrew for the therapists. The session was highly charged, and several times she burst into tears. For the most part, the therapists sat silently and listened.

The goal at this point was to start the writing process and thus give Maria a channel to communicate her feelings and perceptions. Maria continued to write intensively and reported that the writing process brought great relief from her pain and sadness. Parallel with the letter writing to her father, she wrote to her mother and, at the therapists' recommendation, she also wrote to the doctor who had treated her father. This letter was not meant to be sent but rather to express her feelings of anger and aggression. Maria's letters summed up her life since her immigration to Israel, revealed her inner world, her special relationship with her parents, and her dependency on them. She described her strong guilt feelings over the years for having left her elderly parents. In particular she wrote of her last visit to South America, a year before these events, and of finding her mother ill with a difficult, depressing, physical illness. Maria cared for her mother devotedly, but nonetheless, her mother's physical condition deteriorated and she died shortly after Maria had to return to Israel. The therapists connected these guilt feelings to the guilt feelings she harbored at her father's death, for which she blamed herself.

Beginning of the Leave-Taking Work Through the Writing Process Using Metaphors and Fantasies

Maria wrote four to five times a week, and the writing became an integral part of her week. She always sat in the same corner of the house and at the same time in the evening. She sometimes combined poems and songs with her writing—for example, a classic poem of a man who separates from his friends and acquaintances before his death. Maria read the poem to the therapists, sobbing, and saying that the poem expressed her emotions. The therapists suggested a different interpretation: Perhaps the poem expressed ending, but this was not the ending of her life but rather the ending of a specific phase of her life: her past and the period of her life in South America. They emphasized that her need, in contrast to the poem, was not to separate from the living but to separate from the dead. Maria was not about to die; she was about to begin to live again. The therapists used the metaphor of a caterpillar which, for a certain period of its life, is covered with cobwebs and looks from the outside like a chrysalis, a static, inanimate body, while inside there is dynamic metamorphosis and change until a beautiful colorful butterfly emerges.

Maria listened intently and uncharacteristically made no comment. It was evident on her face that the metaphor had been absorbed. Through these poems and metaphors, the patient was able to gently and indirectly begin the process of leave-taking, with emphasis on change and transformation (Witztum et al., 1988).

Coping With Anger and Aggression

At this stage there was a break in therapy because of the therapists' reserve duty and travel. One of the therapists made a special effort to call Maria regularly on the day of therapy. Despite the continuous telephone contact, Maria responded badly to the separation. She stopped writing, developed severe headaches and dizziness, and felt as though "her father was calling her to join him." She felt full of anger and aggression. She did not know why; the feelings were not directed toward the therapists but toward the doctors whom she believed caused her father's death. The therapists made a connection between the separation and the anger and aggression that were evoked and the episode of her father's death and separation from him. This offered an opportunity to work through the anger. Until now Maria could only feel guilty and deserving of punishment. She had preferred to remain with those feelings, instead of coping and trying to separate from her father.

The next meetings were difficult for both Maria and the therapists. Feelings of anger and rage erupted against the family, and when the therapists "dared" to ask Maria to leave something of her father's to which she felt strongly attached, she lashed out at them. The therapists began to raise the question of the household, which had been dysfunctional since the father's death. At this stage the therapists used another metaphor to describe their perceptions to Maria:

> Maria is standing on a narrow bridge, which is stretched over a valley between two mountains. One mountain is bright and green while the second mountain is dark, lofty, and cold. Maria is standing on the bridge, hesitating and not knowing where to go. Each side has something attractive and seductive and she doesn't want to be pushed.

Maria's emotional response to the metaphor was powerful. She began to shake and said that she saw an identical picture. Maria and the therapists started to speak in the language of the metaphor. She observed, "I feel that I've moved several steps to the bright side but my face remains turned to the dark side."

Return to Daily Functioning

Many changes in the life of Maria and her family were noticed during therapy and in the writing. Maria was highly trained musically and would play different instruments for at least an hour a day. She also sang in a choir. When her father died, she totally stopped her musical activities. She barely cooked and refused to make foods that reminded her of her father. For example, she would not make omelets, which had been her father's favorite food. She was known for her delicious cheesecakes, but the last cheesecake she had made was during her father's illness. Since her father's death, she had totally stopped cooking and baking, and her children complained that something was missing.

Therapy at this stage focused on a return to daily functioning. Maria was asked to start playing her instruments again. At first she played her father's favorite melodies, then sad tunes, and gradually she returned to her daily playing. The return to functioning in the house was a great struggle. Maria refused to bake, particularly her father's favorite cheesecake. She made a great effort and baked a cake, which she brought as a surprise to therapy, insisting that the therapists taste it. The therapists agreed, on condition that she, too, eat the cake (which was really delicious!).

The shared eating of the cake became a transition ceremony. (See the biblical description of the covenant on bread and wine.) Afterward, Maria was able to bake and resume her general functioning.

Coping With Linking Objects

Linking objects are one of the characteristics of what used to be called pathological grief (Volkan, 1972, 1981). In this case, the father's hat and scarf, which were described earlier, were the linking objects.

Maria was asked to bring them to therapy and leave them with the therapists. The request evoked anger and rage. Five sessions focused on working through this topic. At first, Maria refused the request absolutely. Afterward she agreed in part and brought the hat and scarf, commenting, "It looks like I am crossing the bridge." However, in the course of the session she regretted her earlier decision and asked permission to take the objects home. The therapists agreed after she promised to bring them to the next session. Yet, she "forgot" to bring the objects to the third session and clarified that the hat and scarf symbolized separation from her father. She did not bring the objects to the fourth session, because she wanted them with her on her father's anniversary of the death. She half joked that she was afraid the therapists would convince her to leave the objects with them. In the fifth session she brought only the hat and not the scarf in an effort to compromise, and only at the sixth session did she bring the scarf, admitting to a surprisingly great sense of relief. The objects were deposited with the therapists until the end of therapy.

The struggle with the objects was actually a symbolic struggle for separation. Maria tried to gain time and to compromise, but in the end she decided to move in the direction of the "bright side." At this point, her writing was minimal. She explained that if she had written, she would have had to tell her parents about her painful separation from the scarf and hat and so she preferred not to write.

Working Through Anger and Aggression

In this period, the symptoms reminiscent of Maria's deeply depressed period reappeared. The therapists felt as though she were carrying a heavy burden on her shoulders. Maria was asked to go into a field and find a heavy stone to reflect the heaviness she felt. Her initial response was surprise and great antagonism. In the session, she began to talk about positive aspects of her life, but she remained angry and demanding. At the end of the session, she promised to consider the matter of the heavy stone. A week later, Maria appeared, bowed down under the weight of a heavy stone, which was well wrapped in a plastic bag. She could barely carry the stone but had chosen it to reflect her mood. She was asked to take it along wherever she went for the whole week, to be aware of its weight and interference in her life. She soon exchanged the stone for a lighter one and reported how much she had begun to enjoy different activities, such as concerts. However, she added that she also hated and disdained herself for having begun to go out and enjoy herself.

At the end of this period, she wrote an angry letter (which was not to be mailed) to the doctor responsible for her father's care. She also took the stone to an old quarry and, using their tools, smashed it into little pieces and particles of dust.

The stone symbolized the paralyzing anger and guilt she was carrying around. At first, she chose a stone she could not carry; when she became aware of this, she exchanged it for a lighter stone and at the end of this process, she pulverized it to dust. She then articulated her anger in a letter to her father's doctor. During this whole period, she struggled valiantly to preserve a reasonable level of functioning.

Return to Work and Termination of Therapy

Successfully pulverizing the stone was accompanied by a big change in the therapeutic environment, which became less emotional and more pragmatic and relevant. Maria decided not to return to her work at the hospital, which she associated with guilt and the negligent care her father had received. She decided to look for work elsewhere and, to her surprise, found good work effortlessly. Both the therapists and Maria felt the need to separate between the old and the new, the past and the future. This need was also felt by the staff members in her former workplace, who gave her a farewell party. Although she found it difficult, Maria attended the very successful party; afterward she was greatly relieved.

Slowly but surely, Maria began to remove her father's clothes. First the heavy coat disappeared, then the sweaters and shirts, and finally only the socks remained. At this stage the therapists asked humorously if she needed the socks to remember her father. Maria laughed and the socks disappeared. This signified the end of treatment. The depression and inner restlessness disappeared. She returned to the stable healthy functioning of the time before her father's death.

Maria decided to fly to South America and sell her parents' home, which was empty and desolate. The therapists viewed the sale of the house as the final part of the leave-taking process and recommended a final session on her return.

The final session was very moving. In agreement with the therapists' promise, Maria's father's scarf and hat, which had been left with the therapists for several months, were returned to her. It was suggested that these objects not be placed in the middle of the guest room but in a special memorial corner dedicated to her father. Her return to full functioning as wife, mother, and working woman closed the circle. The writing stopped. Maria felt that she had written all that she needed to say to her parents. The notebooks were put into a box which would be placed in the memorial corner. The therapists felt that Maria had indeed crossed the bridge to the bright side and hoped that the sun would add warmth and illumination to her life.

REFLECTION

After her father died in the hospital, the client, Maria, suffered from severe resistant depression that did not respond to any antidepressant medication and was sent to a mental hospital for admission and electroconvulsive therapy (ECT) trial.

We described the stages of therapy in full detail based on the Two-Track Model of Bereavement. Therapy began with trying to instate the inner dialogue with the deceased father (Track II) as a way to reorganize the relationship with him. This was followed by attending to component of Track I—returning to daily functioning and her family duties as wife and mother and finally returning to work. This is a demonstration of an integrative strategic intervention, which could be called "classical," with the participation of Van der Hart, who is one of the innovators of this approach (Van der Hart, 1983).

The next case illustrates the use of letter writing combined with behavioral strategies to intervene in the biopsychosocial difficulties associated with Track I of the TTMoB. It conveys how clinical work and therapeutic practice utilize formulation and reflection according to the TTMoB work.

CASE TWO: SUDDEN LOSS IN AN ALIEN COUNTRY

David, a retired 73-year old male, widowed some 9 months previously, is the father of three children. David came to treatment because he was suffering from serious distress, lack of appetite, disturbed sleep, and great sadness, which all began suddenly after his wife passed away.

Past History

David was born in Jerusalem and grew up in a very poor family, one of many children. He had worked all these years in one place. He had been married for 50 years and had enjoyed a very good marriage. His wife had a non-life-threatening heart condition.

While traveling in one of the Balkan countries and in their hotel, his wife complained in the early morning hours that she was short of breath and was feeling weak. She fainted. He called the doctors but by the time they arrived, she had died. This sudden death while on vacation away from home was a very traumatic experience. He stayed behind to take care of the arrangements and ran into many confounding bureaucratic difficulties when he wanted to transport the body home by air, but made efforts to overcome them. He was barely able to surmount these difficulties, for he was hit hard and was left completely exhausted. By the time he came for therapy a year later, David's situation was one of complicated grief. He showed signs of withdrawal, reduced functioning, and severe anxiety. He had stopped driving, he became clinically depressed, and he suffered from sleep disturbance and a loss of appetite. As for the relationship with the deceased, he described yearning and preoccupation with memories of his wife, thinking about how much he missed her, and the difficulties he experienced in remaining alone at night.

Since the death of his wife, David has been unable to sleep alone in his home. He remains secluded at home and has developed a dysphonic and anxiety syndrome, which has been described.

Assessment of distorted thinking that increases emotional distress revealed that David saw no purpose in continuing to live without his beloved wife. The yearning he felt has became unbearable and painful (a secondary symptom). Not only was life without his wife painful, David was also continuously reexperiencing the circumstances of the sudden loss of his wife while on holiday and remembering the dreadful arrangements he had to make to fly back home with the body.

FORMULATION

From the perspective of the Two-Track Model of Bereavement we can make an initial assessment and identify components from both Track I (biopyschological functioning) and Track II (relationship with the deceased). From the perspective of Track I, David describes experiencing severe distress. There is a marked sense of sadness, with depressive symptoms like lack of appetite and disturbed sleep. From the perspective of Track II, David describes yearning and preoccupation with memories of his wife, thinking about how much he misses her, and the difficulties he experiences in remaining alone at night. In fact, since the death of his wife, David has been unable to sleep alone in his home.

The Intervention

It was assumed that a combined intervention of correction of distorted thinking and creating a "sensible" narrative through continuous letter writing would be effective in David's case. In the process of assessment, it became clear that strategic restructuring of distorted thinking that increases emotional distress into a more functional way of interpretation would be a preferred mode of intervention. It would explain and clarify to David what he was experiencing following the loss of his beloved wife, and it would facilitate a more adaptive bereavement process.

David's problem consisted of at least two components representing the two tracks: The first was his depression, which was at the level of clinical depression and could have been treated effectively with appropriate antidepressant medication, and the second was related to his relationship to his deceased wife, which also necessitated active participation. Asked by the therapist (EW) about the possibility of taking medication, David replied that he would like to consider medication as a way to treat his depression, but concerning the second suggestion that he write letters to his deceased wife, he wanted to know exactly what the purpose of this intervention was. Thus, providing information about letter writing was crucial.

Letter Writing as Part of the Therapeutic Process

After explaining the letter-writing assignment and its goals, we discussed it and agreed that its purpose was to help him to experience a more adaptive grief process that would help him improve his functioning so he would be able to maintain his independence and social contacts. The idea of continuous letter writing was introduced and explained to him, and he was requested to try writing to his wife. He agreed, but he was afraid that he would be instructed to sever his emotional connections from his wife.

Second session: A week later. During the session, he says that he wrote his initial letter to his wife, in which he expressed his yearning for her, how difficult it is for him without her, and how much he misses her. He reported that it had been very difficult for him to write the initial letter, but upon completion of the task he felt relieved. He decided that he would use antidepressant medication, and treatment was initiated.

David expressed the feeling that he needed time between sessions and asked that the interval be 2 weeks. His request was accepted by his therapist, but he received an additional task, which was to resume driving as homework. He promised to continue writing, agreed to the additional homework, and agreed to come to the next session in his own car.

Reorganization

Third session: The client reported that he had successfully resumed driving, and indeed he drove his own car to the session. He continued to write to his wife, and during the session he read the letter that described his symptoms and how difficult this period was for him, especially the yearning and loneliness without her.

Fourth session: Two weeks later (by then he had already taken the prescribed dose of medication for 4 weeks), he reported that the drug was working and he felt better. After assessing the improvement of David's function (Track I), the therapist decided to refer to the traumatic element and to touch upon the circumstances of that "horrible night." While the therapist and David were discussing the events of the death on that "horrible night," David suddenly remembered a forgotten memory from his childhood. At the age of 8 years, he went to visit his old grandfather who was lying in bed. His grandfather fell out of bed, and when

David tried to get him back into bed he saw that he wasn't breathing. He tried to shake him, but his grandfather wasn't responding. He understood that something terrible happened to his grandfather, who was motionless, and it turned out that he was dead. David was shocked and became very frightened and sad. While recalling the story, David remarked in amazement that he had forgotten the story all these years and recalled it only now. To the therapist's question if he understood the connection between the two episodes, David replied that he did indeed.

Fifth session: David came in his car to the session 2 weeks later, in a better mood, able to be alone, even for a short period at night, with a significant improvement in functioning around the house.

Sixth session: David reported that he felt better and was capable of staying alone during the day. David reported that lately, without any obvious reason, he had stopped writing to his wife. He promised to resume writing and said he would try to write to her about the difficulties he is having after her death. At his request, the sessions resumed once a month.

Seventh session: David felt better, his anxiety had completely disappeared, and he was more independent during the day. He wrote a letter to his wife about the difficulties. He brought the letter to the session and read it aloud.

Eighth session: David reported that he continued to feel better; his anxiety and depressive fears had almost completely disappeared. The only remaining sign is his inability to sleep alone at night, and he requested his son to come stay with him overnight, and the company of his son enables him to go to sleep. He has brought the letter, and at the therapist's request he reads it out loud. He wrote to his wife that he is suffering and still cannot sleep alone; he thought that he would shortly be all right, but he missed her and spoke of her with the children; he felt sad with a need to cry; he was unable to be separated from his son, who had to sleep over.

Ninth session: The situation was improving; the son was late on two occasions, and David didn't wait but went to bed alone. He hopes that he is on the way to being independent. This is the only vestige of his problems that remain.

He would return 2 months later.

Tenth session: David reported that he continued to be fine, and although the son still slept over, he no longer depended on him to do so. David said that he was done with letter writing.

Eleventh session: David looked better and said he felt well and that he was indifferent to whether or not the son slept over; the son often does not come home. In the meantime, David has met a woman who is about 60 years old and a relationship is forming; he, of course, has not forgotten the deceased wife but wants to alleviate his loneliness. He will come for a follow-up in 2 months time.

Follow-up: The next session was a follow-up, and David said he felt better and had resumed singing in the choir. During therapy, the first anniversary of the death had taken place. David told the therapist that the memorial ceremony had gone smoothly and that nothing unusual had happened.

Second follow-up: David looked and felt better. He reported that he is sleeping by himself, his son got married, and David feels more energetic.

REFLECTION

This is a representative example of an aged widower who lost his wife under traumatic circumstances and developed complicated grief. In terms of the Two-Track Model, Track I is dominant, with symptoms of clinical depression, reduced functioning, and inability to stay alone at home at night. Track II (relationship to the deceased) components are also present: David described yearning and preoccupation with memories of his wife.

The intervention strategically addressed both tracks: Track I with antidepressant and antianxiety medication and cognitive behavior intervention (correction of distorted thinking) and Track II with continuous letter writing, which allowed David to express his feelings. He responded positively to the interventions, recovered from depression, and regained functioning; in a relatively short time, he was able to stay alone at nights and release his son from the duty.

In this final presentation of this therapeutic model, we describe a case that emphasizes work with the relationship to the deceased, Track II, in the intervention.

CASE THREE: THE DAFFODILS ARE BLOOMING AGAIN

Iris, a 60-year-old widow and mother of three, does not work as a result of an accident at home when she fell off a chair and broke her hand.

Main complaint: Iris complained of anxiety with a decreased appetite and problems sleeping, but her mood was normal. Because of her broken hand, she had difficulties in functioning.

Past History

Iris was born in Israel, the youngest of eight children; the parents came to Israel from Turkey. She was a good student and was sent to elementary school but did not go to high school. She did not serve in the army (which is obligatory in Israel) for religious reasons. She felt she had missed opportunities in life and felt bitterness and anger toward her parents, who held her back. Iris married at 18 to get away from home and, in her words, picked a "good" husband, a successful man, who was a building contractor. Later on in life she studied at the Open University. Then, 10 years ago, her husband became ill with cancer and passed away. Over time, there were additional losses: a brother who died 1 year later and a sister to whom she had been much attached, who passed away 4 years ago.

ASSESSMENT AND FORMULATION

Assessment with the Two-Track Model highlighted that components from both tracks were problematic. The client's feelings of sadness and anxiety, coupled with difficulties in sleeping and functioning at home, represented elements of biopsychological functioning difficulty that are characteristic of Track I. There were also marked features of Track II, the relationship to the deceased, mainly concerning the relationship prior to the loss as well as the circumstances of the death: in Iris's case, sad memories of how her husband became ill with cancer and passed away. She felt ambivalent with negative feelings toward her husband, who had left her in such a mess, but she also felt strong yearning and longing for him. Her distress was augmented by the additional losses of her brother and her sister.

The Intervention

Iris's grief can be described as complicated. Utilizing Rubin's model, Iris's breaking her hand resulted in her stopping work and made her feel fragile and helpless and reminded her how she felt when her husband died (Track I); this leads us to Track II. We can see that in Iris's case, her life completely collapsed—familially (she was ignored by the extended family), financially (they were almost bankrupt), and psychologically (she felt depressed and emotionally broken).

An analysis of the information revealed that the issue of grief and difficulties in adapting to the multiple losses is a central issue. Of particular importance were the familial and economical complications that occurred after the death of her beloved husband. He was a wealthy person, and following his death, the economic situation worsened noticeably. Also, her husband, as the firstborn son, was the authority of the extended family, and his death created a vacuum and confusion within the family where his brothers were competing for leadership.

Iris's reaction was one of devastation. She told herself that she should have acted differently in handling financial matters and that she should have listened to the advice given her by her children. The losses of her beloved husband, her sister, and brother were painful and too much for her.

Letter Writing as Part of the Therapeutic Process

The therapist (EW) expressed empathy and explained how he understood the situation while emphasizing the difficulties she had experienced following the loss. Then the therapist suggested that she write to her husband in order to continue her dialogue with him and make him aware of her struggles and her feelings. Iris agreed.

First session: Iris had begun writing; her letters interweave the family's narrative. Another complication evolved when she chose to write about what happened after her husband's death. As mentioned earlier, there were severe difficulties in the family, as the two brothers-in-law had passed away. After her husband's death, it also turned out that much of his business had been based on oral agreements and that many business associates who owed him money denied their debts. Many of them even claimed that he had owed them money. As she explained in her letter to her husband, her way of honoring and maintaining his reputation made her reluctant to declare bankruptcy.

Second session: Iris continued to write and in her writing she dwelt on the issue of the blackmail by former partners and employees who claimed that her husband owed them money and continued to demand money, threatening and intimidating her. She felt guilty because she had refused to declare bankruptcy. Much of the pressure fell on the eldest son, who had worked in the company and had tried to help her deal with the financial expenses after his father's death.

Third session: Iris spoke about her anxiety and her dependency upon her husband even today. Together, we concluded that part of her recovery was also an "occupational rehabilitation." The therapist reminded her how important it was that she get out of the house and involve herself in other activities. She told the therapist about her excellent reputation for taking care of children. For many years she was very successful at working in a nursery school. In the course of events the director had changed, and there was tension and competition between her and the new director, and after she broke her hand she decided to resign (Track I).

Fourth session: Iris continued to write, and after being encouraged to do so by the therapist, she also wrote for the first time about the anger she felt toward her husband because of the way he worked and did not leave records in an organized manner. Her children argued bitterly about whether or not to pay the father's debts, some of which were false claims (the beginning of elaborating the relationship with the deceased—Track II).

Fifth session: The letters Iris wrote and read aloud each session suggested that there is a problem of boundaries with her children and the difficulties she faces in expressing herself. She wrote the following: "I feel guilty particularly regarding my relations with my sons, where I gave in, even when I knew I was right." We analyzed that aspect in terms of thinking errors and searched for alternative ways of thinking.

Reorganization

Sixth session: This was a special session dedicated to the difficult relations that developed with Iris's husband's family after his death, as a result of the financial problems. The result was sad estrangement from this side of the family and her feelings of being rejected. She thought that the family was ungrateful to her husband, and she was angry with them.

Seventh session: Iris recounted a dream she had about her deceased husband; she couldn't remember details but only the feelings. Then, suddenly she recalled a dream in which two of her cousins had visited; she was probably substituting her late husband, which actually points to her feelings of yearning and her wish that he would visit her in her dream.

The session was emotionally intense and toward the end of the session, Iris asked that sessions be reduced to once every 2 weeks.

Eighth session: Iris said she felt fine. She found she had very little to write. Apparently she's "wrung out," she can't decide about what direction to take with regard to work, and she thinks about traveling abroad with her son, who was offered a job abroad.

She asked to change the frequency of the therapy sessions to once every 3 weeks.

Ninth session: Iris decided to try to be a cosmetician. She had decided to stay in Israel. Her son would travel abroad alone for work. She shared with the therapist the emotional upheaval she experienced as the 10th anniversary of her husband's death approached. She hinted to the therapist that she would like to cope with the upcoming event by herself.

The next session took place a month later.

Tenth session: Iris told the therapist that she was at the memorial service for her husband. Afterward, she says that she would like to share with the therapist a special dream. She dreamed that she was walking in her garden which was full of flowers, and she added: "Daffodils are my favorite flowers." The dream was so vivid that she ran to the garden to check if the daffodils had indeed bloomed. Together with the therapist, Iris concluded that blooming of the daffodils represented a return to life. She said that for the first time after a long period, she felt more optimistic. And then she added that she had started to fix up a room (in her house) and begin working as a cosmetician.

Follow-up: One year after therapy had been completed, Iris was invited for a follow-up session. She looked and said she felt better. She reported that she tidied up the room in her house so it would serve as an office, and she reported working successfully at home. Although she still had to cope with many problems with her late husband's family and with her sons, she felt she had the strength to cope with them.

REFLECTION

This is an example of a middle-aged widow whose husband died, followed by more recent multiple losses in her life. The circumstances of her husband's death and her total dependence on him left her very anxious, with ambivalence and strong negative feelings like anger, guilt, remorse, and disappointment. According to Track I of the TTMoB, her symptoms were those of anxiety. As for the relationship with the deceased (Track II), she was ambivalent with negative feelings toward her husband, who had left her in such a mess, but also a strong yearning and longing for him. The symptoms of each track were handled strategically—the first with cognitive restructuring and the second with continuous letter-writing homework and use of metaphors to express her feelings. The client responded well to the interventions and overcame her anxieties and feelings of dependency. She regained her functioning and, in a relatively short time, succeeded in becoming more assertive. She was able to create a space for herself as well as resume working.

CONCLUDING REMARKS

This chapter presented a strategic integrative therapeutic model that employs a combination of letter writing, leave-taking rituals, and metaphors to help clients who suffer from complications of grief (Rubin et al., 2008). In all too many cases, these clients develop a variety of psychiatric syndromes, such as severe anxiety, depression, or somatic difficulties (representing Track I). Interventions for complicated grief can take place during the process of grief or at any other time that the bereaved experiences distress related to the loss event. The chapter illustrates the therapeutic process and the application of the model through case vignettes of loss of parent and loss of spouse.

The strategic interventions are aimed at identifying sources of distress and their consequences. By the employment of a variety of strategic interventions, change occurs and the sources of difficulty become less stressful and an adaptive course of grief is facilitated. The applications of letter writing were shown to be suitable, powerful strategies that facilitate construction of a coherent and adaptive narrative. At its core, the letter writing facilitates a renewed inner dialogue with the deceased and changes in that relationship (Track II). All of the interventions involved went beyond the treatment phases to examine change during a follow-up component following the interventions.

11

Systemic Family Grief Therapy

INTRODUCTION

U p to this point, we have primarily discussed grief and bereavement as experienced by the individual. Recognizing the importance of the family context in bereavement and how it affects the individual bereaved, however, has become increasingly more widespread as an issue to be explored empirically and clinically (Benbow & Goodwillie, 2010; Malkinson, 2007; McBride & Simms, 2001; Rosenblatt, 2005; Walsh & McGoldrick, 2004).

As we have discussed throughout this book, mourning is an ongoing process of reworking the relationship with the deceased, which includes reworking relationships with surviving family members as well as reorganizing life without the deceased. From this perspective, grief that follows loss through death is both an intrapersonal and interpersonal process (Rubin & Malkinson, 2001). Moreover, it is an inner experience that occurs within a context of which the family, its members, and their unique legacy and culture are part. There is a continuous interplay between individual grief and the family. In other words, intervention following a loss through death, whether or not conducted with the individual or with multiple clients physically in the room, is always a family affair. Therapists' lenses should be wide enough to consider the family system as a source and resource toward understanding how the individual bereaved and the family are adapting to life after loss.

In this chapter, we introduce a family systems approach to assist us in viewing the multiple levels of relationships within a family, which have been unfolded as a result of the loss. The effects of the death on the family as a whole, its effect on the relationships between the surviving members, as well as each one's individual relationship with the once-living member now deceased, are relevant. The Milan Model of Systemic Family Therapy will be used to explain how death in the family affects relationships within the family. The Two-Track Model of Bereavement framework, which was described and applied to case examples in previous chapters, will be adapted to assess the family as a system. Paying attention to death as a factor in the family life cycle and formulating questions to explore the relationship from a systems perspective are valuable. Case illustrations of various losses at different stages of the family life cycle will be presented. A systemic assessment and an intervention of constructing a ritual for the family will be discussed.

THE FAMILY AS A SYSTEM

A word about general systems theory: It is an integrated interdisciplinary approach based on the concept of a system "as an organized unit determined by the reciprocal interaction of its components. The distinguishing feature of a system is totality: the whole is greater than the sum of its parts" (Burbatti & Formenti, 1988, p. 7). The elements of relations between family members, the way the family is organized, and what communication forms are used are central to understanding and assessing a family from this perspective. A systems approach maintains that families are dynamic entities moving through phases that involve transitions in relationships (marriage, birth, and death), each transition requiring adaptation. Different theoretical schools of systems approaches emphasize various elements crucial for adaptation, such as open communication, cohesion, ability to maintain relationships, and expression of emotions (Davidson, Quinn, & Josephson, 2001). The Milan School of Systemic Family Therapy focuses on relationships within the family and how these are reorganized when the system experiences changes (Selvini Palazzoli, Boscolo, Chechin, & Pratta, 1978), such as the loss of a family member.

A central notion in the systemic perspective is that all family members are viewed as interacting with each other and interdependent. Changes that occur within the family, positive or negative, desirable or undesirable, affect relationships between its members and the family as a unit. A dynamic process of reorganization and accommodation begins, parallel with the family's immediate response to maintain equilibrium. A loss to death in the family is one such transition.

> Death, or threatened death, is only one of many events that can disturb a family. A family unit is in functional equilibrium when it is calm and each member is functioning at a reasonable efficiency for that period. The equilibrium of the unit is disturbed by either the addition of a new member or the loss of a member. The intensity of the emotional reaction is governed by the functioning level of emotional integration in the family at the time …. A well integrated family may show more overt creativeness at the moment of the change but adapt to it rather quickly. A less integrated family may show little reaction at the time and respond later with symptoms of physical illness, emotional illness or a social misbehavior. (Bowen, 2004, pp. 50–51)

A loss of a family member tears the fabric of relationships among the surviving family members, and the grief that follows is experienced in various ways by each member. Under such circumstances the family's resources to support its members are temporarily shaken, and external help might be needed (Malkinson, 2007). From a systems perspective, two contradicting tasks are most apparent in the transition following the death of a family member: searching for ways to accommodate to the changes resulting from the loss while at the same time striving to continue with life as a functioning unit (Shapiro, 1994, 1996).

ASSUMPTIONS

1. A family is an organized system of relationships, interactions, roles and rules.
2. Transitions in the family life cycle are inevitable and are likely to cause stress.
3. Family relationship patterns are understood in their context where the history and intergenerational relationships are presented as a central source of information.
4. The history and legacy of the family are transmitted inter-generationally in the form of systems beliefs, to which loyalty (and commitment) is expected.
5. Family interactions are conveyed through verbal and nonverbal communication which is cognitive, emotional, and behavioral.
6. The family is a dynamic entity which struggles to maintain its structure.
7. A loss in the family shatters the systems beliefs as well as each individual's ones.

(Based on Walsh & McGoldrick, 2004)

A DEATH IN THE FAMILY

A family approach expands our understanding of the multilevels and the complexity of adjusting to a negative transition in the individual and the family (Carter & McGoldrick, 1999; Walsh & McGoldrick, 2004). Viewing loss from a systems approach is similar in many ways to drawing a map. Each detail is significant, but only by assembling them together does one get the full picture. In family work as in mapmaking, the whole is greater than the sum of its parts, but requires them all. A systems approach provides a resource to explore and reveal important information about relationships in the past, present, and future as a result of the death of a family member. It can also help explore how grieving family members restructure relationships and construct meaning from the loss. Additionally, loss of a family member not only implies a loss of relationships (Bowen, 2004), but it indicates that deceased family members remain part of the family and, in a unique way, become part of the family history, story, tradition, or legacy. At the same time, each individual member constructs personal memories of the deceased that reflect the type of relationship (parent, child, sibling, spouse, grandchild, or cousin) the way the relationship was perceived in actuality as well as how each member wished it to be.

Even though grief is an individual process of reorganizing the inner relationship with a person who is no longer alive, the bereaved are also social beings and part of a family. Regardless of their quality, relationships are being formed from the moment of birth and continue until death—"from cradle to grave." Similarly, inner relationships with the deceased continue to preoccupy members of the family along the life cycle as long as they are alive (Malkinson & Bar-Tur, 2004–2005).

When a loss is experienced by a family, its process of reorganization to continue as an entity begins in parallel but is not necessarily in synchrony with the individual process of reorganization. The individual and the family are searching for ways to accommodate the multiple levels of the meaning of the loss, and understanding and assessing the interconnection between the two is crucial. Each family member's grief is individually based on a unique relationship with the deceased. Although grief is an intrapersonal process, it nevertheless involves relationships between the bereaved and the deceased and between other grieving family members. Each relationship held with the deceased is unique.

On another level, the loss of a family member affects the relationships among living members and is followed by a search for an alternative balance. In the opening chapter, we described the biblical figure of Jacob, from the book of Genesis, who was mourning the purported loss of his beloved son Joseph to illustrate the impact of a loss of a child. From a family perspective, we can see the complexity of relationships and how the relationship between Jacob and his beloved son Joseph affected those between the favored child and his siblings. Spurred by jealousy and hatred of Joseph and possibly anger toward their father, Joseph's brothers sell him into slavery and give their father Joseph's bloody coat, leading the father to believe Joseph is dead. There is a secret that is known to the siblings only. A new reality has been formed within the family. The story goes on to tell us about Jacob's response: He mourned the loss of his son, and although all of his living children knew that Joseph was not dead, they tried to comfort him. But Jacob refused to be comforted and mourned Joseph for many years. Jacob's immersion in his grief probably caused further distance between him and the rest of the family, especially Joseph's siblings. The experience of a loss of a brother or a sister is often experienced by the living siblings as "a double loss": the loss of a sibling and "loss" of the parent(s) who mourns the deceased child (Worden, Davis, & McCown, 1999). The "missing child," as was the case with Joseph, is very much present in the family and echoes of his presence reverberate across relationships and the role he played within the family prior to the loss. Jacob's prolonged grief over his lost child both shapes the dynamics among family members and is influenced by those dynamics. (Bowen, 2004). The secret kept by the brothers further interferes by isolating the children from their father. A system approach to understanding a loss in a family will take into consideration the multilevel interactions and the idea of connectedness: How to retain connections with the deceased, the relationships of each member with the deceased, interactions between living family members, and the family as a unit with its legacy, tradition and myths that are trans-generational.

A SYSTEMIC APPROACH TO FAMILY GRIEF THERAPY

The systemic view of a family, especially following loss through death of one of its members, focuses on the multidimensionality of relationships, those of each family member with the deceased and those between living members. Assessed beliefs, tradition, and legacy also play a significant role in how mourning is experienced. In previous chapters we elaborated on the ways individuals organize their relationship with the deceased, stressing that inner attachments continue to be central to the bereaved's life and continue to influence the family. The way a family organizes its life following a loss may take many forms depending on other variables in its life-cycle stage (Selvini Palozzoli et al., 1978).

A referral to therapy, whether for an individual or a family, can take many forms in the way of the presenting problem as well as the choice of its timing, for example, immediately following the loss or years later (Gelcer, 1983; Malkinson, 2007). We will illustrate these points with short case examples (all are based on real cases that have been modified).

How to Mourn and Continue With Life: The Davis Family

(Malkinson, 2007)

The Davis family requested therapy a few weeks after the loss of their 3-year-old daughter under traumatic circumstances. The parents were very anxious about the well-being of the family, especially the two boys. They were asking how they should manage their life and what the right way to grieve was. They wanted to know what to say and what not to say to the boys, what the right way was to talk about the loss, or whether it was preferable to refrain from too much talking about it as it caused too much pain.

The family—father, mother, two sons (aged 7 and 5), and the little girl—were enjoying a weekend afternoon together on the playground. Father was playing football with the sons and the little girl was running on the playground with the mother watching her. Father kicked the ball too strongly and it landed in the street. As the father ran to catch the ball, the little girl followed him and before he could stop her, she was run over by a car and was fatally injured. She was taken to the hospital where the medical team tried to save her life, but she died. They were all shocked and devastated and yet felt that life must go on. They decided not to delve into the circumstances of the death of their daughter.

REFLECTIONS

The conflict between continuing with life and mourning the death is apparent. The parents fear that the death of their daughter under tragic circumstances is what might be a death of the family as well. Their fear leads them to make the decision to continue with life, as they understand it. They also wish to protect family members from unbearable pain. Avoidance is the behavioral consequence of their appraisal to prevent being immersed in mourning, only to realize that that was not possible.

The Shadow of the Dead Child: The Traumatic Death of Nadir

(Rubin & Nassar, 1993)

The Flanns, a working-class family, made a referral to a local mental health center. It was the mother who requested therapy. The presenting problem was that Reem, their 3-year-old daughter, was exhibiting symptoms following the sudden death of her brother, Nadir, 4 months earlier. The symptoms included sleep difficulties, frequent and uncontrollable bursts of crying, and continuously looking for her brother. Reem witnessed the death of Nadir, aged 10, from a fall while he was playing with her at a nearby construction site. Reem was told that her brother was in the hospital. The Flann family consists of mother, father, Reem, and two older children.

After a short time in therapy, Reem's father shared his active suicidal thoughts, communicating his intent to rejoin his son Nadir in the next world. This response was anathema to Muslim religion, which the Flanns adhere to. Reem's mother found it hard to function. She explained that she did not have the strength to deal with her son's death and the children's response. As a result, she was telling the children, and herself, that her son had not died but instead was the new child growing in her belly. We return to consider this case in Chapter 12, which addresses social-cultural contexts of loss.

REFLECTIONS

The sudden and unexpected death of a child shatters the life of the family and initiates a period of crisis for all its members. The death of the brother witnessed by the sister (in the case of the Flann family) was followed by a number of symptoms characteristic of response to a traumatic event.

The parents' significant role in protecting their family and their children while they are going through their own grief produces a heavy burden: The father's declaration of his wish to rejoin his son and the mother's difficulties in mourning the death while continuing to parent the surviving children emerged as aspects of the family system's dysfunction in the wake of Nadir's death.

A Delayed Grief: The Story of Joe

The story of Joe, a student enrolled in an elective course on loss and bereavement, introduced to the reader in Chapter 1 is an illustration of how a death of a parent impacted the family. As a student, 10 years later, Joe describes the death of his mother to cancer and recalls his experiences as an adolescent who was the youngest of three children. In a very sensitive and honest way, we learn about his parents' decision not to talk about his mother's illness and instead refer to her disappearance for treatment as going on "vacation." The shock of being told about the mother's death and the father's remarrying a year later were very confusing to Joe, who, as a teenager, could not fully grasp and grieve the loss. From a family perspective, the message conveyed was that "life goes on" but that some things are not to be shared. Joe's grieving the death of his mother was made possible in therapy years later, but the family members remain emotionally distant from each other.

REFLECTIONS

Avoidance is a noticeable pattern of interaction in this family, which resulted from not discussing the mother's illness and death. The family's myth regarding its survival is to refrain from what is assumed to be too painful, that is, grieving the mother's death. Joe can see how, as an adolescent and the youngest of three, his response to the event was one of disengagement from experiencing grief. Years later, Joe realizes his "stuckness" and, in therapy, relives his memories and emotions related to his mother's death. In the eyes of Joe, 10 years after his mother's death, he reevaluates the avoidance as his father's choice to protect the family.

The Effects of the Loss of a Child on a Marital Relationship: The Case of Mr. and Mrs. Jonas

(Malkinson, 2007)

Mr. and Mrs. Jonas came for therapy 8 months after their son Jonathan died from cancer. Jonathan was the youngest of three and was 9 years old when he died. Mrs. Jonas, who initiated therapy, said that although Jonathan's death was expected as a result of his critical condition, they were shocked when he died and could not believe it. Mrs. Jonas sensed that everything fell apart and was too painful and thought they should seek professional help. Mr. Jonas expressed his reservations about therapy, fearing that it would block returning back to life, which was most important for them as a couple and as parents to the living children. In his words: "I keep telling my wife that life must go on. Talking about it will never bring Jonathan back. I can't stand it as she goes over and over it." He responded to his wife's insisting they come to therapy by agreeing to come just once. Each was mourning the loss of their son in a different way and, although each expected support from the other, the differences resulted in a growing distance between them.

REFLECTIONS

The loss of a child has the potential to impose stress on the marital relationship for several reasons. The loss of a child is always untimely and disrupts the natural order of the family life cycle (Christ, Bonnano, Malkinson, & Rubin, 2003). For parents, it injures their parental role, and in many ways they continue to be parents of the dead child forever (Malkinson & Bar-Tur, 2004–2005). It also reflects gender differences in experiencing grief. Couples grief therapy, unlike general couples therapy, focuses on assisting each one's own way of searching and maintaining inner involvement with the dead child so that it becomes a source of intimacy.

The Loss of a Grandchild

(Malkinson, 2007)

The Oldamns, in their late 60s, requested help after their son lost his eldest daughter in a terrorist attack and said in a very apologetic manner, "We feel that life has become a long dark night" (Malkinson, 2007, p. 206). They were concerned about their "right" to grieve along with their duty as parents to their son who lost his daughter. They felt their son needed their support and by grieving, they assumed they betrayed their parental role. Therapy sessions were the only place they "could afford" to cry and not be criticized as weak. They were very confused about how to grieve the loss of their granddaughter and support their son at the same time. The two seemed to contradict each other. They further wanted to explore the issue of loyalties to their son, as parents, and their loyalties to their beloved granddaughter, as grandparents.

REFLECTIONS

The natural course of life has been shattered because grandparents are expected to predecease their children and grandchildren. It is what Reed (2003) called "the dual loss": that of mourning the death of their grandchild and grieving their adult child's suffering (p. 1; see also Reed, 2000).

From a family perspective, the grandparents avoid expressing their grief for the sake of their child. They feel they are required to help him, be strong rather than crying, so they hide their grief in an effort "not to become an additional burden" on their mourning adult child.

ASSESSMENT OF THE FAMILY

The purpose of assessment of the family is to assess the process of mourning and adaptation to life following the loss of one of its members. Similar to an individual one, assessment of the family involves factors related to the deceased, factors related to an individual member of the family, and factors related to the family and its sociocultural context. Special attention is paid to the family's stage in the life cycle, relationships of each member with the deceased and those between family members, and the family's past experiences with losses. Additionally, assessment will include the family's beliefs system concerning how the individual and the family grieve as well as family rituals. From a systemic perspective, an important question is the timing of requesting or being referred to therapy as a way to assess the family's oscillation between change and stabilization (Shapiro, 1994, 1996).

WHAT TO ASSESS?

Factors related to the deceased: Who died? Circumstances of the loss: anticipated, sudden (illness), traumatic (disaster, road accident, suicide), violent (murder). Ambiguous loss, missing body (Boss, 1999). Information with regard to burial (funeral).

Factors related to individual member: Age, gender, personality variables, relationship to the deceased.

Factors related to the family: Loss and stage of family life cycle, previous losses, sociocultural and religious factors, financial issues.

The type and nature of relationship of surviving family members will greatly affect the process as experienced by each bereaved family member. Both the degree of closeness with the deceased as perceived and experienced by each family member and the way each views others as part of the process will influence the process.

Assessment of Relationships Using Circular Questioning

Systemic family therapy views interaction between family members, and the meaning attributed to it, as a way to understand relationships. Formulating a hypothesis is a way to gather information with regard to relationships (past, present, and future). The use of circular questions to elicit information about relationships was developed by the Milan team Selvini, Boscolo, Chechin, and Pratta (1980). Exploration using circular questioning of cognitions, emotions, and behaviors following a death in the family reveals the complexity and richness of relationships among family members and their impact on each member's inner relationship with the deceased.

CATEGORIES OF CIRCULAR QUESTIONS ABOUT RELATIONSHIPS

Questions about differences in perceptions of closeness of relationships: "Who was the closest to mother when she was ill?" "Who would agree with/object to your opinion?"

Questions about cognitions, emotions, and behaviors about relationships: "When you think about mum and feel sad, who in the family notices? Who doesn't?"

Hypothetical questions about the deceased: "If mother were here, what would she have said about the family's reaction?" "If we were to ask her about it, how do you think she would have felt? What would she have done?"

Hypothetical questions about the future: "In 2 years time, what would the family look like?" (Boscolo, Chechin, Hoffman, & Penn, 1987)

Family Assessment Based on the Two-Track Model of Bereavement

Throughout the book we have elaborated the application of the Two-Track Model as applied with individuals as a source to assess the process and level of adaptation to loss on the axes of functioning and relationship to the deceased. Additional assessment of some of this model's elements from the tracks of biopsychosocial functioning and relationship to the deceased applied to the family will allow a wider prism for the understanding of individual and family processes. Each track contains relevant components to assess the family as a

TABLE 11.1   Family Assessment Based on the Two-Track Model of Bereavement

Track I: Family Functioning	Track II: Relationship With the Deceased
Familial relationship: How do you see relationships in the family? Are there any changes in these relationships? What has been changed the most?	**Family imagery and memories:** To what extent does the family have openness to talk about the deceased? Who wants to talk most about the loss and who least?
Interpersonal relationship: What changes, if any, have occurred in the family with regard to interpersonal relationships? Do people feel closer or more distanced from each other?	**Features of loss:** What characteristics associated with the bereavement process are present in the family?
Family meaning structure: Are there any changes in the family's views about life and death since ____ died?	**Pre-loss relationship:** What is characteristic to the description of family members of the pre-loss relationship? What is remembered most, and what is being avoided? How are these described (words, pictures, stories)?
Investment in life tasks: Are there any changes in the way the family functions, for example, things the family used to do but stopped doing, and things that weren't done that are now done?	**Memorialization and transformation:** What are the ways the family set as memorials? How did the family decide about it? Whose idea was it? Did all agree?

system. Table 11.1 shows system-relevant components that can be used to assess the family by asking questions related to the individual and the family.

THERAPEUTIC ALLIANCE

Therapeutic alliance when working with couples and families includes alliance with the system (the couple or the family) and the concurrent alliance with individual members who comprise the system. Alliance with the family will focus on aspects such as the family stage of life cycle, myths about death, attitudes toward grief, and ethnocultural and religious mourning customs, whereas alliance with individual members requires attentive listening to differences in how each describes his or her personal response to the loss, including his or her choice of words as well as choosing to be silent. Provision of information about grief, its components, courses, and outcomes will refer to both the collective and shared grief and the individual response to the loss (Witztum, 2004). Similarly, normalizing the process and stressing the system's way of responding to the loss and the individual's idiosyncratic response is useful; although all members go through a similar process, each one experiences it differently. Similarly, it is important to normalize the process while stressing differences between the system's way to respond to the loss and the individual's idiosyncratic responses (Malkinson, 2007).

INTERVENTION: CONSTRUCTING A FAMILY RITUAL

The loss of a loved one, especially under sudden, unexpected, and traumatic circumstances, often increases both the individual's and family system's inability to function. A sense of "collective" dysfunctional guilt is one such example and can take a number of forms, such as the following:

1. The guilt-provoking event is frozen, everything remains intact, and nothing is being moved.
2. The event is avoided, as if trying to erase its occurrence by moving to another place, taking away all the deceased's belongings to avoid reminders, or leaving the belonging untouched as if nothing happened.
3. One can become overinvolved in one's daily routine (many times extending it), such as spending longer hours at work, which helps one to be immersed in the here and now and avoid "facing" the past.

In the case of dysfunctional guilt, the family may develop a set of ritualistic, repetitive behaviors as a way of protecting itself from facing the pain. In such cases therapeutic rituals such as those described in Chapters 9 and 10 can be effective interventions (Burbatti & Formenti, 1988; Malkinson, 2007; Van der Hart, 1983; Witztum & Roman, 2000). Rituals can either be structured similarly to traditional mourning or can be based on existing family rituals (meals, doing things together, etc.).

In the Davis family described earlier, the conflict between continuing with life and mourning the death was apparent. The parents feared that the death of their daughter under tragic circumstances might mean the death of the family as well. Their fear led them to make the decision to continue with life, as they understood it, and to use that as a way to protect family members from unbearable pain. Avoidance was their device to prevent themselves from being immersed in mourning, only to realize that this was not possible.

A family ritual was constructed for the Davis family and with their involvement. As the first anniversary of the death of their daughter was approaching, the ritual was aimed at addressing the issue of avoiding the discussion of the death and its tragic circumstances.

The ritual was constructed in a session with the parents only, in order to legitimize grief and pain as part of the family experience following the loss. It was constructed after the father revealed that from time to time since the loss, he would take the albums out and peek at the pictures without anybody else seeing him do it.

THE CONSTRUCTION OF A FAMILY RITUAL

A ritual is a structured assignment focused on the specific difficulty encountered by the family as a way to introduce a change through prescribing an assignment to be jointly performed by its members. The purpose of the ritual is to change inflexible rules with regard to existing beliefs held by the family. (Based on Burbatti & Formenti, 1988)

The parents were instructed to plan a time they could gather together with the children, take out the albums, and look at the photographs and share memories of the deceased daughter. Together with the therapists, the parents planned in detail how they were going to tell the children about the gathering and the sharing of the memories and looking at the photographs in the albums. This was the first stage in preparing the family to plan the first-year ceremony at the grave.

The session following the family gathering was a joint session with the children. A sense of relief mixed with pain was shared by all family members as if to say that the deceased daughter has rejoined the family and it was all right to talk about her and how much she was missed.

A SYSTEMS APPROACH: CLINICAL ISSUES TO BE CONSIDERED

In many ways, grief in the family parallels the individual process of loss. Inasmuch as individuals get stuck in the grief process, so do families.

Similar to the individual process, a family's adaptation to the new reality includes assimilation of the loss into the existing family belief system, and past experiences with losses, while accommodating the system to its outcomes through the adoption of new beliefs, roles, and relationships. The family's grief process is a compound of individual responses to loss based on the family history, belief system, and intergenerational relationships that have evolved throughout the years. From a systemic perspective, family schemas are formed and transformed throughout the years and are combinations of family-of-origin schemas (family tradition) and schemas developed jointly by members of the family. A loss of a family member causes an unbalance in existing patterns of relationships and shatters the family's belief system.

Family therapy combines individual and systemic strategies to help the system regain functioning and regain its sense of being a family with memories of the deceased being part of it and not the physical presence.

Therapeutic Goals of Family Therapy

1. Assist the family to deal adaptively with issues of grief and pain.
2. Reorganize in a more functional way the present relationship among family members so the system can experience grief and minimize avoidance of loss-related emotions.
3. Help the family become a constructive source of support to its members.
4. Help the family re-create a story wherein the loss is woven and becomes part of the family's narrative.

CONCLUSIONS

The systemic perspective described in the chapter highlighted how frequently a loss *in* the family is perceived and experienced by families as a loss *by* the family and potentially *of* the family. Clearly, the death event conveys a sense of finality never to be regained, to which the system's initial response is to protect itself so as to survive. Although in many ways something has been lost and the family changed forever, not all is lost; the family as a system continues to evolve, with new roles being formed and relationships being transformed in a different way. Most of all, memories and legacy remain, and internal relationships with the deceased are transformed and reshaped.

The loss of a family member has many voices. The experience of each member affects the family no less than the family as a whole has an effect on its individual members. The two are connected and interrelated. The echoes of continuing bonds with the deceased, when heard from a family perspective, have many sounds: sounds that may change their intensity and their volume with the passage of time but will never disappear. These sounds are there and will remain so as each member of the family and the family as a whole continue to maintain bonds with the deceased.

Family therapy from a systemic perspective provides an opportunity to widen the lenses in working with bereaved individuals as well as with families in a way that facilitates understanding how relationships evolve and shape around the deceased and weave "the presence of the absent" into the family life story in a more constructive way so life can continue.

Section *IV*

Expanding Horizons: Culture, Clinical Challenges, and Facilitating Resilience

Figure S4.1   Anthropoid coffins, Pottery, Deir el-Balah, Late Bronze period. Photo © The Israel Museum, Jerusalem.

Section IV addresses contexts of mourning and bereavement. We share what we believe the clinician must know, and what the bereaved still need to learn, in order to work more effectively. In the first chapter of this part (Chapter 12), we address the majority and minority aspects of cultural worldviews. The meaning paradigm or *Weltanschauung* (worldview) of a culture is relevant for understanding the broader matrix of the context of mourning and adaptation. As in the rest of the book, clinical material is included liberally to bring home aspects of culture, with a primary focus on the United States and Israel. Next, in Chapter 13, we address how to strengthen the secure base of the counseling and therapy encounters by discussing the situations and cases that most trouble clinicians. In so doing, we touch upon psychiatric and other acute complications that may require attention to suicidal risk, medication, and other aspects of crisis intervention. The chapter is not a substitute for professional training and experience in mental health, but it is a useful synopsis of some of the more important issues to keep in mind.

Chapter 14 focuses on facilitating growth and resilience outside the clinical office through attention to the potentials inherent in activity, being connected to others, spirituality, dialoguing with oneself, self-help groups, and techniques such as mindfulness. The chapter concludes with attention to therapist self-care and completes the circle of how one can take better care of the other by not neglecting to pay proper attention to ourselves as caregivers.

12

The Social–Cultural Contexts of Loss
Considerations for Culturally Sensitive Interventions

B ereavement following the loss of a loved one is known to be universal, normal, and quintessentially human. Individuals' grief responses with their biopsychosocial components as well as culturally sanctioned responses vary tremendously. The duration and magnitude of such responses are mediated by the identity of the person who has died, the history and person of the griever, and the religious and cultural context of the bereaved.

For example, following the death of a spouse or a child, the lens through which the bereaved views him- or herself and the world may be characterized by a fundamental bias—that there is no value to a life without the deceased who was so loved (Witztum et al., 2001). The determination of how to understand that perspective is not only related to the nature of the loss but also to the amount of time since the death and numerous other variables that have received attention in the literature (Stroebe et al., 2008). Additionally, the cultural lens is critical. In the individualized Western societies, seeing the world as devoid of meaning during the first weeks after the loss may be seen as an expression of normal grief. In many Islamic cultures, however, such a response may be considered highly unusual and deviant—because of the culture's worldview that emphasizes a return to adaptive functioning within days after a death (Rubin & Yasien-Esmael, 2004).

In addition to the universal aspects of the grief and bereavement process, there are specific symbolic and behavioral characteristics unique to different cultures. For example, one of the major characteristics common to cultures and religions is the issue of assisting the transition to another dimension—from the living world to the world of the dead (*rite de passage;* Van Gennep, 1960). One of the functions of ritual and religion for the bereaved and for society is to set up a structure that addresses how the deceased can make this transformation successfully. At the same time, religion and ritual are also sources of social solidarity, emotional support, and community unity (Palgi & Abramovitch, 1984).

In this chapter we will elaborate on cultural aspects in the process of bereavement and how to use them in culturally sensitive grief therapy. The variation among peoples, stemming from religion, culture, language, and history, is staggering. In this chapter, we have chosen three ethnic groups familiar to North Americans to illustrate some of the variations of culture there. We then present three case examples to illustrate clinical interventions in Israel that involved sensitivity to Jewish, Christian, and Islamic variations on culture. Ultimately, the importance of learning about the customs, rituals, belief systems, and social constructs of varying religious and ethnic groups allow one to practice with the necessary respect for the differences that shape important aspects of the response to grief.

EXAMPLES OF DIFFERENT CULTURAL TRADITIONS OF GRIEF AND MOURNING

Cultural approaches to dealing with death are embedded in larger and well-articulated aspects of culture and society. Each culture has its own approach to dealing with loss. To fully understand each culture's way of dealing with death requires extensive knowledge of its history and social structure, economic and political sectors. Beliefs and practices concerning death and mourning are extremely important in a person's life. In many societies, death rituals are far more elaborate and protracted than those prevalent in Western societies. To outsiders, they may require actions that seem pointless and even destructive or unpleasant (Witztum et al., 2001). Without sufficient recognition and understanding of these cultural variations, clinicians will not be able to properly evaluate and intervene with clients from different cultural and ethnic groups.

Countries that are absorbing significant numbers of immigrants, such as the United States, Britain, France, Germany, and Israel, have become increasingly diverse. In the United States, for example, an increasingly large percentage of the population consists of individuals of various ethnic and racial backgrounds. As America's culturally diverse population continues to increase rapidly, the need for a more culturally competent caregiver workforce also rises. According to the U.S. Census Bureau, the population of Asian and Pacific Islanders in the United States increased by 87% from 1981 to 1991. Similarly, Hispanics increased by 50%, American Indians, Eskimos, and Aleuts by 42%, Blacks by 5%, and Whites by 7%. The bureau went on to project that in the 21st century, the greater number of people living in the United States will belong to groups now referred to as "minorities" (Esposito, Buckalew, & Chukunta, 1996). Similarly, in Britain, in the 2001 census minorities accounted for 4.6 million people or 7.9% of the total population; this represents a growth of 53% between 1991 and 2001. Half of the total minority ethnic population considered themselves as Asian of predominantly Indian, Pakistani, or Bangladeshi origin. A quarter described themselves as being Black, 15% of mixed ethnicity, 5% Chinese, and 5% other ethnicity (Carey & Cosgrove, 2006).

The cultural tapestry is often a central mediator of many clinical interactions. Knowledge about how patients experience and express pain, maintain hope in the face of a poor prognosis, and respond to grief and loss is relevant for healthcare professionals. As a country's population increases in cultural and ethnic diversity, the recognition and provision of culturally sensitive health care increases in importance as well (Skaff, Chesla, Mycue, & Fisher, 2002).

CULTURAL AND ETHNIC GROUPS

Schermerhorn (1978) has defined an ethnic group as "a collectivity within a larger society having real or putative common ancestry, memories of a shared historical past, and a cultural focus on one or more symbolic aspects defined as the epitome of their peoplehood. A necessary accompaniment is some consciousness of kind among members of the group" (p. 12). A bereaved person's ethnicity is determined not only by the person's country of origin but also by who he says he is, what he does and with whom, and how he feels about it. Behavioral dimension of ethnicity means that the person has learned distinctive values, beliefs, behavioral norms, and languages that serve as the basis of interaction within the group and also of participation in mainstream social institutions (Eisenbruch, 1984).

In approaching a bereaved person belonging to a particular ethnic group, it is helpful to realize that there may be more variation within the group than between groups of other ethnic origin. Typically, ethnic groups share a historical tradition that encompasses both the meaning of death and the way in which the individual within society deals with bereavement. The evolution and emergence of subcultures adds to the mix by extending the span of a particular culture's worldview and behavioral variation.

In the next section, we present a brief synopsis and description of beliefs and coping behaviors of people from three cultures within the American mosaic. Although presented briefly, they exemplify and illustrate the types of information needed for the mental health professional to become culturally sensitive and aware when approaching a family's grief needs and orientation in these cultures.

Before embarking on an intervention plan, the therapist should relate to these basic questions (modified and expanded from the National Cancer Institute, 2010):

1. What are the culturally prescribed rituals for managing the dying process, the body of the deceased, the disposal of the body, and commemoration of the death?
2. What are the beliefs about what happens after death?
3. What does the client consider an appropriate emotional expression and integration of the loss?
4. What does the client consider to be the gender rules for handling the death?
5. Do certain types of death carry a stigma for this group (e.g., suicide), or are certain types of death especially traumatic for that cultural group (e.g., death of a child)?

EXAMPLES OF CULTURAL AND RELIGIOUS VARIATION IN NORTH AMERICA

English-speaking persons in North America make up the vast majority of the residents there. Beneath the language matrix shared by this majority, however, are many subcultures with incredible divergence. These groups have differences in political beliefs, religious principles (including an absence of same), languages spoken at home, social class, orientation to individual and collectivist principles, gender-specific behaviors, and the list can go on for many pages. Uniting these American peoples in their shared life space, however, is a basic commitment to living together with respect, tolerance, and equality before the law. The indigenous inhabitants, the European settlers, the Africans brought to the country against their will, as well as the succeeding waves of Asian and other cultures both influence and are influenced by the bubbling culture of the United States. An underlying theme often associated with Americans is their belief in change and in moving forward (Goodwin, 2005; Isaacson, 2003; Larson, 2003). We consider three strands within this amazing fabric of a developing people.

Native American People

Native Americans, often referred to as American Indians, are not one people or culture. Defying the stereotype, the beliefs, traditions, rituals, and ceremonies among these indigenous tribal groups vary widely. Influencing the original native culture of each group are the influences of assimilation and acculturation, much of which reflects the influence of relocation and education at boarding schools and competing missionary efforts (Clements et al., 2003). Many Native American children grew up without the traditions of their ancestors. The majority currently practice several Christian religions, such as Catholicism, Presbyterian, and Jehovah's Witness (Esposito et al., 1996).

Lawson (1990) defines the term *Native American* as encompassing diverse tribal groups with distinct characteristics and styles. Native American cultures have absorbed varying degrees of influence from contemporary American culture. Stroebe and Stroebe (1987) have described the mourning practices of the Navajo peoples as limited to 4 days. After this period, the bereaved are expected to return to normal life. Excessive emotion is not encouraged during these 4 days. The Navajo people believe speaking of the deceased or of their emotions concerning the loss can do harm to the living because of the power of the deceased individual. In family life, children have great value and may be the only achievement in life. Religious ceremonies are based on living with nature; wakes are long, with food and memorial gifts distributed. The Navajo, similar to many Native Americans, believe that the spirit of the dying person cannot be freed unless the family is with that person.

The definitions of what is normative and what is complicated bereavement are things to consider when considering the course of therapy. S. I. Miller and Schoenfeld (1973) explored the occurrence of the pathologic grief-work hypothesis, which postulates that without grieving openly, there will be poorer adjustment. Among the Navajo people, the cultural norms do not endorse the grief-work hypothesis that expression of grief is adaptive. In that culture, the evidence is doubtful that suppression of open grief may result in depression for the grieving individual. Often suspicious of individuals of European descent, Native Americans require an approach that communicates sensitivity and respect for their spiritual beliefs. The Navajo are private grievers, and expressing grief is believed harmful to the spirit of the deceased. With the Navajo, grief assessment should include the entire family. Attending to the response of the family or community is preferable to an individual interview paradigm.

> Navajo cultural norms do not endorse the grief-work hypothesis, and encouraging people to express their grief goes against the tradition and is believed to be harmful to the deceased and bereaved alike.
>
> The mental health professional's grief assessment should include the entire family. Listening and providing support to the family or community may be more effective than use of an individual interview paradigm.

African American Grief

The term *African American* often is used as a brushstroke description for many groups, subcultures, and countries of origin for the large community who have original ties to the African continent. In traditional African culture, death is certainly not the end. In fact, in African culture, death is called "transition": It signals the end of one existence and the beginning of another. In addition, African American individuals have a number of distinctive religious and secular ceremonies and traditions (Holloway, 2002).

The African American population, through history, has experienced tragic and unexpected deaths. They achieve support through their religious beliefs. The memorial service and funeral, which may be one and the same, usually occur within 1 week of the death and are the only religious ceremonies to acknowledge the death. However, African heritage and traditions extend beyond the simple confines of Christianity's view of death (Esposito et al., 1996). The presence of a growing Muslim representation among Blacks in North America encompasses immigrants from Africa as well as converts and persons born into the variety of American traditions. A mix of African, Christian, and Muslim traditions may characterize various subcultures of grievers.

The relatively high proportion of traumatic loss in this population, combined with the harsh realities of life and the limited nature of both material and social resources structures, can be significantly moderated by religion because of the support of the belief system and the community of the faithful.

> A strong community and church support system exists.
>
> Initial reactions to grief is accepted; however, prolonged grief is not tolerated.
>
> The concept of being "strong" is held in high regard in the cultural guidelines of grief.

The African American typically will rely upon his or her family and church for support and avoid organized, professionally run groups (Esposito, Buckalew & Chukunta, 1996).

Latinos

Although the religious beliefs and preferences of their countries of origin determine the rituals involved in the grief and bereavement process for Latino individuals, the rituals also vary within the Latino culture, depending on the level of acculturation into the mainstream society. First-generation Latino immigrants tend to be much more traditional than successive generations. The customs described in this chapter are very traditional.

When working with grieving Latino families, healthcare professionals must understand the concept of *respeto* (i.e., rules that guide social relationships). In traditional families, a strict hierarchy exists and must be honored. Status typically is ordered from oldest to youngest and from men to women. Mental health professionals should greet family members with a handshake and address them formally.

Usually, Latino individuals express their grief by crying openly, which is considered a healthy and appropriate emotional response (Parry & Ryan, 1996). People who were emotionally closest to the deceased are expected to grieve openly and are offered the comfort and support of family and friends. Whereas it is not unusual to hear Latina women wailing loudly, calling out the name of the deceased, and fainting, machismo plays a significant part in the lack of emotional response among adult Latino men. Latino men are expected to "be strong" for the family and usually do not grieve openly. Religion and spirituality are very important for Latino individuals who practice Catholicism, the dominant religion for this group (Parry & Ryan, 1996). Many Latino families believe in spiritual and psychological continuity between the living and the dead and usually continue a relationship with the deceased through prayer and visits to the grave.

Latinos grieving sudden death have a significantly greater grief intensity than Latinos grieving expected death and greater than Anglos grieving either kind of death. In the Latino population, the intensity of grief is not affected by funeral rituals, closeness of relationship, time since death, or participation in novenas. Puerto Ricans place great importance on resolving conflicts, seeing the dying relative, and completing relationships that will free him or her to enter the afterlife. Curses and visions of the deceased are common within this culture. Feelings of guilt or unresolved issues in the relationship between the deceased and survivor will manifest themselves in the bereaved. For example, in some Hispanic families the father is expected to pick up or display attention to the child upon returning home from work; if this is not done, it is believed that something will happen to the child. In the case of SIDS (sudden infant death syndrome), it is important to assess if guilt feelings arise from a deviation from the expected belief.

Formal mourning begins with an open-casket service, during which a Rosary is said, using beads. Group prayers for the soul of the deceased are recited for one or two evenings prior to the day of the funeral. This is also a time for family members and friends to pay their respects to the body of the deceased and offer condolences to the immediate family members. A funeral mass usually is held at a church, followed by a procession to the burial site. There a graveside service is recited, and the grave is blessed before burial with holy water by a priest or a deacon (Clements et al., 2003).

The healthcare professionals must understand the concept of respeto (i.e., rules that guide social relationships). In traditional families, a strict hierarchy exists and must be honored. Status typically is ordered form oldest to youngest and from men to women.

Mental health professional should greet family members with handshake and addressed them formally. Latino individuals express their grief by crying openly, which is considered a healthy and appropriate emotional response.

Latinos grieving sudden death have a significantly greater grief intensity than Latinos grieving expected death.

Religion and spirituality are very important for Latino individuals who practice Catholicism.

CULTURAL AND RELIGIOUS VARIATION IN ISRAEL

In this section, we consider the combination of ethnic and religious variations that impacted the response to loss in three cases. In keeping with our intent to make this examination of culture and religion useful to clinicians in various settings, we will give a brief introduction to the religions involved that are generalizable elsewhere and we will attend to the requisite material that is specific to the location and features of the particular cases.

Israel is a country of over 7 million whose citizenry is approximately 80% Jewish, 19% Muslim, and the remainder Christian. The history of the Jewish people in their ancestral homeland is as old as the Bible or Torah. That history involves God's promise of the territory (hence the term *The Promised Land*) to the descendents of Abraham, Isaac, and Jacob. After the exodus from Egypt, the Jews exercised dominion over their territory until the destruction of the Second Temple in the year 70. The exile of the majority of the Jews from Judea and their dispersal around much of the world was inspiring in their carrying on of tradition and horrifying in the extent of discrimination and anti-Semitism encountered. Beginning in the 19th century, the return to Zion theme began to take on concrete reality with the moving back, or Aliyah, to the ancestral homeland. In this area, controlled first by Turkey and after World War I by Britain, the immigration served to catalyze the Arab residents and increasing conflict emerged between the immigrants and the residents. By the 1930s and the rise of Nazism, the need for a Jewish homeland became acute. In the absence of a haven for Jews, the Holocaust, or *Shoah*, of World War II served as a watershed and collective trauma (Berkowitz, 1979; Malkinson & Witztum, 2000; Rubin, 2010; Witztum & Malkinson, 2009).

The establishment of the State of Israel in 1948 has been a matter of great consequence for Jewish persons all over the world. The waves of Jewish immigration to Israel from all over the world have greatly influenced Jewish and Israeli culture (Witztum et al., 2001). Refugees from the ashes of Europe in the 1940s, Jews fleeing Arab states in the 1940s and 1950s, the Russian immigration of the 1970s and 1980s, and the Ethiopian immigrants of the 1990s have all contributed to the molding of Jewish society in Israel.

At the same time, Israel is home to a sizeable group of indigenous Arab citizens whose lives were changed dramatically and tragically during the period of the establishment of the State. The vast majority remains culturally, linguistically, and religiously part of the broader Arab world while at the same time maintaining their citizenship, ties, and lives within Israel. A large Palestinian Diaspora exists today, and Arab citizens of Israel may have relatives scattered across the globe as well as living in the Palestinian territories. This situation often complicates the experience of participating in loss rituals for the broader family even in the best of circumstances.

Israel in the second decade of the 21st century is a country both united and divided by religion, ethnicity, and history. The Arab–Israeli wars of 1948, 1956, 1967, 1973, and 1982 as well as the first and second Intifada have made Israel a country aware of bereavement, trauma, and terror. Today, Israelis continue to have control over the West Bank and Gaza territories, and a stagnant peace process remains contentious. How to balance Israel's legitimate security needs and the political aspirations of the Palestinian people continues to defy attempts at solutions.

Against this backdrop, we look at three cases that demonstrate the importance of cultural understanding and the dangers of mismanagement with clients from different subcultures. The first describes Jewish immigrants from Russia, and the second describes immigrants from Ethiopia. Finally, in the third, we consider a bereaved Muslim family and their response to the tragic death of a son.

Judaism

A small proportion of both Western and the world's population, the Jews have claimed a disproportionately large place in the religious and intellectual history of the world for over 2 millennia. Judaism has had a pronounced influence on the two largest monotheistic religions that followed it: Christianity and Islam. The world's Jewish population is estimated at 13.4 million (Mandell L. Berman Institute, 2010) with the majority residing in Israel and North America. Considered both an ethnic community and a religion, the majority of Jewish persons do not practice the tenets of the religion (Kellner, 2006). The largest Jewish religious movements are Orthodox Judaism, Conservative Judaism, and Reform Judaism. The movements differ in their approaches to traditional practices, gender differences, and Jewish law. The rabbis who are consulted on matters of theology and practice differ in how they interpret the vast sacred texts, religious law, and its interface with modern life (Telushkin, 2008). The notion of life after death, resurrection of the deceased, and the vision of the end of days are present in Jewish tradition but are not well articulated or clear to most members of the faith (Reimer, 1974).

All Jewish communities traditionally view burial of the dead and the support of the bereaved as among the most central of communal obligations. The tradition prescribes rituals for burying the dead, how to conduct the funeral, and the subsequent social mourning rituals (Lamm, 1974). Centered around the cycle of life, the bereaved observed a week-long mourning period labeled *Shiva* (Hebrew term designating the English word *seven*) where they grieved, recited the traditional Kaddish prayer at services, and were comforted by visits from the broad social community (Wieseltier, 1998). For the remainder of the first month, or *Shloshim* (Hebrew for thirty), the family observed a less strict degree of mourning. At the conclusion of the first year, the mourning period and mourner status ended. Prayers for the memory of the deceased continued to be recited either at least several times a year in the Ashkenazic holiday *Yizkor* services or weekly in the Sephardic Sabbath services. These rituals encouraged reworking of the relationship to the deceased. Despite the vast differences among members of the Jewish majority in Israel, matters relating to bereavement and burial have been ceded to the ultra-Orthodox, whose interpretation of Jewish law privileges such things as an immediate and speedy burial—often within hours of the death (Greenberg & Witztum, 2001). At times, the mismatch between the bereaved and those who are entrusted with the responsibility for burial can be exceedingly problematic.

Swift burial is in accord with Jewish tradition, but it may not meet the needs or expectations of the bereaved.

The idea of everlasting soul and an afterlife are often inchoate ideas and are often not associated with imagery of any kind.

Recitation of the Kaddish prayer by the mourner and observance of the *Shiva* allow for expression of community support as well as for the bereaved to experience a sense of attending to the needs of the deceased.

A recurring tradition of memory and reconnection with the deceased across the life cycle is part of the Jewish legacy.

Christianity

For most people in the West, Christianity is the religion they are most familiar with. With over a billion and a half adherents in the world, variation within the faith tradition is decidedly pronounced. In Smith's (1994) view of Christianity as a wisdom tradition, he emphasized that the religion was centered around the life of Jesus of Nazareth. "Jesus saw social barriers as an affront to Yahweh's compassion ... made him a social prophet... advocating an alternative vision of the human community" (p. 209). The theme of resurrection and the identification of Jesus with God became central themes for Christianity. The decisions of the Nicene Council in 325 CE concluded that Jesus was God incarnate and "true God and true man." Christianity incorporated the Jewish scriptures into the faith tradition as the Old Testament and, combining them with the Gospels called the New Testament, wove together particularistic and universalistic themes that were compelling for individuals, cultures, and societies that had heretofore adopted more animistic or polytheistic approaches.

Over time, Christianity divided into three branches: Roman Catholicism, Eastern Orthodoxy, and Protestantism. The rituals, prayers, and manner of attending to death, dying, and bereavement vary greatly. Belief in the continued existence of the soul after death, faith in the resurrection of the dead, the idea and expression that the dead "are with God," and the presence of a faith community and religious leadership all have the potential to provide support and solace to the bereaved. In the Eastern Orthodox tradition of Russia and Eastern Europe, the pomp and ceremony involved in death included an extended time period for viewing the body and paying last respects, as well as ornate and stylized funerals that endowed the funeral with a great deal of ceremony that was considered the proper way to honor the dead. In the Russian Orthodox tradition, commemorations on the 3rd, 9th, and 40th days after death, and on anniversaries thereafter, continue ancient Christian practices and have been observed for most of the history of Christianity (Sveshnikov, 2010). As the dominant culture in the former Soviet Union, the Russian traditions in conducting funerals influenced the death and mourning rituals of the Jewish minority and other religions within this region whose own religious traditions were suppressed.

> The centrality of Jesus in the Christian tradition places death and coming back to life squarely in the forefront of this religion.
> In many Christian traditions, honoring the deceased by display of the body for a period of several days is traditional.
> The degree to which the deceased is memorialized at various time periods varies between and among Christian denominations.

We now turn to the first bereavement case vignette involving a Russian-Israeli family.

The Story of Marina

(Witztum et al., 2001)

Marina, 64 years old, emigrated from Russia to Israel 10 years ago. She lost her husband 2 years prior to emigrating to Israel. She had four children. When two of them—a son and a daughter—decided to leave Russia and move to Israel, she followed them to what she regarded as the Promised Land.

After arrival, the family members lived together in the same apartment in a town in the south of Israel. Marina helped her children with housekeeping as well as in taking care of her grandsons and granddaughters.

Two years later, she became ill and was diagnosed as suffering from lung cancer. Following a long bout with the disease, she was admitted to a hospital for treatment but expressed a wish to die at home. Back at home, the children arranged a special room for her where her loving, caring family surrounded her. Her health continued to deteriorate. One day when her son and daughter were at work and the children in kindergartens and schools, alone at home, she felt very ill and barely managed to call a neighbor. The neighbor called for an ambulance. The physician accompanying the medical team certified her death and she was taken to a funeral home.

The paramedic contacted Marina's children and told them about their mother's death. They were informed that in accordance with Jewish custom, the funeral would have to be held the same evening. They were asked to come as soon as possible so that the Hevra Kadisha (religious burial society) could make arrangements.

The family, in a state of a shock, was unable to understand the rush. In accordance with the custom in their homeland, they expected to take the body back home so that a proper separation from their beloved mother and grandmother could take place. Their protests and appeals were rejected, and the funeral was held that evening. As a protest, they decided to refuse to sit *Shiva* (the 7-day period to receive consolation), and instead they chose to hole up in their apartment and refuse to mourn. Their behavior was interpreted as bizarre and along the lines of a "Folie à deux" or as a kind of family-shared delusion. This caused a great deal of concern among social workers and mental health agents. Nonetheless, family members refused any contact with any authorities. One of the authors (EW) was requested to make a home visit and to do an emergency assessment.

An Intervention Based on a Culturally Sensitive Evaluation

(Witztum, 2004)

Assessing the family's desperation and anger, it was considered appropriate by the consultant to take action and help the family find an alternative way to mourn and express their feelings.

The intervention was attempted 10 days after Marina had died. I arrived at their home and behind the closed door presented myself as an independent physician and gave the name of a common acquaintance (a Rabbi) who sent me. Only then did they agree to open the door and let me in. Family members were extremely upset and complained about the way the funeral was conducted. They felt bitter and wounded. They had suffered a severe insult to their honor, having been deprived of the possibility of proper separating from Marina, their beloved mother and grandmother. This was why the family refused to sit *Shiva* (a religious ritual) or talk with the social workers who were sent to them.

In the intervention, I listened empathetically to their complaints and helped them to process their feelings of frustration and anger. The family members talked at length about the customs in their hometown in Russia and explained how different they were from those they had experienced with Marina's death. They said that the body would have been washed, the deceased's face would then be cleaned and embellished, her hair combed, and the body would be placed in a beautiful casket. The casket would be decorated with flowers and put in the middle of the room where all members of the family would have the opportunity to kiss and to hug the deceased, crying as they parted from her. After a while, in accordance with prior planning, the funeral procession would begin, leaving the deceased's house toward the cemetery, possibly accompanied by an orchestra, depending upon the family's financial situation.

In Russia, burying the dead and the mourning process were considered private issues, and every bereaved family had to handle this in their own way according to the family's tradition and custom. Many who were secular did not keep all the funeral customs (like *Shiva*), and the service was more influenced by the culture of their Gentile neighbors. When the new immigrants from the former Soviet Union arrived to Israel, they were surprised, shocked, and humiliated to discover that all "last rites" business was "confiscated" by Jewish religious services.

Later I suggested an alternative ritual that would take place on the day of *Shloshim*, the 30-day anniversary of the death during which they would share memories of the deceased. Together we negotiated and constructed a complex ritual that included reminiscences and expressions of their difficulties and feelings, in addition to the religious part that was to be kept briefly.

After the *Shloshim*, the Rabbi reported to me that the ceremony had been very moving and that the family also set up the gravestone. The family wanted to thank me. Follow-up showed that family members resumed normal functioning and, after a year had passed, they performed a secular ceremony. This incident is a classical example of culture-based misunderstanding that could have led to highly severe consequences. The clinical intervention represents a good example of a culture-sensitive crisis intervention.

Ethiopian Mourning Customs

A second example would be the immigrants from Ethiopia who preserved their cultural integrity, observing the rituals and traditions of their faith, especially the Sabbath and the rules of ritual purity, including detailed customs of mourning and burial rituals (Grisaru, Malkinson, & Witztum, 2008).

According to this custom, when an Ethiopian dies not in his house but, for example, in a hospital, the message is delivered to one of the neighbor families, who serves as a middleman, first bringing the bad news to the elders who then tell the close relatives, usually in the afternoon when people return from work or early in the morning before work. In no case is the tragic news to be delivered directly to the family, but always through the middleman who volunteers to take upon himself the difficult mission of purveying the sad news. This custom enables the beginning of the funeral ritual and lamentations immediately following the family's reception of the message, with the participation of numerous people. Another important aspect for Ethiopian Jews is the strict rules of purity.

Unfortunately, in Israel there is frequently a lack of awareness of the proper, culturally sensitive way to break bad news, particularly in this culture. There are cases when families with a fallen soldier of Ethiopian origin were informed directly of his death, as is customary in the Israeli army. In such incidents, the shocked bereaved family members fainted, wailed, and screamed vigorously. One mother who heard of her loss immediately tried to jump out of the fourth floor window but was saved only by the quick response of an Ethiopian middleman. One of the explanations for this vigorous response is that such behavior serves to recruit the support system of neighbors and friends who would be expected to rush to see what happened and to deal with the mourner's hostility and anger (Grisaru et al., 2008).

Ethiopian Jews also make great efforts to maintain burial and memory rituals. In Israel, involvement in these rituals is seen as extremely important, even for distant family members. At work, employers may find it difficult to understand why an

Ethiopian Jew would miss work in order to take part in such a ritual or to offer condolence to a seemingly distant relative. In Israel, the final memorial service is of particular significance for those who have learned that a family member died in Ethiopia. The service enables surviving family members to part from the deceased in an honorable manner, especially as they did not participate in the burial and mourning rituals (Witztum et al., 2001).

Breaking Bad News: An Intervention Based on Culturally Sensitive Evaluation

What is advisable is to pass news of the death to a fellow Ethiopian, who is then asked to find a proper community member to convey the sad message to the family. If an Ethiopian youth is studying at a boarding school, and someone close dies at home, it is best to send the youth home with a fellow Ethiopian, without imparting any information.

Concerning the military situation, after a number of serious incidents, the psychology department of the Israel Defense Forces (IDF) decided to create a special team for informing families in cases of loss. The team includes an Ethiopian as a permanent member whose task would be to recruit the Ethiopian elders, and then the "right" relatives could be present while breaking the bitter news. The Ethiopian team member was expected to translate discreetly and in a culturally sensitive manner the officer's official announcement in appropriate Ethiopian language. It is stressed that the informer (the cultural broker, who is always a male) is not allowed to embrace a grieving female parent, which is usually forbidden by religious law.

The culturally insensitive announcement of a death may also cause complicated traumatic grief. As one deceased's mother stated bitterly: "We were killed twice: once when our beloved son died, and then when we were informed in the wrong way."

Islam

The Islamic approach to death is organized into a set of rituals and communal norms that structure the initial response to death, the funeral, and the formal mourning periods. Central to Islam is the notion that how the Prophet Muhammad responded to loss, how he counseled others to respond, and what he said is worthy of emulation points the way for believers to behave (Rubin & Yasien-Esmael, 2004). Funeral and burial practices differ somewhat among the wide variety of cultures in which Islam is practiced, but there are general patterns based on the advice given by the Prophet. When death is very near, someone is called to read verses of the Qur'an at the bedside. Muslims are advised to mourn communally for 3 days while verses from the Qur'an are usually recited. The Islamic religion sets forth a clear period during which one can mourn. This is generally 3 days and is known as *Hidad* (mourning). During this period, the religion allows one to express grief, but the expression is modulated within the bounds of tradition (Yasien-Esmael & Rubin, 2005). It is advisable to bury the dead body as soon as possible after death. In Islam, burial represents the human being's return to the most elemental state, since the Creator formed humans from earthly materials. Therefore, cremation, preservation, interment in above-ground mausoleums, or other methods are not permitted in Islam.

Muslims are advised to comfort the bereaved person by visiting them, strengthening their faith, offering them food, and reciting the Qur'an. Although grieving may never fully end, the period of outward mourning lasts no more than 3 days. Muslims believe that all suffering, life, death, joy, and happiness are derived from Allah and that Allah is the one who gives us strength to survive. These beliefs are usually sources of comfort and strength that aid in the healing process (Mehraby, 2003). Wikan (1988) suggested Islamic practice is integrated and perceived differently in different societies and different countries.

> The Islamic approach to death is organized into a set of rituals and communal norms that structure the initial response to death, the funeral, and the formal mourning period.
>
> Muslims are advised to comfort the bereaved person by visiting them, strengthening their faith, offering them food, and reciting the Qur'an. Although grieving may never fully end, the period of outward mourning lasts no more than 3 days.
>
> Muslims believe that all suffering, life, death, joy, and happiness are derived from Allah and that Allah is the one who gives us strength to survive. These beliefs are usually sources of comfort and strength that aid in the healing process.
>
> It is advisable to bury the dead body as soon as possible after death. In Islam, burial represents the human being's return to the most elemental state, since the Creator formed humans from earthly materials. Therefore, cremation, preservation, interment in above-ground mausoleums, or other methods are not permitted in Islam.

A case that exemplifies aspects of the complicated mix of culture, language, religion, and bereavement in Israel is the Flann family mentioned in the previous chapter. This case involved a Muslim family, a Christian therapist in training, and an American-Israeli Jewish supervisor (SSR). In the case analysis published, important aspects of the fault lines of ethnicity, language, and national aspirations were addressed (Rubin & Nassar, 1993). The significance of the Muslim tradition and the family's behavior in disregard of that tradition are what makes this case relevant to this chapter.

Reem Flann had witnessed her brother Nadir's death, and her mother had taken her to a mental health clinic for assistance. From a family perspective, there were many indications that the grief process had gone seriously awry. Within a short time after beginning therapy, Reem's father shared his active suicidal thoughts and communicated his intent to rejoin his son in the next world. Reem's mother was barely functioning. She explained that she did not have the strength to deal with her son's death and the children's response. As a result, she was telling her children, and sometimes herself, that her son had not died but instead was the new child growing inside her belly. What did worry her was what would happen if the child was a girl. Reem was traumatically reenacting the moment of her brother's death. In addition to her general restlessness and difficulty settling, she played out her experience of the events through her behavior. She seemed to typify the moment of her brother's death by throwing herself off the therapy table and shouting, "I will not recover; I will not survive."

The case intervention was ultimately successful, although it came within a hair's breadth of unraveling. From the perspective of multicultural interventions, there is something inspiring in the ability of Muslim, Christian, and Jewish people's ability to work together to assist the one in need. Part of what proved very important was the exploration of the relative importance of the Arab-Israeli conflict in the issues, potentially derailing the case. What emerged as the most difficult aspect of the case for therapist and family, however, was actually the pain and sense of helplessness felt in response to Nadir's death.

Ultimately, the family, together with the therapist, reached a turning point. Going beyond the safety of the therapy room, the therapist made home visits. In these visits, the story of the bereavement, the journey to the site of the accident and the grave, and the connection to the linking objects representing Nadir allowed for the normal grief process to reassert itself. The case also served as a catalyst for the supervisor to learn and study Islamic and Arab responses to death with a select group of graduate students (Yasien-Esmael & Rubin, 2005).

By the time the case was reported, many of the cultural questions that the non-Islamic therapeutic team had considered were answered in the negative. Was the denial of death acceptable in Islam? No. Was the idea that the child was being reborn into his mother acceptable to Islamic thinking? No. What is the expectation for the active grief response (which is generally isomorphic with the prescribed mourning ritual, that is, 3 days)? Was a prolonged grief period acceptable in Islamic practice of theology? "No, but ..." (The last response takes into account the veritable loss liturgy surrounding child death from the Middle Ages acknowledging that the pain of child death continues exceedingly beyond the 3 days prescribed.) Was it acceptable to delay building the memorial for the deceased child? Not exactly. The answer to that is less theological and more sociological—with the reality being that most Islamic peoples in Israel (as well as Jewish Israelis) complete the monument in a relatively short period of time. Perhaps the most basic message of Islamic response to loss might be distilled as follows: What happens is to be accepted as the will of God.

While the successful outcome of the case is heartening, the same supervisor would respond a tad differently with the benefits of knowledge and experience. At the time, the intervention options seemed limited. Today, the options for adding additional tools to the therapist's toolkit are somewhat clearer. From the cultural-religious side, and from an intervention point of view, the value of bringing in a responsible kadi clergyman for assistance is an option that might have been considered. There is great variation in Islamic thinking about what is acceptable and who the family's religious authority might be. The religious leader also has a community of persons who may become involved. From the perspective of linking objects and leave-taking rituals, the pictures and things linked with Nadir could have been incorporated into the therapeutic plan of intervention. Not only the construction of a monument on the gravesite of Nadir, but also the use of these objects in a combined psychological and religious ritual of grief and burial could have been helpful. It would have been helpful to know that what supervisor and therapist perceived as highly dysfunctional and maladaptive grief responses were also highly deviant both culturally and religiously. Whereas today the additional literature and the World Wide Web make information sources available virtually on demand, the value of seeking out local representatives of the religion and culture could have been done even in the pre-Internet days.

CONCLUDING REMARKS

As the vast majority of therapists are generally aware of the tremendous variation in individuals and families, as well as variation in the significance of relationships, they are often quite good at learning from their clients about the needs and uniqueness of their lives. Applying this approach to culture, however, is most appropriate when the clinician is reasonably familiar with the broad parameters of the culture in question. Professionals need to adopt a cultural-sensitive perspective when treating individuals or families from different cultural backgrounds than their own. Moreover, it is important to emphasize that when differences in practices and traditions do exist, the perceptions of the culturally aware clinician can still be useful. Even when rejected (such as the help offered by the consultant to verify the fact of the suicide, and the Ethiopian family's choice to reject it), *the family's cultural needs are essential and have to be considered in planning the intervention.*

In order to plan sensitive culture assessment and intervention with ethnic minority or specific cultural group, the clinician should be able to:

A. Recognize the specific cultural rituals for managing the dying process, the body of the deceased and the disposal of the body, and commemoration of the death in the culture.

B. Understand the beliefs about what happens after death in this group.

C. Evaluate what the client and client's culture consider an appropriate emotional expression of the loss in the framework of that culture.

13

Emergencies in Complications Following Loss

*T*he modern world is replete with natural and man-made disasters that include earthquakes, tsunamis, hurricanes, and floods, as well as wars and terrorist incidents. No less important are the personal "disasters" that encompass automobile accidents, work accidents, homicide, suicide, and a variety of other difficult events that cause injury and death. In many cases of sudden death, there is a traumatic element that exposes family members and friends to difficult features that can exacerbate the sharpness of their response and can precipitate difficult conditions of emotional distress.

Consider the following: It is a Sunday morning and the phone rings. On the other end is a request for assistance. The 50-year-old woman who has lost her mother 2 days ago is calling about her 85-year-old father. In the brief telephone consultation, you learn that the woman's parents were married for 55 years, were living in an assisted living facility, and the mother had fallen and died shortly thereafter. The father is crying constantly, shouting, and repeatedly voicing his wish to die. He has been on antidepressant medications for several years and had been considered stable, but the physicians monitoring the drug did not know him well at all. In response to his acute response, the medical officer at the living facility had given him an intramuscular injection of Valium which calmed him only briefly.

Whether you are the treating clinician or considering to whom to refer the case, what are some of the things to address? These are some of the things we consider in this chapter.

Competent professional mental health counselors encounter these acute cases and should be familiar with the evaluation and intervention strategies for such particular losses. In this chapter, we present a model of intervention, a type of crisis intervention, in acute and traumatic bereavement. The first stage makes much use of support and evaluation. In addition, we will look at three areas of preparation for work with acute bereavement: elevated emotional distress, suicidal ideation and potential, and indications for medication.

We return to one of the pioneers of work and bereavement discussed in Chapter 1, Eric Lindemann, whose work has often been cited as a paradigmatic model for crisis intervention (Parad, 1965, 1966). The five responses to acute grief Lindemann (1944) described are (1) somatic distress, (2) preoccupation with the image of the deceased, (3) guilt, (4) hostile reactions, and (5) loss of patterns of conduct. Our adaptation in work with the bereaved in cases of traumatic loss is an active one, characterized by support as well as by attention to screening and evaluation. The purpose of screening and evaluation is to determine what, if any, intervention format is indicated. Many times, more than one meeting will be required before it will be clear what is indicated.

Particularly acute and difficult responses to subjectively and/or objectively perceived traumatic loss, as well as highly distressed responses to bereavement of any sort, include some of what Lindemann (1944) described. Among the highly distressed responses are those characterized by elevated and acute anxiety, elevated and extreme depressive responses, acute mixed anxiety and depressive responses, responses that appear to be pre-psychotic or acute psychotic, and acute confusional states. The acute confusional states can also be seen in responses to a variety of traumatic events such as assault, life threat to the individual, and similar events (Herman, 1992).

We recommend that in all such cases it is important to address potential suicidality. Direct questions include specifically asking about the bereaved's thoughts regarding harming himself or herself. In particular, inquiry regarding any concrete plans for "joining" the deceased or leaving the pain of loss behind can be sensitively raised. Statements such as "I wish I were dead" or "Why didn't God take me?" are not in and of themselves indications of suicidality. It can be useful to label such statements for the bereaved as expressions of their pain and distress as well as to indicate that many people feel this way at such times for awhile and that it is a response to the upheaval they experience. At the same time, however, the clinician can make it clear that concrete thoughts or plans regarding ending one's life are important to discuss, as they cross the line between emotional distress and danger to oneself. When evidence for concrete plans for taking one's life is present, it is important to conduct a more thorough evaluation for potential suicidality such as that conducted by specialized mental health professionals in psychiatry, clinical psychology, and psychiatric social work. Depending on the results of the evaluation, it may be necessary to consider continued observation in situ and/or hospitalization. Making sure a proper evaluation has been conducted and documented is expected from all competent practitioners, although there may be legal and clinical reasons to conduct a formal psychiatric consultation.

Bryan and Rudd (2006) have argued against both extremes—excessive cautiousness ("better safe than sorry") as well as underestimating suicidal risk as a result of a dismissive attitude or poor assessment. At the same time, we have documentation in the literature that indications of complicated bereavement substantially heighten risk of suicidality independently of major depression and post-traumatic stress (Latham & Prigerson, 2004). Formal training in mental health and suicidal assessment risk are valuable additions to clinical competence, but the reality of the field is that there are decided limits to what can be done. Orbach (2001) has written eloquently and sensitively on the importance of maintaining empathy both with the person who has suicidal thoughts and with the suicidal aspects of the client as a way of fostering connection and forging rapport and a base for change. It is important to help clients choose life. Understanding their thoughts and accepting their feelings regarding the choice of death can facilitate their reconnection to life.

EVALUATION OF SUICIDAL RISK IN BEREAVEMENT: VARIATIONS ON A HIERARCHICAL APPROACH

1. Symptoms of dysfunction—From what you've described so far, it sounds like you have been feeling depressed. Can you tell me what areas of your life have been affected (sleep, appetite, anxiety, ruminative thoughts)?

2. Hopelessness—It's not uncommon after a loss to feel that things are terrible now and won't get any better. Are there times when you feel that way? What makes it worse? What makes it better?

3. Guilt—Sometimes people feel so responsible for a loved one's death, or they feel so badly about how they failed in the relationship; they feel a strong sense of guilt. Is that something you experience? How often? What makes it worse?

4. Suicidal ideation—There are times after a loss, when the bereaved may feel depressed, hopeless, and stressed, or when they think about the person they miss so much, they sometimes think about death and dying for themselves. Does that describe you? Could you say more?

5. Purpose of suicide—What do you think about when you think of dying? For some people at a low point after loss, it might feel like an escape from pain or a terrible situation without hope. For others, they might think of it as a punishment for themselves or for others. And sometimes, people might think of it as a way to be close to the person who died. Can you say something about this and how it is for you?

6. Protective factors—What are some of the things that distance you from thoughts of self-harm? Do you have access to family and friends who you can talk to? What about religion and clergy? What are your reasons for living? What beliefs do you hold that keep you alive and involved in life?

(Modified from Bryan & Rudd, 2006.)

In cases where suicidality and lethality have been ruled out to the best of the clinician's estimation, there still may be a reason to refer the individual for psychiatric evaluation and consideration of the use of medications. Whereas the individual psychotherapist may consider referral to an outside expert for medication consultation, often in teams dealing with mass disaster a multidisciplinary model may be in place.

Whether or not a medical model and medical hierarchy are employed, the relevant questions remain: Are medications useful, recommended, or deemed critical to assist the bereaved at this time? For example, in cases where an individual who has suffered from major depressive disorder is bereaved, medication aimed at alleviating depression should be considered. Despite the proven effectiveness of medication, overuse of medication and provision of drug treatment as a substitute for listening to our clients are exceedingly problematic (Salzman, Glick, & Keshavan, 2010).

> Medication groups that may be of assistance in acute response to loss include the following:
>
> Antianxiety: Benzodiazepine in fixed dose according to needs
> Antidepressant: Selective serotonin reuptake inhibitor (SSRI) or serotonin-norepinephrine reuptake inhibitor (SNRI) if there are signs of major depressive episode or history of dealing with confusion, pre-psychotic, and/or psychotic phenomena
> Antipsychotic medications in small doses (e.g., quetiapine, commercial name Seroquel)

When the response of the bereaved to either objectively traumatic or subjectively perceived traumatic bereavement triggers the acute responses of anxiety, depression, confusion, and/or variations along the psychotic continuum, short-term intervention focused on this acute response is indicated. In our experience, responses that do not resolve within 24 to 48 hours should be considered cause for concern. Despite the general tolerance for the variations and fluctuations in functioning during acute bereavement in its early manifestations and later on as well, behaviors that suggest extremes or a collapse in ego functioning should not be attributed to normal variation in loss. The careful clinician will attend to the importance of limiting decompensation and stabilizing the response to loss.

In general, working with the response to traumatic loss in its earliest days contains a strong supportive element. In addition, during the acute phase of response to loss, the bereaved's ability to exercise freedom of choice may be significantly compromised. Cultural variations often share a master of ritual who directs the "proper" mode of responding to loss, burial, and grieving, which serve important functions of organizing the external structure of the griever. Secular mental health professionals can also assist by structuring, directing, and providing an environment of holding (Winnicott, 1965), food, a place to sit, and an ear and heart open to what may be a repetitive grief story in the initial hours and days following loss.

To return to the initial consultation that we began the chapter with, the response to the case might include the following:

1. Prescribing physician—Despite the individual's use of antidepressant medications, the physician–client relationship was virtually nonexistent. This left the consultant with greater responsibility. Involving the treating physician in the case and follow-up would be important.

2. Prescription for family—The father's response was described to the family as strong but not outside the bounds of response to acute grief and bereavement. The recommendation was made for the family to take him to their home for the initial days following the death. This would allow for the family to provide support, to place him in familiar surroundings, and also to give them the opportunity to observe the progress of his acute response. The importance of listening to him, as well as observing his response over time, was communicated.
3. The medication recommendation would include the avoidance of benzodiazepines and consider increasing the dose of the SSRI antidepressant medication that he had been taking. In addition, the use of a major tranquilizer like Seroquel (quetiapine) at a low dosage would serve to calm him and help him to adjust to his difficult situation.
4. The cultural variant, the 7-day *Shiva* period in which many people were coming to visit, was considered, and the family planned how to bring father home in a way that would allow him to have privacy without isolation.
5. The importance of contact with the clinicians on a daily basis was recognized until stability returned.

As can be seen in the initial case description, it is useful to consider the use and application of supportive work with directive aspects of treatment. The use of medication, behavioral intervention, relaxation techniques, as well as mobilization of natural supports in the family and community, can all be employed in crisis intervention with complications of bereavement even in the early stages of response to loss. The principles involved and the range of intervention possibilities will be further developed in the following two cases.

A CASE OF SUDDEN ACUTE TRAUMATIC LOSS

Baruch, a 30-year-old Israeli male from a religious background, was married, with a wife in the latter stages of pregnancy, and was employed as a postman. He was seen shortly after the loss of his mother.

Principal Complaint

Referred for urgent counseling by his family physician following a complaint of chest pains, sweating, and acute anxiety, Baruch completely stopped functioning within 1 week of his mother's death.

Past History

Baruch was the second child of a family of six children. As a child he suffered from paralysis and was operated on many times. He completed primary and secondary schools, served in the army service as a volunteer, and got married. His wife is now pregnant after a long course of fertility treatment. He describes himself as having been very attached to his mother since childhood. His mother had cancer for 10 years and had received painful therapy. He knew that she was very ill and had cared for her devotedly.

After she died and during the *Shiva*, he felt unable to cry and express his feelings. When the *Shiva* period was over, he experienced a severe panic attack with chest pains, dizziness, and an inability to cope with noise. He went back to work but was unable to manage, was unfocused, and argued with his colleagues and with his boss. Finally he was told to take a vacation. Then all at once, without any explanation, he turned on his sister and beat her up. He was shocked at what he had done. Full of guilt, he couldn't understand what was happening to him. All of this information was obtained within the first session.

Intervention as Crisis Intervention

At the end of the first treatment hour, the therapist told Baruch that he was suffering from an acute bereavement response. This served as both explanation and means of support. Baruch had difficulty expressing his emotions because he thought that crying would detract from his masculinity. He was also unable to express negative emotions.

On exploration, it became apparent that he was very angry with his mother, who had left him with her death. Eventually, it would be helpful for him to release his pent-up emotions. Despite his having been with her through hard times and her terminal illness for many years, she had nonetheless abandoned him. The explanation further clarified for him that it was only reasonable that his deep sorrow prompted his outburst of disturbed behavior, since he and his mother had such an intense relationship. Listening to this supportive explanation, Baruch gradually became more relaxed. In the therapist's construction of the events, he used the additional information that had emerged to shape a coherent narrative that would minimize stigma and help Baruch regain a sense of coherence regarding his own behavior. He was told that a significant source for his aggressive behavior toward his sister was related to their relationship with their mother. Whereas during childhood, there had been normal sibling competition for their mother's love, when she fell sick Baruch was the one to bear the burden of looking after her. This had made him very angry and thus served as an explanation for his displays of anxiety and anger. By the end of the session, Baruch was encouraged to express the emotions that he was unable to previously. Furthermore, he was encouraged to have his wife act as "a big sister." By telling her his feelings and getting her support, he would be benefiting from the natural support system that can be mobilized for dealing with a crisis situation. Lastly, Baruch was offered an antianxiety drug to help him overcome his feeling of panic.

At the second session, Baruch appeared more relaxed and said that he had cried a lot and had gotten through the hardest part of those emotions. As a result, he had visited his mother's grave for the first time, something that he was unable to do previously. Also, as suggested in the previous session, Baruch had asked his wife to share his experiences. During this second session, preparations were made to help him adjust to the separation from his mother. The significance of detachment from expectations of their interaction was balanced by an explanation of the continuing relationship with his mother's memory and his recollections of her. In terms of his functioning, his colleagues had requested that he return to work, but he was concerned that their response was motivated by pity. This was to be discussed further in the next session.

Baruch missed his third appointment. He called to say that he went back to work the day after the second appointment, he is managing well, his wife is due to give birth any day, and therefore he missed his appointment because he was doing better.

Follow-up

An appointment was made 2 months later. At this session, Baruch seemed relaxed and mentioned that all of his physical symptoms and anxious feelings had disappeared and that he was "back to equilibrium." He thanked his therapist for the treatment and apologized for not coming to the third meeting.

> **REFLECTION**
>
> From the perspective of a crisis intervention, Baruch's problematic behavior was characterized by significant difficulties related to both axes of the Two-Track Model of Bereavement. The active intervention of the therapist was designed to offer a coherent explanation of what had transpired to the client, to link it to the loss he had suffered, and to utilize to the fullest the resources of the pre-loss personality, family support system, and the reassuring construction of the therapist. In the present case, this intervention was successful and served to relocate a dysfunctional response to loss and place it on an adaptive trajectory.

A CASE OF ACUTE GRIEF FOLLOWING PREGNANCY LOSS

Anne was a 34-year-old married woman with a 3-year-old child who was in the seventh month of pregnancy with a normal child. She had terminated a previous pregnancy in the fifth month for medical reasons. She was a social worker by profession.

Principal Complaint

Anne experienced emotional problems, depression, and a major reduction in vitality after following her gynecologist's recommendation to abort the fetus, which had a cardiac abnormality.

Past History

Anne was a native-born Israeli and the eldest of four children. Her father had been a day laborer, and her mother had been a homemaker. Economic conditions were difficult and the home atmosphere was described as hard. Anne completed technical high school. During military service she was a security guard and this was a very good time in her life. After the army service, she traveled abroad, then worked for a year and saved money to train as a social worker. She reported her marriage to be a happy one and enjoyed her daughter. She became pregnant according to plan but then learned at ultrasound that the baby had a serious heart defect that was inoperable. It was decided to terminate the pregnancy by Boero's method of induced premature labor.

The abortion–birth took place in the fifth month of her pregnancy. She prepared herself and envisioned the procedure, the parting from the dead child that she would hold in her arms after it was born and say goodbye. The labor lasted 10 hours. She felt that the midwife was heartless and aggressive and wanted her replaced, but the medical team told her that this was an experienced midwife and they refused to replace her. The birth was very slow and the baby was a breech presentation. The midwife became impatient and started to pull on the baby's legs with force, and then what she regarded as a catastrophe happened—the baby became torn with its head stuck in the womb. She was rushed into surgery and it took them 2 hours to free the head.

Both the recall and the analysis of what happened in front of the hospital staff and students depressed her and worsened her mood. This was particularly so since the head of the department claimed that this was not an unusual complication and with this, he tried to belittle the significance of the loss.

Anne complains of moodiness, anhedonia, bouts of crying, suicidal thoughts, and cringes at the prospect of the forthcoming birth.

The Intervention

During the session, reframing of her situation was attempted. The positive aspects were emphasized, such as the fact that she was in advanced pregnancy with a normal baby and was soon to give birth. We talked about the great pain of her loss and the negative attitude that the medical staff had adopted. These had provoked the anger and loss of confidence that Anne experienced. We decided not to prescribe antidepressants for the present and put off the possibility of litigation until a time when it would not feel as if she were "holding the baby in her arms."

REFLECTION

In both of these cases, the intervention was one of short-term duration. In the first case, there were three consultation sessions and in the second, one. The subject of traumatic loss was central to both cases. The therapist adopted a most empathic attitude, performed a reframing of their situations, and encouraged them to reconsider their negative feelings of anger and disappointment. Despite the distinct possibility of prescribing drugs in such acute cases, there was no need except for using an antidepressant on one occasion in the first case.

CONCLUDING REMARKS

We have addressed three areas whose mastery can assist the therapist: assessment of suicidal ideation; medication possibilities in response to loss; and crisis intervention.

These involve providing information, support, and directive organization for particular derailments of adaptive grieving. In earlier chapters devoted to theory and therapy, we made use of assessment and intervention models suited to both short- and long-term therapies. In this chapter, we focused on aspects of clinical complications and emergencies that may present in screening, evaluation, or brief consultations as well as emerging in more traditional longer term clinical situations. The background materials and the clinical cases used to illustrate the points in this chapter demonstrate a number of principles that the clinician may find of use in any number of situations. The options to use educational, supportive, and directive aspects of intervention in crisis interventions may lend themselves particularly to short-term interventions seen in traumatic losses where traditional therapy modes may not be possible. Having the ability to respond with some of the tools presented here can expand the clinician's range of effectiveness.

14

Growth and Resilience
Considerations for Clients and Therapists

*H*uman beings are resilient, and there are many ways in which their resiliency is manifest. The Oxford English Dictionary (1989) defines resiliency as "the capacity to recover quickly from difficulties; toughness." We all recognize that loss and bereavement can interfere with many areas of the bereaved's life. All too often, these are not self-limiting temporary responses to loss that respond to the balm of time alone. Throughout the book, we have focused on the importance of maintaining a bifocal approach to bereavement via the examination of both tracks of the Two-Track Model of Bereavement (Rubin, Malkinson, & Witztum, 2011). In this chapter, we wish to address the individual's capacity to self-repair, to grow, to find ways to integrate life changes into the narrative of the life story, and to manage adaptively to respond to the challenges and traumas of life. All of what we address in this chapter is relevant for the client as well as for the therapist. In line with our responsibilities, however, we begin with a client focus before returning to the clinician.

The idea behind the continuing relationship to the deceased includes the notion of growth and change (Tedeschi & Calhoun, 2004), and we have addressed those points in earlier chapters of the book. At the same time, interventions dealing with difficulties in biopsychosocial functioning have been the traditional bailiwick of the mental health professional. For now, however, we turn to consider a different aspect of the biopsychosocial functioning, one that is associated with well-being. In the same way that medicine can focus on repairing illness or on promoting health and well-being (Ryff & Singer, 1998), some aspects of medicine and psychology focus on helping persons address deficits in function, and other aspects focus on helping people develop and grow. Of course, function and growth are not neatly separated, but they do reflect differences of goals and emphases that are important to distinguish and clarify. We believe that the option for living well after loss can be an integral part of the support provided by the ongoing relational bond to the deceased.

Our point, however, is that whether or not the relationship is involved here, the things we address in this chapter can assist the bereaved in their post-loss living.

> For the bereaved, the idea of continuing a relationship with the deceased involves finding ways to integrate the loss in the narrative of the life story. Managing adaptively is a life-long task that includes the individual's capacity for self-repair and self-growth in life. Often, the taking care of oneself can be interwoven with the relationship to the deceased as in "he would want me to be strong and effective in life" or "I feel her support as I do these things." The areas considered may reflect Track I biopsychosocial functioning, but the rationale and narrative may well be interwoven with Track II's ongoing relationship to the deceased.

In recent years, the positive psychology movement has developed and matured to the point that it has both a research base and an evolving theoretical worldview of the human individual (Csikszentmihalyi & Csikszentmihalyi, 2006; Gilbert, 2007; Lyubomirsky, 2008). Many of the tools of the traditionally trained therapist have focused on assisting persons in their struggles with difficulties in therapy: Sharing and exploring in a safe environment the difficulties of one's struggle with the processes of loss and mourning is important. Verbalizing one's despair or wish to give up on life and express the difficulties of one's struggle with the processes of loss and mourning is important. In the therapy relationship, the bereaved can deal with waves of anxiety, pain, and guilt that may accompany loss. Therapy is also that place where one can talk about relief at the death and anger at the deceased. Ultimately, it is a special relationship where a caring and attentive professional is there for the bereaved. Some of these functions are well served by contacts with peers and self-help situations, but for the more complex cases, professional assistance is advised.

We recognize the value of the psychotherapies that devise interventions targeting psychosocial dysfunction, including both intrapsychic or inner psychological conflicts as well as variations in the nature of the establishment and maintenance of interpersonal attachments. Now we turn to consider additional avenues that can be incorporated into the therapeutic purview of an intervention. We include them here as part of the therapist's consideration of the needs of the bereaved. The interventions available to the therapist, directed toward those things that clients can do for themselves, have value. They can increase the effectiveness of an intervention by supplementing the work of more traditional therapies. Whether conceptualized as independent things a therapist can encourage clients to do, or whether incorporated into a structured part of the treatment of loss that is part of the therapeutic regimen, it is helpful to consider a short list of interventions and how to use them in work with the bereaved. To quote Martin Seligman (2006), "So one thing that clinical psychology needs to develop in light of the stubbornness of the dysphorias is a psychology of dealing with it: developing interventions that train people how to be functional in the presence of their dominant dysphorias" (p. 232).

We list six areas that we recommend therapists be familiar with. At a minimum, therapists should have sufficient familiarity to be able to refer clients to individuals and places providing services in these areas. From the perspective of the Two-Track Model of Bereavement, all of these strategies may initially engage those aspects of response to loss associated with the biopsychosocial engagement in life (Rubin & Prigerson, 2008). Interventions may weave the narrative of the ongoing relationship into the fabric of the treatment rationale. This can be used to explain why adopting some or all of what we discuss next not only is good for the individual but also serves to carry out the wishes of the deceased for the bereaved's welfare.

ACTIVITY AND PHYSICAL ACTIVITY: THE IMPORTANCE OF REMAINING ACTIVE

Individuals who remove themselves from life for prolonged periods do so at their own peril. Avoiding avoidance is one of the more important strategies that we can communicate to our clients. It is no coincidence that in the treatment of the traumas in many paradigms, including the prolonged exposure techniques favored by Foa and colleagues (Foa, Keane, Cohen, & Friedman, 2008), the engagement with, rather than the avoidance of, the feared and anxiety-provoking stimuli are central to the intervention. Of course, engagement that only produces distress and that "further traumatizes" the individual is neither the goal nor the technique advocated. But by attending to pacing, by encouraging and explaining to the client why one will need to be engaged and confront stimuli, and by assisting the individuals in titrating their distress, the stage is set to encourage and build on the policy of engagement.

One of the simplest and easiest modes of engagement is the use of the human body to carry one forward. Physical activity, exercise, and movement are examples of basic activities that often give a sense of mastery, control, and some degree of power and sense of self-control and efficacy to the individual performing this task. The value of this in health benefits and in affording areas where one is in control of certain aspects of his or her way of moving in the world is important (Salmon, 2001). But all activity, rather than inactivity, gives a sense of purpose and can link to meaningful existence.

Encouraging clients to join a gym, to walk, to jog, to run, or to do tai chi is a way of encouraging the physical, which has the added benefit of increasing social involvement. Research on the benefits of physical activity and exercise regimens for the treatment and prevention of depression and anxiety are generally positive (Lawlor & Hopker, 2001; Penedo & Dahn, 2005). Despite the voluminous literature, however, more carefully conducted research is still needed to delineate in greater detail and specificity, the conditions, type, dosage, and various contributions of different physical exercise regimes. What one can be very clear about, however, is that the inclusion of physical activity into one's lifestyle has psychological and health benefits for both emotional and physical well-being and survival. Being involved with age-appropriate physical activity is participation in life and, as such, deserves attention in working with the bereaved.

Activity is not limited to the physical. The idea that one has to be doing things, even when one does not feel much like doing them, is based on the importance of activity. Much as medicine has learned to get patients moving as soon as possible after repair of injury and surgery, aware that much damage can be secondary to inactivity, such is true also for life activity in a variety of areas. Encouraging activity is not the same as encouraging one to return to all of the previously enjoyed activities used in the past. Nonetheless, it is important to encourage persons to choose to remain active and, its companion, to remain engaged in life.

Being involved with others and involved in social networks sets in motion a virtuous cycle. Involvement often begets more involvement, and persons who find they are important to others and validated as such tend to feel connected and alive. Despite this generally positive scenario, however, it can be important for the clinician to monitor progress. Distorted interpretation of the experience, unrealistic expectations, negative feedback, and inappropriate selection of social frameworks for activity can all undercut or sabotage the positive effects of social activity. We will return to this point shortly when we address remaining intertwined with others.

CONTRIBUTING TO THE WELL-BEING OF OTHERS: REMAINING RELEVANT AND ENGAGED

Continuing the theme of remaining open to self and others and remaining connected to life takes on an additional link when one seeks to encourage the bereaved to go outside of himself or herself to the outside world. By encouraging the bereaved to find ways to matter to other people, one encourages the connection to the fabric of life. The additional benefit of being engaged in helping others is according to Riesman's (1965) helper principle, "When you help you are being helped" (p. 28). It is a consistent feature of life that by finding ways to give to others, many people feel that they receive a great deal more than they have given. Part of the focus here is to get people involved in other aspects of life as a way of being helped. To be involved with the fabric and community of life outside oneself has many benefits. While giving to others can be a powerful mobilizing force within the individual to meet the responsibilities and opportunities of life, there are times when it seems to be beyond the capability or scope of the bereaved. Remaining connected to others, and finding ways to be connected, are worthy and complete goals within themselves.

For those individuals who may be relatively isolated, the idea is to find ways to increase their connections to others without necessarily furthering a focus on helping others. Social support and face-to-face recognition, where one is "seen" and his or her personhood acknowledged, are powerful validating forces. Self-help and support groups are places where this can occur, but there are many others. For example, elderly persons may have limited opportunities for interaction with others, and it is valuable to help them find ways to maximize opportunities for contacts. For those whose use of technology extends to social networks online, this, too, is an area worth encouraging. Similarly, individuals with limited social circles may lose the very person who helped them engage and interact with other persons. Assisting them in finding ways of being involved with others can provide a necessary human environment and web of connectedness.

For those who are connected in social webs that may be highly demanding of their active participation, negotiating additional dimensions of involvement may require something different. For example, a widowed young mother with infants or very young children may find herself constantly engaged in caretaking tasks that keep her involved with her children and their lives. Although involved in care, these activities may engage her in a deep and meaningful but relatively narrow band of connection. Attending to ensuring opportunities for other avenues of connection can provide an important balance to life after loss. Adult relatives caretaking for older adults may be in an even more restricted place. It is not unusual for one elderly parent to die and for the other parent's difficulty in functioning to make intense physical and emotional demands on a surviving child, who becomes heavily involved in caretaking. In such situations, the grief for the deceased may be joined to a different grief for the living compromised parent, as well as the depletion of resources that may come with caretaking. Attending to involvement and the nature of the involvement are both important tasks. In the next section, we take up one of the internal and external sources of support and involvement that affords many people solace and care (Sacks, 2006).

SPIRITUALITY AND RELIGION

The human tendency to have beliefs, religions, and rituals is among the earliest and most powerful features associated with human civilization and culture. From primitive society to the most evolved civilizations, the human tendency to look for meaning and spiritual forces at work has been interwoven with a multitude of approaches to the questions of the implications of life, death, and the hereafter. With the rise of secular societies in the Western world, issues of spirituality have broadened to include a variety of philosophies of meaning that are not associated with religion per se, but include personalized and organized belief systems of incredible variety and degrees of articulation and inarticulation. Whether dealing with members of organized religions or of individually constructed meaning structures emphasizing spiritual or secular elements, all humans deal with the meaning of life and death.

In modern psychology, the definition of spirituality and its overlap with religious and religion is still evolving (Emmons, 2006). The English term *spirituality* comes from the Latin *spiritus,* relating to the breath or animating or vital principles of a person. As used in psychology, it is defined in human terms. Emmons (2006, p. 64) quotes a number of definitions, including these: "'a deep sense of belonging, of wholeness, of connectedness, and of openness to the infinite' (Kelly, 1995, pp. 4–5), as that which 'involves ultimate and personal truths' (Wong, 1998, p. 364)." For the bereaved, the importance of understanding their experience of the spiritual provides both a place to stand and a potential point of leverage that can alter and reorganize the meaning of life, the relationship with the deceased, the deceased's life, and the meaning of the loss. This truism has been central to religion and part of its role in helping the bereaved transition from the relationship with a living person to one who is now deceased.

We need not expect that religious or spiritual approaches to loss are always successful to still value their contributions. Clinicians identifying particular difficulties of response to loss can move to supplement the spiritual with their psychological interventions.

Whether in the time frame prior to death, or in the time frame following loss, the significance of the spiritual-religious-personal meaning worldview with regard to the loss is an area that is relevant (Sacks, 2006). Clinicians should be open to this dimension, with a curiosity and willingness to learn and include it in their attempt to empathize and understand the bereaved.

The more intriguing aspect of spiritual and religious issues may relate to their relatively late entry into the worldview of the therapy room at both practical and theoretical levels. The fact that many therapists are not very spiritually and religiously inclined or identified is only a part of the story. The justifiable wish to benefit from the meeting of individuals who represent the full range of a pluralistic society also adds to a reticence to include religious doctrine or spiritual sensibilities in encounters with persons who may not share one's worldview. The reticence to accept those with noticeable characteristics of "otherness" is intertwined with religious, national, ideological, and ethnic features. More than balancing this concern, however, is a belated recognition of the value of spiritual and religious resources for adjustment. Clinicians need to understand and find ways to help clients use their internal resources and beliefs in ways that encourage them as they confront the aftermath of bereavement and the challenges of life.

The religious status and beliefs of the clinician would seem to be less important than the ability to maintain a respectful position toward the belief system of the client. Thinking together with clients about how to mobilize their view of the spiritual and/or religious in the pursuit of engagement with life can allow them to engage and utilize this powerful and ubiquitous source of strength. At the same time, we would caution the spiritual or religiously engaged therapist against using his or her own belief system and worldview to unduly influence bereaved clients, whose vulnerability does not always allow them the freedom to assert their individuality and free choice in the consulting room. There are plenty of religious clergy and informed lay persons available, and the therapist would do well not to confuse his or her role as a clinician with that of the clergy.

DIALOGUES WITH ONESELF: JOURNALING, BLOGGING, WRITING IN ONE'S DIARY, DICTATING TO A COMPUTER PROGRAM OR TAPE RECORDER

Writing occasionally to give a place to thoughts and emotions so that they are formulated outside of oneself is a powerful force for supporting oneself and allowing for change. In this section, we are talking about something different than the letter writing and structured tasks we discussed earlier in the book (see Chapter 10 in particular). Therapy and support groups build on the healing features of sharing thoughts, feelings, and emotions with others who are sympathetic. Indeed, the presence of a supportive and accepting figure as a listener is one of the shared and common elements in many forms of individual and other psychotherapies (Reid, 2010). What is no less important, however, is an appreciation that the mere process of putting the information outside of oneself has positive effects even when nothing further is done. Putting one's thoughts outside of oneself, whether in organized fashion or stream of consciousness, whether spoken or written, has been shown repeatedly to have positive effects. The fact that one can do this in total privacy, at any time of the day or night, in virtually any feeling state, has the benefit of providing a self-contained and 24/7 accessible mode of helping regulate one's cognitive emotional state. This activity offers one the opportunity to unburden and also to give permission for a release of a flow of thoughts and feelings that is preferable to their being left inchoate and bottled up.

Pennebaker (1997, 2004) has demonstrated how writing about painful experiences in and of itself, without having the material read by another, can have beneficial effects for the writer. Writing in a diary, journal, or blog (whether public or not) and taking time to express, and perhaps make sense out of, one's experience allow for the expansion of a dialogue with oneself that can have beneficial effects.

Writing and communicating from ourselves to ourselves, our loved ones, friends, colleagues, persons we know, persons in cyberspace, Twitter space, and Facebook space, as well as to God or spiritual forces often serve to continue the unfolding of a narrative. In many cases, the narrative can develop and evolve to reflect and simulate the changing perspectives of the narrator. When directed to other people who can respond, the narrative can become a dialogue that can also take on additional aspects by virtue of the interaction. This taps into a number of important strands of experience.

Turning passivity into activity, in the form of communication, blogging, and journaling is also one of the ways that one's progress and coping with life events can be assessed, followed, and ultimately reviewed.

There are any number of poignant diaries that reflect the writer's grief or feelings of loss; one of the most famous is C. S. Lewis's account of his experience in his book *A Grief Observed,* which encompasses both his Christian faith and his touching grief. From Lewis's writing, we have the combination of literary talent and straight look at the pain of loss of a spouse: "No one ever told me that grief felt so much like fear" (1961, p. 15). Leon Wieseltier's *Kaddish* (1998) is a special kind of diary that tracks the author's experience in saying the traditional Jewish prayer for his dead father for the religiously mandated 11-month period. Following his musings and thoughts, one gets a sense of the ebb and flow of the pain of parent loss in the mature adult. The number of books, blogs, and postings written on this topic is long and often distinguished. But one looks not for literary talent in this area as reflected in published work; rather, one seeks the emotional power that serves the writer and that is available to all (Kasher, 2004).

MINDFULNESS

Learning to allow oneself to experience the ebb and flow of one's being in the moment, allowing thoughts and emotions to just be rather than to expend effort trying to control them, is at the heart of this way of thinking about adaptation and functioning. Mindfulness, which often involves using a body focus, enhances one's presence in the here and now with free floating openness to one's changing body states, thoughts, feelings, with the intention to remain open and nonjudgmental. Often, it can be understood as intertwined with yoga or the physical activities of tai chi and many other forms of Eastern movement regimens. These serve to liberate one from falling into previous patterns of cognitive and emotional mind-sets that increase the likelihood of experiencing emotional distress. The popularity and empirical support for this approach are impressive (Hofmann, Sawyer, Witt, & Oh, 2010; Tsang, Chan, & Cheung, 2008).

There is some irony in following up the Western notion of activity and taking control with aspects of the more Eastern traditions. And yet, there are benefits in the pursuit of learning to tolerate and be sensitive to the ebb and flow of emotions and thoughts that wash over us without translating them into anything else. In line with positive psychology and Eastern traditions, mindfulness is focused on awareness of the moment instead of being spurred to action or to complicated intellectual and emotional analyses. Rather, it is the charge of merely taking note of what is occurring and being in the moment with it. The focus on mindfulness is a paradigm shift that has stressed a significantly different aspect of what needs to be altered. Forsythe and Eifert (2007), in their own field of cognitive behavioral therapy, began to reframe psychological difficulties such that the kinds of thoughts and feelings that had been the target of intervention were not always the best place to direct intervention. Instead they recommend therapists "help people bring acceptance, compassion and gentleness to their unpleasant thoughts, feelings, memories, and even sense of self. In short, stop struggling to feel and think better, and instead start living better with whatever you may be feeling or thinking" (p. 7).

There are many variations on these themes, and they may be interconnected with other emphases. For example, the acceptance and commitment therapies of the Association for Contextual Behavioral Science (http://contextualpsychology.org) or the Center for Mindfulness in Medicine, Health Care, and Society (http://www.umassmed.edu/content.aspx?id=41252) are ways to become more familiar with the principles involved. By allowing the bereaved to be where they are and to reorder the context and approach to how their thoughts and emotions are experienced, there are opportunities for assisting them in connecting to aspects of their life, their pain, their body sensations, their surroundings, and their place in the world.

Many approaches to mindfulness include focusing on one's experience in the moment. As in meditation, with which mindfulness shares many characteristics, there is time set aside for the individual to relax, focus on something such as one's breath, and leave the mind empty of thoughts. The idea of not focusing and following thoughts but trying to leave one's experience open to what drifts in and out of one's thoughts, and remembering to return to the focus on breathing or whatever is the declared focus of one's attention when possible, provides an alternative to some of the more ruminative patterns of thinking.

A parallel component of this approach includes an accepting and gentle position toward the self. This is important, as the natural tendency not to remain open to the point of focus for more than a brief period can seem daunting. The recurring deviations from one's focus is matched by encouraging the acceptance of this reality. Acceptance of the distance between the ideal attained after time and practice, and the reality of the beginning practitioner, is a challenge to be met with compassion. In the stance embodying openness to the flow of thoughts and feeling that course through the person practicing mindfulness, opportunities for reframing occur. For the bereaved, this means that thoughts about the deceased, the death, life, and so on can be experienced as waves of thoughts and feelings that make no demands upon the bereaved for the moment. If one treats them as thoughts and feelings unanchored in reality and unencumbered by expectation for evaluation, action, or consequences, the pressure is lessened.

In the sadness, anxiety, longing, or other emotions that may wash over the bereaved, there is value to breaking the associational cycle that is attached to the thoughts, feelings, and conclusions the bereaved may draw from another encounter with the cognitive-emotional pattern of loss. For some bereaved, adding this mode of response can help. Mindfulness is generally not seen as a treatment for acute depression, but for the milder forms of sadness and depression, it has much value (Z. Segal, personal communication, October 14, 2010). When added to the life organization of the recently bereaved, we believe mindfulness can serve as an additional force for strength and resilience.

SELF-HELP GROUPS AND MUTUAL SUPPORT

The value of self-help groups as supplementing therapy as well as being an independent intervention following loss and bereavement are well documented. Silverman's (2004) pioneering widow-to-widow program was among the earliest to make use of the potential for people who have undergone personal experiences of loss to assist others in similar circumstances. Klass's (1996) description of the impact of the Compassionate Friends bereaved parents group broke new ground not only with regard to the ongoing bonds to the deceased but also for the powerful nature of bereaved parents' ability to assist each other in the context of a self-help group. These works and others like them provided in-depth exposure to the ability of persons who had gone through similar experiences to be of help and support to each other. The resilience and wisdom available in groups of persons who have shared difficult bereavement experiences, and the ability of these lay persons to help each other with little or no support from professionals, is no longer an idea to be questioned.

One such representative group, known as the Compassionate Friends, was founded by Simon Stephens, an English chaplain whose work exposed him to the value of bereaved parents supporting each other. The Compassionate Friends was later established in the United States and grew mightily. With more than 600 chapters in the United States, and branches in 30 countries around the world, the organization focuses on assisting bereaved parents, siblings, grandparents, and other family members during the "natural grieving process" after a child has died. In addition to the Compassionate Friends (http://www.compassionatefriends.org/home.aspx), the CRUSE group in England has become very well known and influential in the field of loss, bringing together volunteers and others who wish to be part of the helping and being helped communities around the United Kingdom. (http://www.crusebereavementcare.org.uk)

There is no single model for peer support groups. Not all self-help groups insist on independence or the absence of professionals. What characterizes bereavement self-help and support groups in the 21st century is the rise of the online communities, chat rooms, and blogger options, alongside the face-to-face real-life interactions that go on in various locations. These options are not mutually exclusive, and many persons who make use of one option also use the other. The upshot is that persons may be in a peer-led bereavement group meeting formally or informally, an online support group or chat room, and individual therapy and feel that each has something to provide for them.

Here is how one online self-help group presented itself:

> Our groups operate 24-hours/day, 365 days/year. Members participate when they wish and are able to, not at a set time. When one member of a group sends an email message to the group, everyone in the group receives a copy. This allows many people to respond with love and caring to the thoughts and feelings of an individual, day and night, year-round. (http://griefnet.org/support/sg2.html)

The potential for connecting to one's areas of strength and growth following loss and grief are enhanced in the following ways:

1. Activity and physical activity: It is important to remain active.
2. Contributing to the well-being of others: It is valuable to remaining relevant and engaged.
3. Addressing spirituality and religion: Involving these aspects in one's life contributes to well-being.
4. Dialogues with oneself: Journaling, blogging, writing in a diary, dictating to a computer program or tape recorder have effects that are positive.
5. Practicing mindfulness: The practice of meditation, mindfulness, or other ways of experiencing oneself and the world around one can be beneficial.
6. Joining self-help groups and sources that offer mutual support: Being with people who understand what you have been going through by virtue of their own experience can provide unique support.

LAST BUT NOT LEAST: THE THERAPIST'S SELF-CARE

We cannot take leave of this book without addressing the needs of the therapists who work with bereaved individuals, families, and groups. In their lives as human beings, therapists, like their clients, encounter death and experience losses and the grief that follows (Witztum, 2004). It is not only our clients who can benefit from attention to the positive aspects of a life focus. Therapists as caregivers working with bereaved are vulnerable to the accumulated effect of strenuous work and of being exposed directly or indirectly to traumatic events; this is known as *compassion fatigue* or *secondary traumatization* (Figley, 1995; Malkinson & Geron, 2002). The awareness that it is not only our clients who can benefit from attention to the positive aspects of a life focus deserves attention. All of us, bereaved clients and therapists alike, can benefit from finding ways to remain balanced and engaged in life (Rubin, 2000).

The pain, sadness, and anguish of dealing with death, dying, and bereavement in our encounters with others are a source of meaningful engagement with another as well as a source of stress and emotional depletion. To be effective and present in the human encounter, we need to be available and vulnerable. Yet in listening and in engaging with persons dealing with their hurt, fear, and pain, our own emotional responses of empathy, sympathy, anxiety, angst, and sadness are stimulated and activated.

The areas mentioned above, in the context of avenues the bereaved can use to manage a balanced and positive engagement with life, are relevant (with some modifications) for therapists as well. Although there are additional specific needs and alternative avenues for the therapists and counselors to attend to themselves, first and foremost the strategies and directions described above are also relevant.

Activity in general and physical activity in particular are relevant for therapists. The entire therapy enterprise functions as part of remaining engaged and helping others. There is a depletion of emotional resources that occurs when giving and caring for others and deriving too much of one's "value" from that role alone without it being balanced by emotional attachments, relationships, and sources of engagement that are outside of the world of therapy. In parallel to the risks of the bereaved being too focused on the deceased, therapists can and do become too focused on their work and clients; in doing so, they increase the risk to their own psychological well-being as well as effectiveness for others. The mental health benefits of spirituality and religion are generally insufficient to sway those who are not open or drawn to these approaches. For those who do connect with the spiritual and religious, they are valuable and add levels of meaning and connection to meaning matrixes that are emotionally enriching.

For therapists, the benefits of writing, whether professionally or personally, conform to all the expectations that Pennebaker and others have found in them. Mindfulness, the various ways of stilling the mind and reconnecting to the body as a unique base, reflects directions that are of use to therapists at all stages of development. Finally, therapists' choices with regard to support are many. These include professional supervision, peer group supervision, and the entire range of therapies that characterize the training and preparation of mental health professionals for their professional practice (Wiseman & Shefler, 2001).

Perhaps it is not surprising that working with bereaved not only is strenuous but opens opportunities for therapists to experience positive changes about self with a sense of mission about life and death and a meaningful experience of growth (Calhoun & Tedeschi, 1999; Malkinson, 2007).

CONCLUSION

In the human encounter of therapist and client, the pain of loss cannot be confined to one or the other. If connection is to be successful, empathy, openness, and honesty with regard to one's own emotional life guarantee that the experience is not limited to the client. Both are participants in the therapeutic and human encounter around loss, and both are changed by the meeting. Ensuring proper support for both parties outside the therapy room leads to exploration of directions that bear remarkable similarities.

We close this chapter on being attentive to caring for self and others with a thoughtful quote from Hillel the Elder. Close to 2 millennia old, the wisdom of his words ring true across time and space, and speak to client and therapist alike.

> If I am not for myself, who will be for me? And if I am only for myself, what am I? And if not now, when?
>
> *Ethics of the Fathers, 1:14, Hertz, 1945, p. 25.*

Epilogue

We take our leave from you here. As so many things in life, we wanted to say and communicate more, but we reached the end of our allotted time and space for this volume. For some of you, the messages of the book may continue to reverberate and serve as a bridge or ongoing connection to the ideas, cases, and ways of working that were presented. As in other forms of relationships, the chemistry and connection are highly individual. From our part, writing for you has been significant. Ideas, concepts, and clinical material were rethought, reexperienced, and recast so that even much of what we thought we knew turned into something that we encountered freshly and we wrote from that perspective. Blending old and new, familiar and unfamiliar, creates something that has not been before. We hope that you were encouraged to connect to both the familiar and the unfamiliar in combinations and creative pathways that open, deepen, and truly inform your work and yourselves. Thank you for being with us.

Appendix: The Two-Track Bereavement Questionnaire (TTBQ2-70)

BACKGROUND INFORMATION

THE TWO-TRACK BEREAVEMENT QUESTIONNAIRE ON LIFE FOLLOWING LOSS (TTBQ2-70)

Please complete the following questionnaire, which addresses a variety of questions concerning your life after the loss of a person important to you. Please read the questions and mark the answer that seems most appropriate to you. At the end of the questionnaire is a section where you may add your comments. Thank you.

Information about you	Details about the deceased
Today's date: _____/_____/_____	First Name of the deceased _____
Your Sex: (please circle) Male / Female Your age:_____	Date of death: _____/_____/_____ Age at death: _____
Your Country of birth: _____ Years in this country: _____:	Circumstances of the death: _____ _____
Religion: (please specify):_____ Degree of Religious Observance/Belief: Please circle the number that applies best to you. <table><tr><td>1</td><td>2</td><td>3</td><td>4</td><td>5</td></tr><tr><td>Very little</td><td>Little</td><td>So-so</td><td>Much</td><td>Very much</td></tr></table>	Your relation to the deceased: (please specify how you were related to or involved with the deceased). _____ _____
Languages spoken at home: _____ _____ _____	

In all parts of the questionnaire, unless stated otherwise: 1- true, 2- mostly true, 3- so- so, 4- mostly not true, 5- not true.	For office use only

Part I. All questions refer to the past week unless stated otherwise.

	True		So-so		Not true	
1. My health is very good:	1	2	3	4	5	F
2. My mood is very depressed:	1	2	3	4	5	F-R
3. I feel very anxious:	1	2	3	4	5	G-R
4. Since the loss, life seems very different to me:	1	2	3	4	5	D-R

Please explain briefly and give an example: _____

_____

	True		So-so		Not true	
5. Since the loss, the meaning of my life and of the world around me has changed greatly:	1	2	3	4	5	D-R
6. The direction of the changes in the meaning of my life has been for the worse only:	1	2	3	4	5	F-R
7. Thoughts and feelings flood and confuse me:	1	2	3	4	5	RAG-R
	Several times a day	Almost daily	Almost every week	Almost every month	Almost never	

	True		So-so		Not true	
8. I am involved and participate in various activities and tasks:	1	2	3	4	5	F-M
9. I function very well at work / school: (Circle the X on the right if not applicable)	1	2	3	4	5	F / X
10. Following the loss, how I think of myself (my self-perception) has changed greatly:	1	2	3	4	5	D-R

	True		So-so		Not true	
11. My self-perception this week has been almost totally positive:	1	2	3	4	5	F-M
12. I find it difficult to function socially:	1	2	3	4	5	F-R-M
13. My relationships with close family are very good: (Circle the X on the right if not applicable)	1	2	3	4	5	F X
14. My relationships with close family are a significant source of support for me: (Circle the X on the right if not applicable)	1	2	3	4	5	F-M X
15. Connections with others outside the family are a significant source of support for me:	1	2	3	4	5	G-M
16. My functioning as a spouse is very good: (Circle the X on the right if not applicable)	1	2	3	4	5	F X
17. My functioning as a parent is very good : (Circle the X on the right if not applicable)	1	2	3	4	5	F X
18. My values and beliefs are a significant source of support for me:	1	2	3	4	5	F-M
19. I believe and trust in my abilities to cope on my own with the tasks of life:	1	2	3	4	5	F
20. Following the loss, it is fair to describe my current situation as in great need of help:	1	2	3	4	5	G-R

II. Please read the instructions for the next section and proceed. In the following questions, wherever a line (_____) appears, please answer as if the name of the deceased was written there. The questions refer to the past week, unless stated otherwise.	For office use only

	True		So-so		Not true	
1. I find it hard to recall memories of _____ even when I try to:	1	2	3	4	5	G-R-M

	True		So-so		Not true	
2. Our relationship was such that when I think of _____, I usually remember our disagreements:	1	2	3	4	5	CN-R-M
3. Because of _____'s virtues and unique qualities, it's very hard to have negative thoughts about him/her:	1	2	3	4	5	PC

	Almost never	Almost every month	Almost every week	Almost daily	Several times a day	
4. Occasionally, I behave or act emotionally, as if I don't believe that _____ is gone. This happens to me:	1	2	3	4	5	RAG-M
5. I notice things that remind me of _____. For example, people that look like him/her, voices, or a feeling he/she's around. This happens to me:	1	2	3	4	5	RAG-M

	True		So-so		Not true	
6. I think of _____ all the time:	1	2	3	4	5	RAG-R
7. I've reached a degree of acceptance of the loss of _____:	1	2	3	4	5	RAG
8. When I think of _____, I feel strong guilt and regret that I didn't do things differently:	1	2	3	4	5	RAG-R
9. Thoughts about _____ bring up positive feelings in me:	1	2	3	4	5	G
10. I remember _____:	1	2	3	4	5	RAG-M

	Almost never	Almost every month	Almost every week	Almost daily	Several times a day	

	True		So-so		Not true	
11. I avoid things that remind me of _____:	1	2	3	4	5	CN-R

	True		So-so		Not true	
12. Thinking of and remembering _____ significantly calms me:	1	2	3	4	5	G
13. Life without _____ is too hard to bear:	1	2	3	4	5	RAG-R
14. Since the loss, I've discovered some negative things about _____ that I didn't know before. Those things changed what I thought of him/her for the worse:	1	2	3	4	5	CN-R
15. I yearn strongly for _____ and miss him/her deeply:	1	2	3	4	5	RAG-M
	Almost never	Almost every month	Almost every week	Almost daily	Several times a day	
	True		So-so		Not true	
16. I feel pain whenever I recall _____:	1	2	3	4	5	RAG-R
17. Now I understand people who think about putting an end to their own life after losing a close person:	1	2	3	4	5	D-R
18. I do things to keep alive and maintain the memory of _____:	1	2	3	4	5	RAG

(please give 3 examples of keeping alive or maintaining the memory of _____)

1) _____

2) _____

3) _____

	True		So-so		Not true	
19. Since the loss I've discovered some positive things about _____ that I didn't know before. Those things changed what I thought of him/her for the better:	1	2	3	4	5	G
20. It's possible to define my situation today, following the loss, as suffering greatly:	1	2	3	4	5	RAG-R

III. Please read the instructions for this section and proceed. The following questions relate to the last 2 years of the relationship between you and _____ during his/her life.						For office use only
	True		So-so		Not true	
1. My relationship with _____ was very close:	1	2	3	4	5	PC-R
2. During his/her life, _____ was a major source of emotional support for me:	1	2	3	4	5	PC-R
3. I was emotionally dependent on _____:	1	2	3	4	5	PC-R
4. My relationship with _____ had many and strong ups and downs:	1	2	3	4	5	CN-R
5. My relationship with _____ had much avoidance and distance:	1	2	3	4	5	CN
6. _____ was emotionally dependent on me:	1	2	3	4	5	PC-R
7. My relationship with _____ was characterized by sharp changes between being close to being angry and/or wishing to be distant:	1	2	3	4	5	CN-R
8. _____ was the person closest to me:	1	2	3	4	5	PC-R
9. Overall, my relationship with ___ was based on a sense of mutual trust:	1	2	3	4	5	PC-R
10. The relationship between ____ and I was based on mutual understanding, freedom, and a sense of comfort or "flow":	1	2	3	4	5	PC-R

IV. Please proceed. The next questions ask about your thoughts and feelings today.						For office use only
	True		So-so		Not true	
1. The loss was traumatic for me:	1	2	3	4	5	D-R

	True		So-so		Not true	
2. The loss happened suddenly and unexpectedly:	1	2	3	4	5	D-R
3. The loss took place under circumstances of violence or horror (such as accident, terror, or self-harm) or other difficult circumstances:	1	2	3	4	5	D-R
Please explain: _____						
4. Because of the loss I feel very angry:	1	2	3	4	5	G-R-M
Whom are you angry with and why? A)_____ B)_____						
5. I witnessed the death of _____:	1	2	3	4	5	G-R
6. My life was in danger when ____ died:	1	2	3	4	5	G-R
7. I keep on experiencing the loss as a shocking and traumatic event in my life:	1	2	3	4	5	D-R
Please explain why: _____						
8. Loss of the kind I experienced is usually experienced as a most difficult event:	1	2	3	4	5	D-R
9. The circumstances that caused the loss I've experienced are usually considered as extremely difficult:	1	2	3	4	5	D-R
	Almost never	Almost every month	Almost every week	Almost daily	Several times a day	
10. I see images or pictures from the death scene that enter my thoughts:	1	2	3	4	5	RAG-M

	Almost never	Almost every month	Almost every week	Almost daily	Several times a day	
11. I see images or pictures of ____ in my head:	1	2	3	4	5	RAG-M
12. I find myself actively avoiding thoughts of _____:	1	2	3	4	5	G-M
13. I am tense and not relaxed:	1	2	3	4	5	RAG-M
14. I am flooded by thoughts and feelings about the death of _____ :	1	2	3	4	5	RAG-M
	True		So-so		Not true	
15. People who are not family are aware of how great my loss is:	1	2	3	4	5	G
16. In facing life's difficulties, I usually trust only myself:	1	2	3	4	5	G-R
17. Before the loss, difficult events affected me for a short while only:	1	2	3	4	5	D
18. I am able to talk and share my feelings with other people and to receive their help and support:	1	2	3	4	5	G
19. I have managed to overcome difficult events in my life:	1	2	3	4	5	F
20. I believe that I'm capable of handling my feelings and reactions to the loss without the support and help of others:	1	2	3	4	5	D

If you wish to add information about how you have coped with your loss or to make additional comments, please add them here.

_____

_____

_____

_____

Thank you for your participation.

KEY FOR CLINICIANS AND RESEARCHERS

TTBQ2-70 is copyrighted. Permission is granted to use this measure for clinical and research purposes. We would appreciate receiving a copy of the results of your study. Please consult the Web site of the International Center for Loss, Bereavement and Human Resilience at the University of Haifa for details of where to send your results.

Track I:
F- Functional Difficulties
D- Dislocation and Trauma

Track II:
RAG- Relational Active Grief
PC- Positive/Close Relationship
CN- Conflict in the Relationship

G- General issues

Additional:
R- Reverse score on this item
M- Modified from TTBQ1

RESEARCH WITH THE TWO-TRACK BEREAVEMENT QUESTIONNAIRE (TTBQ2-70)

The interplay and synergy between theory, clinical work, and empirical research about bereavement encourage progress in our understanding of the impact of loss upon the bereaved. In the case of the Two-Track Model of Bereavement, a body of research is evolving that addresses aspects of this approach to conceptualizing and assessing the processes of mourning and the outcomes to bereavement. While virtually any empirical study on loss can be located on a map that will characterize which track and which dimensions are being assessed, it is our intention here to attend to research specifically constructed for the purpose of taking a bifocal approach that is inherent in the model itself. A summary of representative research with the Two-Track Model of Bereavement prior to the millennium was reported in the literature (Rubin, 1999). This appendix focuses on newer research restricted to that using the Two-Track Bereavement Questionnaire (Rubin et al., 2009).

RESEARCH ON LOSS WITH THE TWO-TRACK BEREAVEMENT QUESTIONNAIRE

The Two-Track Bereavement Questionnaire (TTBQ) was designed to assess the response to loss over time from the perspective of the Two-Track Model of Bereavement (Rubin et al., 2009). Developed, piloted, and translated into Hebrew, English, and Arabic, the questionnaire was validated on 354 persons who completed the 70-item self-report questionnaire. The questionnaire was constructed in accordance with the Two-Track Model of Bereavement with questions assessing Track I's focus on the bereaved's biopsychosocial functioning and Track II's focus on the bereaved's ongoing relationship to the range of memories, images, thoughts, and feeling states associated with the deceased (Rubin, 1981, 1999). Factor analysis identified five factors that accounted for 51% of the variance explained. In accord with the theoretical and clinical model, three factors were primarily associated with the relationship to the deceased (Track II): Relational Active Grieving, Close and Positive Relationship, and Conflictual Aspects of the Relationship; and two factors were linked to functioning (Track I): General Biopsychosocial Functioning and Traumatic Perception of the Loss. It should be noted that the relational factors preceded the functioning factors, suggesting that this axis is predominant in the experience of the bereaved.

The first factor, labeled Relational Active Grieving, comprised 16 items and was associated with hardship adjusting to life without the loved one who had died. It involved acute and painful emotions stemming from the loss of a loved one. All items revolved around the response to the loss and combined features of images of the death and the deceased, which often serve to heighten the salience of the grief. In addition, items reflecting preoccupation with and longing for the deceased, the hardship of living without the deceased, and items associated with ongoing grieving were associated with this factor. The next two factors emphasized the nature of the ongoing relationship to the deceased, characteristic of Track II. Factor 2, Close and Positive Relationship With the Deceased, comprised 8 items associated with both the pre-loss relationship with the deceased and the ongoing nature of the relationship. Perceptions of the relationship as a close one, with features of trust and emotional support, and features associated with the soothing presence of the relationship post-loss were present. The third factor, Conflictual Relationship With the Deceased, contained 6 items that emphasized the conflictual and negative aspects of the relationship combining pre-loss and post-loss indications of difficulty.

The final two factors emphasized features associated directly with the nature of biopsychosocial functioning characteristic of Track I. The fourth factor, General Biopsychosocial Functioning, consisted of 14 items encompassing poor coping, difficulties in managing interpersonal relationships with family members and with non–family members, a negative sense of self, meaning change in a negative direction, poor physical health, depressive mood, and anxiety. The fifth and final factor, Traumatic Perception of the Loss, contained 12 items associated with traumatic perception of loss. These included attention to the difficult circumstances of the loss, the experience of the death as sudden and unexpected, and its perception as a traumatic event in one's life. Other items were associated with the magnitude of the change and the difficulty coping, including suicidal ideation and the need for outside help. In all of the factors, as well as in the entire scale, a higher score meant more grief, more hardship, and more intense involvement with the deceased.

To demonstrate the value of this type of analysis of the various elements in the measure, we compared three types of kinship responses to see how persons bereaved of parents, spouses, and children coped with their losses. On Factor 1, Relational Active Grieving, and Factor 4, Problems in General Functioning, each kinship group was shown to score significantly different from the others. On both of these factors, those bereaved of children showed the greatest amount of difficulty. Loss of spouse or partner was a middle group, and those bereaved of elderly parents showed the least hardship following the loss. On Factor 2, Close and Positive Relationship to the

Deceased, once again each kinship group scored significantly different from the others, only this time the partner loss group reported the closest relationship, followed by those bereaved of children. Adults bereaved of older parents rated their relationships to the deceased as less close and positive. Finally, on Factor 5, Perception of Trauma, the partner-loss and child-loss groups did not differ from each other, although they did show greater difficulties than the parent-loss group.

With regard to the total score of the TTBQ, significant group differences were found. Those bereaved of children demonstrated the greatest amount of difficulty, followed by the partner-loss group, and then by those who lost older parents. Specifying its multidimensional nature remains a challenge (Worden, Davies, & McCown, 1999). Analyses of the distinctions showed that grief over a child was the most pronounced and active (Factor 1), while partners were perceived as the closest of kinship relationships (Factor 2). The intensity of grief over the loss of a child is most strongly reflected in the immediacy of the grief. The intimacy of the relationship with a partner is part of the unique physical and emotional bond reflected on the relational factor and emerges most strongly on the factor associated with the nature of the pre-loss relationship (Bar Nadav, 2007). The strong impact of partner and child loss was visible on the indices of functioning (Factor 4) and perception of trauma (Factor 5). On all the indices, the loss of a parent yielded lower scores than did spousal or child loss. On total score measures, each of the three kinship groups differed on the overall score for the TTBQ.

Research with the TTBQ analyzing the impact of child loss considered how agreement or refusal to donate organs or tissues might influence the bereavement experience. Analyses according to status of donation and by type of death (brain versus heart criteria) established that the loss of a child was so overwhelming that no differences were found for either type of death or for donation decision (Ashkenazi, 2010; Freiberg, 2008; Rubin & Ashkenazi, 2003). In other words, despite the added sensitivity of the TTBQ as compared to other measures of bereavement, the impact of continuing difficulties and involvement with the memories of the deceased child in the years following bereavement were pronounced and predominant (Adres, 2011).

The availability of the TTBQ as a self-report measure assessing functioning, relationship, and need for assistance is a logical outgrowth of the Two-Track Model of Bereavement. It is a useful measure and an important addition to the evolving set of measures addressing the domains of response to loss.

ATTACHMENT AND THE TTBQ

The attachment classification sorts persons into several different categories of insecure attachment. These have been shown conclusively to be important to understanding loss and bereavement. Dependent persons, those with disorganized attachment, and those who were highly fearful have been shown to have particular difficulty following bereavement. (Adres, 2011)

In working with the TTBQ, the self-report measure is of general clinical interest. The individual items, factor scores, and total scores are excellent measures of how the bereaved is responding at any chosen point in time. For purposes of evaluation, it is possible to use the questionnaire for assessment on its own as well as to use it for gauging progress in therapy at different points in time. By adding measures of attachment, it is possible to consider how the secure attachment style differs from the insecure variations of fearful-avoidant relationship, the dismissive attachment style, and the preoccupied variations of attachment. It is important to keep in mind that the dismissive attachment style often looks similar to secure attachment on self-report measures because their evaluation of themselves and others is relatively split off from awareness of anxiety and from interpersonal feedback.

In several studies of the impact of child death on parents, as well as the contribution of attachment style to outcome, the results were quite striking. On the TTBQ, it was possible to document the continuing problems within the bereaved parent group as compared to the matched nonbereaved sample. When the attachment lens was added, however, several findings took on an additional color. In particular, the group functioning best were securely attached while the group feeling the worst with bereavement were those classified as fearful. In this research as well, the dismissive personality style showed up as problematic despite the fact that on measures of self-report they look similar to the securely attached. In contrast to self-report measures, interview and written tools that allow for nuances of the interpersonal relationship to be explored show the dismissive group are severely limited in their ability to convey a complex and deep relationship to another or to recognize the relatively narrow and limited nature of the relationships they form.

The assessment of how the deceased is recollected and organized at conscious and unconscious levels is central to the assessment of outcome to bereavement and should be equally central to clinical assessment and research in the field, but it is not (Field, 2006; Malkinson et al., 2006; Rubin, Malkinson, & Witztum, 2008). Relationship as a concept is much broader than the yearning or pining that the bereaved experiences and which shows up in relational active grief. Bereavement clinicians and researchers continue to make progress on the understanding and specification of the relationship to the deceased (Rubin et al., 2008). Memories of the deceased may be limited, occasionally accessible, or highly intrusive (Horowitz et al., 1997). The affect associated with these memories may result in distress, a sense of well-being, or a mixture (Bowlby, 1963, 1973, 1980; Main, 1991). Focusing on dysfunction addresses one aspect targeting the symptomatic effects of response to loss. Focusing on pining and acceptance of death address progress in the transition from relationship with a living person to a meaningful relationship with someone who is no longer alive. Even when research indicates that dysfunction is no longer present and the death has been accepted, much remains to be learned. Included in the TTBQ are questions about the organization and function of relationships with the living and how these are similar to and dissimilar from relationships with the deceased. Memories of interactions with both the living and the deceased are part of one's inner world and are connected to moods, thoughts, and feelings.

The content and structure of the narrative underlying the bereaved's thoughts and feelings about a relationship with the deceased can be facilitative or deleterious to the bereaved. Therapy often focuses on the content and context of these memories when they interfere with the bereaved's ability to meet life adaptively. Research on the attachment network and the activation of the recollected connections to significant others has documented the nature of these cognitive-emotional processes (Mikulincer & Shaver, 2003, 2008). The way in which the bereaved thinks, remembers, and feels about the deceased is gradually becoming a greater focus of both quantitative and qualitative research, but much remains to be done in this area (Field, 2006; Horowitz et al., 1980; Klass et al., 1996; Saldinger, Porterfield, & Cain, 2004; Silverman et al., 2003).

Ultimately, the bifocal approach of the Two-Track Model of Bereavement combines the behavioral-empirical perspective with the relational focus on the dimensions directly associated with connection to the deceased. The model assists the conceptualization and specification regarding the overt and covert aspects of bonds to those they love. Whereas "until death do us part" conveys the reality of the physical separation, it is not enough for one partner to die for the bond with the loved one to end. As long as there is someone who remembers, the relationship has not ended. Following functioning and relationship to the deceased over time, we can learn much about the impact of loss and its processing. The Two-Track Bereavement Questionnaire long form (TTBQ2-70) can assist clinicians and researchers with this task.

References

Adres, I. (2011). Attachment and the Two-Track Model of Bereavement in parent loss: The contribution of the relationships with spouse, a living child, and "God" to outcome. Unpublished doctoral dissertation.University of Haifa, Haifa, Israel.

American Psychiatric Association. (1994). *Diagnostic and statistical manual of mental disorders* (4th ed.). Washington, DC: Author.

Ashkenazi, T. (2010). The ramifications of child organ and tissue donations on the mourning process and parents' adjustment to loss. Unpublished doctoral dissertation. Tel Aviv University, Tel Aviv, Israel.

Attig, T. (1996). *How we grieve: Relearning the world.* New York: Oxford University Press.

Balk, D. E. (1996). Attachment and the reactions of bereaved college students: A longitudinal study. In D. Klass, P. R. Silverman, & S. L. Nickman (Eds.), *Continuing bonds: New understandings of grief* (pp. 311–328). Washington, DC: Taylor & Francis.

Balk, D. E., & Cook, A. S. (Eds.). (1995). Ethics and bereavement research [Special issue]. *Death Studies, 19*(2)

Bar Nadav, O. (2007). *Partner loss and the Two-Track Model of Bereavement: The long term consequences of bereavement for young women.* Unpublished doctoral dissertation, University of Haifa, Haifa, Israel.

Bar-On, D. (1991). *Legacy of silence: Encounters with children of the Third Reich.* Cambridge, MA: Harvard University Press.

Beauchamp, T. L., & Childress, J. F. (2001). *Principles of biomedical ethics* (5th ed.). New York: Oxford University Press.

Beck, A. T. (1976). *Cognitive therapy and the emotional disorders.* New York: International University Press.

Benbow, S. M., & Goodwillie, G. (2010). Think family: Systemic family therapy in later life. In N. A. Pachana, K. Laidlaw, & B. Knight (Eds.), *Casebook of clinical geropsychology* (pp. 91–106). Oxford, England: Oxford University Press.

Berkowitz, E. (1979). *With God in hell: Judaism in the ghettos and deathcamps.* New York: Sanhedrin Press.

Berman, E. (2004). *Impossible training: A relational view of psychoanalytic education.* New York: Routledge.

Berzoff, J., Flanagan, L. M., & Hertz, P. (Eds.). (2007). *Inside out and outside in: Psychodynamic clinical theory, practice, and psychopathology in multicultural contexts* (2nd ed.). Northvale, NJ: Jason Aronson.

Berzoff, J., & Silverman, P. R. (2004). *Living with dying.* New York: Columbia University Press.

Beutler, L. (2009). Making science matter in clinical practice: Redefining psychotherapy. *Clinical Psychology: Science and Practice, 16*(3), 301–317.

Bibring, E. (1953). The mechanism of depression. In P. Greenacre (Ed.), *Affective disorders.* New York: International University Press.

Blatt, S. J. (2004). *Experiences of depression: Theoretical, clinical and research perspectives.* Washington, DC: American Psychological Association.

Boelen, P. A., Kip, H. J., Voorsluijs, J. J., & van den Bout, J. (2004). Irrational beliefs and basic assumptions in bereaved university students: A comparison study. *Journal of Rational-Emotive & Cognitive-Behavior Therapy, 22*(2), 111–129.

Bollas, C. (1987). *The shadow of the object.* New York: Columbia University Press.

Bonanno, G. A. (2004). Loss, trauma, and human resilience: Have we underestimated the human capacity to thrive after extremely aversive events? *American Psychologist, 59,* 20–28.

Bonanno, G. A. (2009). *The other side of sadness.* New York: Basic Books.

Bonanno, G. A., Boerner, K., & Wortman, C. B. (2008). Trajectories of grieving. In M. Stroebe, R. Hansson, H. Schut, & W. Stroebe (Eds.), *Handbook of bereavement research and practice: Advances in theory and intervention* (pp. 287–307). Washington, DC: American Psychological Association.

Boscolo, L., Chechin, G., Hoffman, L., & Penn, P. (1987). *Milan systemic family therapy.* New York: Basic Books.

Boss, P. (1999). *Ambiguous loss.* Cambridge, MA: Harvard University Press.

Bowen, M. (2004). Family reaction to loss. In F. Walsh & M. McGoldrick (Eds.), *Living beyond loss: Death in the family* (2nd ed., pp. 47–60). New York: W. W. Norton.

Bowlby, J. (1969). *Attachment and loss: Vol. 1. Attachment.* London: Hogarth.

Bowlby, J. (1973). *Attachment and loss: Vol. 2. Separation: Anxiety and anger.* London: Hogarth.

Bowlby, J. (1980). *Attachment and loss: Vol. 3. Loss: Sadness and depression.* London: Hogarth.

Breuer, J., & Freud, S. (1955). On the psychical mechanism of hysterical phenomena: Preliminary communication. In J. Strachey (Ed. & Trans.), *Standard edition of the complete psychological works of Sigmund Freud* (Vol. 2, pp. 3–17). London: Hogarth Press (Original work published 1893).

Breslau, N. (2002). Gender differences in trauma and posttraumatic stress disorder. *Journal of Gender Specific Medicine, 5,* 34–40.

Briere, J. (2004). *Psychological assessment of adult posttraumatic states: Phenomenology, diagnosis, and measurement* (2nd ed.). Washington, DC: American Psychological Association.

Brom, D., & Kleber, R. (2000). On coping with trauma and coping with grief: Similarities and differences. In R. Malkinson, S. Rubin, & E. Witztum (Eds.), *Traumatic and nontraumatic loss and bereavement: Clinical theory and practice* (pp. 41–66). Madison, CT: Psychosocial Press.

Bryan, C. J., & Rudd, M. D. (2006). Advances in the assessment of suicide risk. *Journal of Clinical Psychology, 62*(2), 185–200.

Buckley, P. (Ed.). (1986). *Essential papers on object relations.* New York: New York University Press.

Burbatti, G. L., & Formenti, L. (1988). *The Milan approach to family therapy.* Northvale, NJ: Jason Aronson.

Calhoun, L. G., & Tedeschi, R. G. (1999). *Facilitating posttraumatic growth: A clinician's guide.* Mahwah, NJ: Erlbaum.

Caplan, G. (1975). Eric Lindemann. *American Journal of Psychiatry, 132,* 296.

Carey, S. M., & Cosgrove, J. F. (2006). Cultural issues surrounding end-of-life care. *Current Anaesthesia & Critical Care, 17,* 263–270.

Carter, B., & McGoldrick, M. (1999). *The expanded family life cycle* (3rd ed.). Boston: Allyn & Bacon. Family reaction to loss.

Cassidy, J., & Shaver, P. R. (1999). *Handbook of attachment: Theory, research, and clinical applications.* New York: Guilford Press.

Christ, G. H., Bonanno, G., Malkinson, R., & Rubin, S. (2003). Bereavement experiences after the death of a child. In M. J. Field & R. E. Behrman (Eds.), *When children die: Improving palliative and end-of-life care for children and their families* (pp. 553–579). Washington, DC: National Academies Press.

Clements, P. T., Vigil, G. J., Manno, M. S., Henry, G. C., Wilks, J., Das, S., et al. (2003). Cultural perspectives of death, grief, and bereavement. *Journal of Psychosocial Nursing, 41,* 18–26.

Cook, A. S. (2001). The dynamics of ethical decision making in bereavement research. In M. S. Stroebe, R. O. Hansson, W. Stroebe, & H. Schut (Eds.), *Handbook of bereavement research: Consequences, coping, and care* (pp. 119–142). Washington, DC: American Psychological Association.

Crisp, A. H., & Priest, R. G. (1972). Psychoneurotic status during the year following bereavement. *Journal of Psychosomatic Medicine, 16,* 351–355.

Csikszentmihalyi, M., & Csikszentmihalyi, I. S. (Eds.). (2006). *A life worth living: Contributions to positive psychology.* New York: Oxford University Press.

Currier, J. M., Neimeyer, R. A., & Berman, J. S. (2008). The effectiveness of psychotherapeutic intervention for bereaved persons: A comprehensive quantitative review. *Psychological Bulletin, 134*(5), 648–661.

Daie, N., & Witztum, E. (1991). Short-term strategic treatment in traumatic conversion reactions. *American Journal of Psychotherapy, 55,* 335–347.

David, D., & DiGiuseppe, R. (2010). Social and cultural aspects of rational and irrational beliefs: A brief reconceptualization. In D. David, S. J. Lynn, & A. Ellis (Eds.), *Rational and irrational beliefs: Research theory, and clinical practice* (pp. 49–62). New York: Oxford University Press.

David, D., Freeman, A., & DiGiuseppe, R. (2010). Rational and irrational beliefs: Implications for mechanism of change and psychotherapy. In D. David, S. J. Lynn, & A. Ellis (Eds.), *Rational and irrational beliefs: Research, theory, and clinical practice* (pp. 195–218). New York: Oxford University Press.

David, D., Lynn, S. J., & Ellis, A. (2010). *Rational and irrational beliefs: Research, theory, and clinical practice.* New York: Oxford University Press.

Davidson, R., Quinn, W. H., & Josephson, A. M. (2001). Assessment of the family: Systemic and developmental perspectives. *Current Perspectives of Family Therapy, 10*(3), 415–429.

Davies, B. (1999). *Shadows in the sun: The experiences of sibling bereavement in childhood.* New York: Taylor & Francis.

Davies, J. M. (2004). Whose bad objects are we anyway? Repetition and our elusive love affair with evil. *Psychoanalytic Dialogues, 14,* 711–732.

Davis, C. (2008). Redefining goals and redefining self: A closer look at posttraumatic growth following loss. In M. S. Stroebe, R. O. Hansson, H. Schut, & W. Stroebe (Eds.), *Handbook of bereavement research and practice: Advances in theory and intervention* (pp. 309–325). Washington, DC: American Psychological Association.

DellaPergola, S. (2010). World Jewish population 2010. North American Jewish data bank. Mandell L. Berman Institute. http://www.jewishdatabank.org/Reports/World_Jewish_Population_2010.pdf, p 17. Accessed June, 2011

DeSpelder, L., & Strickland, A. (2008). *The last dance: Encountering death and dying* (8th ed.). New York: McGraw-Hill.

DiGiuseppe, R. (1991). Rational-emotive model of assessment. In M. Bernard (Ed.), *Using rational emotive therapy effectively: A practitioner's guide* (pp. 151–170). New York: Plenum Press.

Doka, K. (2002). *Disenfranchised grief: New directions, challenges, and strategies for practice.* Champaign, IL: Research Press.

Doka, K. J. & Martin, T. (2010). *Grieving beyond gender: Understanding the ways men and women mourn.* New York: Routledge.

Dryden, W. (1991). *Reason and therapeutic change.* London: Whurr.

Dryden, W. (2009). *Rational emotive behaviour therapy.* Hove, England: Routledge.

Durkheim, E. (1997). *Suicide* (G. Simpson, Ed. & Trans.). New York: Free Press. (Original work published 1897)

Eisenbruch, M. (1984). Cross-cultural aspects of bereavement, II: Ethnic and cultural variations in the development of bereavement practices. *Culture Medicine and Psychiatry, 8,* 315–347.

Elitzur, A. S., & Omer, H. (2001). What would you say to the person on the roof? A suicide prevention text. *Suicide and Life-Threatening Behavior, 31*(2), 129–139.

Ellis, A. (1962). *Reason and emotion in psychotherapy.* Secaucus, NJ: Lyle Stewart.

Ellis, A. (1976). The biological basic of human irrationality. *Journal of Individual Psychology, 32,* 145–168.

Ellis, A. (1991). The revised ABC's of rational-emotive therapy (RET). *Journal of Rational-Emotive & Cognitive-Behavior Therapy, 9*(3), 139–172.

Ellis, A. (1993). Rational-emotive imagery: RET version. In M. E. Bernard & J. L. Wolfe (Eds.), *The RET resource book for practitioners* (pp. II.8–II.10). New York: Institute for Rational-Emotive Therapy.

Ellis, A. (1994). *Reason and emotion in psychotherapy. A comprehensive method of treating human disturbances* (Rev. & updated ed.). New York: Birch Lane Press.

Ellis, A. (2002). *Overcoming resistance: A rational emotive behavioral therapy integrated approach* (2nd ed.). New York: Springer.

Ellis, A. (2006). Rational emotive behavior therapy and the mindfulness based stress reduction training of Kabat-Zinn. *Journal of Rational-Emotive Therapy & Cognitive-Behavior Therapy, 24*(1), 63–78.

Emanuel, E. J., Grady, C., Crouch, R. A., Lie, R. K., Miller, F. G., & Wendler, D. (2008). *The Oxford textbook of clinical research ethics.* New York: Oxford University Press.

Emmons, R. A. (2006). Spirituality: Recent progress. In M. Csikszentmihalyi & I. S. Csikszentmihalyi, (Eds.), *A life worth living: Contributions to positive psychology* (pp. 62–84). New York: Oxford University Press

Epictetus. (1890). *The collected works of Epictetus.* New York: Longmans Green.

Erikson, E. H. (1950). *Childhood and society.* New York: W. W. Norton.

Esposito, L., Buckalew, P., & Chukunta, T. (1996). Cultural diversity in grief. *Home Health Care Management Practice, 8,* 23–29.

Fachler, A. (2008). *Fatherless fathers: A quantitative and qualitative exploration of the characteristics and experience of attachment, empathy, and fatherhood, in light of father loss.* Unpublished doctoral dissertation, University of Haifa, Israel.

Fenichel, O. (1945). *The psychoanalytic theory of neurosis.* New York: W.W. Norton.

Field, N. (2006). Unresolved grief and continuing bonds: An attachment perspective. *Death Studies, 30,* 739–756.

Fleming, S., & Robinson, P. (2001). Grief and cognitive-behavioral therapy: The reconstruction of meaning. In M. S. Stroebe, & R. O. Hansson, W. Stroebe, & H. Schut (Eds.), *Handbook of bereavement research: Consequences, coping, and care* (pp. 647–669). Washington, DC: American Psychological Association.

Fletcher, L., & Hayes, S. C. (2005). Relational frame theory, acceptance and commitment therapy, and a functional analytic definition of mindfulness. *Journal of Rational-Emotive & Cognitive Behavior Therapy, 23*(4), 315–336.

Figley, C. R. (Ed.) (1995). *Compassion fatigue: Secondary traumatic stress disorders from treating the traumatized.* New York: Brunner/Mazel.

Foa, E. B., Keane, T. M., Friedman, M. J., & Cohen, J. E. (Eds.). (2008). *Effective treatments for PTSD: Practice guidelines from the International Society for Traumatic Stress Studies* (2nd ed.). New York: Guilford Press.

Foa, E. B., & Rothbaum, B. O. (1998). *Treating the trauma of rape: Cognitive-behavioral therapy for PTSD.* New York: Guilford Press.

Forsythe, J. P., & Eifert, G. H. (2007). *The mindfulness and acceptance workbook for anxiety.* Oakland, CA: New Harbinger.

Frankiel, R. V. (Ed.). (1994). *Essential papers on object loss.* New York: New York University Press.

Frankl, V. (1984). *Man's search for meaning: An introduction to logotherapy* (3rd ed.). New York: Simon & Schuster. (Original work published 1959)

Freiberg, R. (2007). Loss and personal growth among bereaved parents. Unpublished M.A. thesis, University of Haifa, Haifa, Israel.

Freud, E. L. (Ed.). (1961). *Letters of Sigmund Freud.* New York: Basic Books.

Freud, S. (1957). Mourning and melancholia. In J. Strachey (Ed. & Trans.), *Standard edition of the complete psychological works of Sigmund Freud* (Vol. 14, pp. 237–258). London: Hogarth. (Original work published 1917)

Furst, S. (Ed.). (1967). *Psychic trauma.* New York: Basic Books.

Gaitini, M. (2009). *The dead mother: On the impact of different types of death and deadness upon the life course of adult women.* Unpublished doctoral dissertation, University of Haifa, Haifa, Israel.

Galea, S., Ahern, J., Resnick, H., Kilpatrick, D., Bucyvalas, M., Gold, J., & Vlahov, D. (2002). Psychological sequelae of the September 11 terrorist attacks in New York City. *New England Journal of Medicine, 346,* 982–987.

Gilbert, D. (2007). *Stumbling upon happiness.* New York: Vintage Books.

Gildin-Kellerman, T. (2010). *Trauma.* Unpublished doctoral dissertation, University of Haifa, Haifa, Israel.

Golan, N. (1975). Wife to widow to woman. *Social Work, 20,* 369–374.

Gonçalves, O. F., & Machado, P. P. (1999). Cognitive narrative psychotherapy: Research foundations. *Journal of Clinical Psychology, 55*(10), 1179–1193.

Goodwin, D. K. (2005). *Team of rivals: The political genius of Abraham Lincoln.* New York: Simon & Schuster.

Goss, R. E., & Klass, D. (2005). *Dead but not lost: Grief narratives in religious traditions.* Walnut Creek, CA: AltaMira Press.

Green, B. (2000). Traumatic loss: Conceptual and empirical links between trauma and bereavement. *Journal of Personal and Interpersonal Loss, 5,* 1–17.

Greenberg, D., & Witztum, E. (2001). *Sanity and sanctity: Mental health care of the ultra-orthodox community in Jerusalem.* New Haven, CT: Yale University Press.

Grisaru, N., Malkinson, R., & Witztum, E. (2008). Bereavement customs, grief and rituals among Ethiopian immigrants to Israel. *Illness, Crisis & Loss, 16*(2), 111–123.

Hagman, G. (1995). Death of a selfobject: Towards a self psychology of the mourning process. In A. Goldberg (Ed.), *The impact of new ideas: Progress in self psychology* (Vol. 11, pp. 189–205). Hillsdale, NJ: Analytic Press.

Herman, J. L. (1992). *Trauma and recovery.* New York: Basic Books.

Hertz, J. H. (trans). (1945). *Sayings of the fathers.* New York: Behrman House.

Hofmann, S. G., Sawyer, A. T., Witt, A. A., & Oh, D. (2010). The effect of mindfulness-based therapy on anxiety and depression: A meta-analytic review. *Journal of Consulting and Clinical Psychology, 78,* 169–183.

Hogan, N., & DeSantis, L. (1996). Basic constructs of a theory of adolescent sibling bereavement. In D. Klass, P. R. Silverman, & S. L. Nickman (Eds.), *Continuing bonds: New understandings of grief* (pp. 235–256). Washington, DC: Taylor & Francis.

Holland, J. M., Currier, J. M., & Neimeyer, R. A. (2006). Meaning reconstruction in the first two years of bereavement: The role of sense-making and benefit-finding. *Omega, 53*(3), 175–191.

Holland, J. M., & Neimeyer, R. A. (2010). An examination of stage theory of grief among individuals bereaved by natural and violent causes: A meaning-oriented contribution. *Omega, 61*(2), 103–120.

Holloway, K. F. C. (2002). *Passed on: African American mourning stories: A memorial.* Durham, NC: Duke University Press.

Horowitz, M. J. (2001). *Stress response syndromes: Personality styles and interventions* (4th ed.). Northvale, NJ: Jason Aronson.

Horowitz, M. J. (2006). Meditating on complicated grief disorder as a diagnosis. *Omega, 52*(1), 67–69.

Horowitz, M. J., Siegel, B., Holen, A., Bonanno, G. A., Milbrath, C., & Stinson, C. S. (1997). Diagnostic criteria for complicated grief disorder. *American Journal of Psychiatry, 154*(7), 904–910.

Horowitz, M. J., Wilner, N., Marmar, C., & Krupnick, J. (1980). Pathological grief and the activation of latent self images. *American Journal of Psychiatry, 137,* 1157–1160.

Humphrey, K. M. (2009). *Counseling strategies for loss and grief.* Alexandria, VA: American Counseling Association.

Isaacson, W. (2003). *Benjamin Franklin: An American life.* New York: Simon & Schuster.

Janoff-Bulman, R. (1992). *Shattered assumptions: Towards a new psychology of trauma.* New York: Free Press.

Jewish Publication Society. (1962). *The Torah: The Five Books of Moses.* Philadelphia: Author.

Jordan, J., & Neimeyer, R. (2003). Does grief counseling work? *Death Studies, 27,* 765–786.

Jordan, J. R., & McIntosh, J. L. (2010). (Eds.). *Grief after suicide: Understanding the consequences and caring for the survivors.* New York: Routledge.

Kabat-Zinn, J. (1990). *Full catastrophe living: Using the wisdom of your body and the mind to face stress, pain, and illness.* New York: Delacorte Press.

Kardiner, A. (1941) *The traumatic neuroses of war.* New York: Hoeber.

Kasher, A. (2004). Life in the heart. *Journal of Loss and Trauma,* 8(4), 247–260.

Kasher, A. (with Witztum, E.). (2007). *King Herod: A persecuted persecutor: A case study in psychohistory and psychobiography.* Berlin, Germany: Walter de Gruyter.

Kassinove, H., & Tafrate, R. C. (2002). *Anger management: The complete treatment book for practitioners.* Atascadero, CA: Impact Publishers.

Kauffman, J. (Ed.). (2002). *Loss of the assumptive world: A theory of traumatic loss.* New York: Brunner-Routledge.

Kellner, M. (2006). *Must a Jew believe anything?* (2nd ed.). Oxford, England: Littman Library of Jewish Civilization.

Kelly, G. (1955). *Principles of personal construct psychology.* New York: W. W. Norton.

Kinzie, J. D., & Goetz, R. R. (1996) Century of controversy surrounding posttraumatic stress, stress-spectrum syndromes: The impact on *DSM-III* and *DSM-IV. Journal of Traumatic Stress.* 9,159–179.

Kirman, H. H. (1998). One-person or two-person psychology? *Modern Psychoanalysis, 23,* 3–22.

Klass, D. (1988). *Parental grief: Solace and resolution.* New York: Springer.

Klass, D. (1996). The deceased child in the psychic and social worlds of bereaved parents during the resolution of grief. In D. Klass, P. R. Silverman, & S. L. Nickman (Eds.), *Continuing bonds: New understandings of grief* (pp. 199–215). Washington, DC: Taylor & Francis.

Klass, D., Silverman, P. R., & Nickman, S. L. (Eds.). (1996). *Continuing bonds: New understandings of grief.* Washington, DC: Taylor & Francis.

Klein, M. (1940). Mourning and its relationship to manic-depressive states. *International Journal of Psychoanalysis, 21,* 125–141.

Kohut, H. (1971). *The analysis of the self.* New York: International University Press.

Kohut, H. (1977). *The restoration of the self.* New York: International University Press.

Koocher, G., & Keith-Spiegel, P. (2008). *Ethics in psychology and the mental health professions: Professional standards and cases* (3rd ed.). Oxford, England: Oxford University Press.

Koren, D., Arnon, I., & Klein, E. (1999). Acute stress response and posttraumatic stress disorder in traffic accident victims: A one-year prospective, follow-up study. *American Journal of Psychiatry, 156,* 369–373.

Lamm, M. (1969). *The Jewish way in death and mourning.* New York: Jonathan David.

Lampert-Tsamert, M. (2007). *"Visible" and "non-visible loss": The experience of loss in the lives of women who have lost their fathers in early childhood.* Unpublished doctoral dissertation, University of Haifa, Haifa, Israel.

Langs, R. (1976). *The therapeutic interaction* (Vols. 1 & 2). New York: Jason Aronson.

Larson, E. (2003). *The devil in the White City: Murder, magic, and madness at the fair that changed America.* New York: Crown.

Larson, D. G., & Hoyt, W. T. (2007). What has become of grief counseling? An evaluation of the empirical foundations of the new pessimism. *Professional Psychology: Research and Practice, 38,* 347-355.

Larson, D. G., & Hoyt, W. T. (2009). Grief counselling efficacy: What have we learned? *Bereavement Care, 28,* (3) 14–19.

Lasiu, G. C., & Hegadoren, K. M. (2006). Posttraumatic stress disorder Part II: Development of the construct within the North American psychiatric taxonomy. *Perspectives in Psychiatric Care, 42,* 73–78.

Latham, A. E., & Prigerson, H. G. (2004). Suicidality and bereavement: Complicated grief as psychiatric disorder presenting greatest risk for suicidality. *Suicide and Life Threatening Behavior, 34*(4), 350–362.

Lawlor, D. A., & Hopker, S. W. (2001). The effectiveness of exercise as an intervention in the management of depression: Systematic review and meta-regression analysis of randomized controlled trials. *British Medical Journal, 322,* 763–767.

Lawson, L. (1990). Culturally sensitive support for grieving parents. *Maternal/Child Nursing, 15,* 76–79.

Lazarus, R. S., & Folkman, S. (1984). *Stress, appraisal and coping.* New York: Springer.

Lehman, D. R., Wortman, G. B., & Williams, A. F. (1987). Long-term effects of losing a spouse or child in a motor vehicle crash. *Journal of Personality and Social Psychology, 52*(1), 218–231.

Levi, P. (1989). *The mirror maker: Stories and essays.* New York: Schocken Books.

Lewis, C. S. (1961). *A grief observed.* New York: HarperOne, p. 15.

Lindemann, E. (1944). Symptomatology and management of acute grief. *American Journal of Psychiatry, 101,* 141–148.

Linehan, M. M. (1993). *Cognitive behavioral treatment of borderline personality disorder.* New York: Guilford Press.

Lyubomirsky, S. (2008). *The how of happiness: A new approach to getting the life you want.* New York: Penguin.

Maciejewski, P. K., Zhang, B., Block, S. D., & Prigerson, H. G. (2007). An empirical examination of the stage theory of grief. *Journal of the American Medical Association, 297*(7), 716–723.

Mahler, M., Pine, F., & Bergmann, A. (1975). *The psychological birth of the human infant.* New York: Basic Books.

Main, M. (1991). Metacognitive knowledge, metacognitive monitoring and singular (coherent) vs. multiple (incoherent) models of attachment: Findings and directions for future research. In C. M. Parkes, J. Stevenson-Hinde, & P. Marris (Eds.), *Attachment across the life cycle* (pp. 127–159). London: Tavistock.

Malkinson, R. (1996). Cognitive behavioral grief therapy. *Journal of Rational-Emotive and Cognitive-Behavioral Therapy, 14*(4), 156–165.

Malkinson, R. (2001). Cognitive-behavioral therapy of grief: A review and application. *Research on Social Work Practice, 11,* 671–698.

Malkinson, R. (2007). *Cognitive grief therapy: Constructing a rational meaning to life following loss.* New York: W. W. Norton.

Malkinson, R. (2011). Cognitive grief therapy: The ABC model of REBT. *Journal Psychological Topics. 19,*(2), 289–305.

Malkinson, R., & Bar-Tur, L. (2000). The aging of grief: Parental grief of Israeli soldiers. *Journal of Personal and Interpersonal Loss, 5*(2/3), 247–261.

Malkinson, R., & Bar-Tur, L. (2004–2005). Long-term bereavement processes of older parents: The three phases of grief. *Omega, 50*(2), 103–129.

Malkinson, R., & Ellis, A. (2000). The application of rational-emotive behavior therapy (REBT) in traumatic and nontraumatic grief. In R. Malkinson, S. Rubin, & E. Witztum (Eds.), *Traumatic and nontraumatic loss and bereavement: Clinical theory and practice* (pp. 173–196). Madison, CT: Psychosocial Press.

Malkinson, R., & Geron, Y. (2006). Intervention continuity in posttraffic fatality: From notifying families of the loss to establishing a self-help group. In E. K: Rynearson (Ed.), *Violent death: Resilience and intervention beyond the crisis.* New York: Routledge.

Malkinson, R., Rubin, S., & Witztum, E. (Eds.). (1993). *Loss and bereavement in Jewish society in Israel.* Israel: Canah/Ministry of Defense.

Malkinson, R., Rubin, S. S., & Witztum, E. (Eds.). (2000). *Traumatic and nontraumatic loss and bereavement: Clinical theory and practice.* Madison, CT: Psychosocial Press.

Malkinson, R., Rubin, S. S., & Witztum, E. (2006). Therapeutic Issues and the Relationship to the Deceased: Working Clinically with the Two-Track Model of Bereavement. *Death Studies, 30,* 797–815.

Malkinson, R., & Witztum, E. (2000). Collective bereavement and commemoration: Cultural aspects of collective myth and the creation of national identity. In R. Malkinson, S. Rubin & E. Witztum (Eds.), *Traumatic and nontraumatic loss and bereavement: Clinical theory and practice* (pp. 295–320). Madison CT: Psychosocial Press.

Margolin, J., & Witztum, E. (2003). Ethical issues in psychiatry. In G. Shefler, Y. Achmon, & G. Weil (Eds.), *Ethical issues for professionals in counseling and psychotherapy* (pp. 516–538). Jerusalem: Hebrew University Magnes Press. (in Hebrew)

Maultsby, M. J., Jr. (1971). Rational emotive imagery. *Rational Living, 6*(1), 24–27.

McBride, J., & Simms, S. (2001). A death in the family: Adapting a family system framework to the grief process. *American Journal of Family Therapy, 29,* 59–73.

Mehraby, N. (2003). Psychotherapy with Islamic clients facing loss and grief. *Psychotherapy in Australia, 9*(2).

Mikulincer, M., & Shaver, P. R. (2003). The attachment behavioral system in adulthood: Activation, psychodynamics, and interpersonal processes. In M. P. Zanna (Ed.), *New York: Advances in Experimental Social Psychology* Vol. 35. New York: Academic Press, pp. 56–152.

Mikulincer, M., & Shaver, P. R. (2007). *Attachment in adulthood: Structure, dynamics, and change.* New York: Guilford Press.

Mikulincer, M., & Shaver, P. R. (2008). An attachment perspective on bereavement. In M. S. Stroebe, R. O. Hansson, H. Schut, & W. Stroebe (Eds.), *Handbook of bereavement research and practice: Advances in theory and intervention.* Washington, DC: American Psychological Association, pp. 87–112.

Miller, L. (2002). Psychological interventions for terroristic trauma: Symptoms, syndromes, and treatment strategies. *Psychotherapy: Theory/Research/Practice/Training, 39,* 283–296.

Miller, S. I., & Schoenfeld, L. (1973). Grief in the Navajo: Psychodynamics and culture. *International Journal of Social Psychiatry, 19*(3/4), 187–191.

Mitchell, S. A. (1988). *Relational concepts in psychoanalysis: Integration.* Cambridge, MA: Harvard University Press.

Mitchell, S. A., & Black, M. J. (1995). *Freud and beyond: A history of modern psychoanalytic thought.* New York: Basic Books.

Mor-Yosef, S. (2010).The influence of combat on the emotional function of combat veterans: Combat, being wounded, and interpersonal loss as a function of attachment and coping style. Unpublished doctoral dissertation. University of Haifa, Haifa, Israel.

Nadeau, J. W. (2008). Meaning-making in bereaved families: Assessment, intervention and future research. In M. S. Stroebe, R. O. Hansson, H. Schut, & W. Stroebe (Eds.), *Handbook of bereavement research and practice: Advances in theory and intervention* (pp. 511–530). Washington, DC: American Psychological Association.

National Cancer Institute. (2010). *Cross-cultural responses to grief and mourning.* Retrieved December 12, 2010, from http://www.cancer.gov/cancertopics/pdq/supportivecare/bereavement/HealthProfessional/page7

Neimeyer, R., Keese, N. J., & Fortner, B. V. (2000). Loss and meaning reconstruction: Propositions and procedures. In R. Malkinson, S. Rubin, & E. Witztum (Eds.), *Traumatic and nontraumatic loss and bereavement: Clinical theory and practice* (pp. 197–230). Madison, CT: Psychosocial Press.

Neimeyer, R. A. (1996). Process interventions for the constructivist In H. Rosen & K. Kuehlwein (Eds.), *Constructing psychotherapist realities.* San Francisco: Jossey-Bass, pp. 371–411.

Neimeyer, R. A. (1999). *Lessons of loss: A guide to coping.* New York: McGraw-Hill.

Neimeyer, R. A. (Ed.). (2001). *Meaning reconstruction and the experience of loss.* Washington, DC: American Psychological Association.

Neimeyer, R. A., & Mahoney, M. J. (Eds.). (1995). *Constructivism in psychotherapy.* Washington, DC: American Psychological Association.

Neria, Y., Gross, R., Litz, B., Maguen, S., Insel, B., Seirmarco, G., et al. (2007). Prevalence and psychological correlates of complicated grief among bereaved adults 2.5–3.5 years after September 11th attacks. *Journal of Traumatic Stress, 20*(3), 251–262.

Nolen-Hoeksema, S. (2002). Ruminative coping and adjustment. In M. S. Stroebe, R. O. Hansson, W. Stroebe, & H. Schut (Eds.), *Handbook of bereavement research: Consequences, coping, and care* (pp. 545–562). Washington, DC: American Psychological Association.

Noy, S. (2000). *Traumatic stress.* Tel Aviv: Schocken (Hebrew)

O'Connor, M., Nikoletti, S., Kristjanson, L. J., Faaai, R. L., & Willcock, B. (2003). Writing therapy for the bereaved: Evaluation of an intervention. *Journal of Palliative Medicine, 6,* 95–204.

Ogden, T. H. (1994). *Subjects of analysis.* Northvale, NJ: Jason Aronson.

Oppenheim, D., & Goldsmith, D. F. (Eds.). (2007). *Attachment theory in clinical work with children: Bridging the gap between research and practice.* New York: Guilford Press.

Orbach, I. (1995). *The hidden mind.* New York: Wiley.

Orbach, I. (2001). How would you listen to the person on the roof? A response to H. Omer and A. Elitzur. *Suicide and Life-Threatening Behavior, 31*(2), 140–143.

Oxford English Dictionary (2nd ed). (1989). Oxford, England: Oxford University Press.

Palgi, P., & Abramovitch, H. (1984). Death: A cross-cultural perspective. *Annual Review of Anthropology, 13,* 385–417.

Paloutzian, R. F., & Park, C. L. (2005). *Handbook of the psychology of religion and spirituality.* New York: Guilford Press.

Parad, H. J. (Ed.). (1965). *Crisis intervention.* New York: Family Service Association of America.

Parad, H. J. (1966). The use of time limited crisis intervention in community mental health programming. *Social Service Review, 40,* 275–282.

Parkes, C. M. (1975). What becomes of redundant world models? A contribution to the study of change. *British Journal of Medical Psychology, 48,* 131–137.

Parkes, C. M. (1986). *Bereavement: Studies of grief in adult life* (2nd ed.). Harmondsworth, England: Penguin.

Parkes, C. M. (2006). Symposium on complicated grief. *Omega, 52*(1), 1–8.

Parkes, C. M., & Prigerson, H. G. (2010). *Bereavement: Studies of grief in adult life* (4th edition). London: Routledge.

Parry, K., & Ryan, A. S. (Eds.). (1996). *A cross-cultural look at death, dying, and religion.* Chicago: Nelson-Hall.

Penedo, F. J., & Dahn, J. R. (2005). Exercise and well-being: A review of mental and physical health benefits associated with physical activity. *Current Opinion in Psychiatry, 18*(2), 189–193.

Pennebaker, J. (1993). Putting stress into words. *Behavior Research and Therapy, 131,* 539–548.

Pennebaker, J. W. (1997). Writing about emotional experiences as a therapeutic process. *American Psychological Society, 8,* 162–166.

Pennebaker, J. W. (2004). *Writing to heal: A guided journal for recovering from trauma and emotional upheaval.* Oakland, CA: New Harbinger.

Pennebaker J. W., & Beall, S. K. (1986). Confronting a traumatic event: Toward an understanding of inhibition and disease. *Journal of Abnormal Psychology, 95,* 274–281.

Piaget, J. (1950). The psychology of intelligence. New York: Harcourt, Brace.

Pollock, G. (1989). *The mourning-liberation process.* New York: International Universities Press.

Prigerson, H. G., Frank, E., Kasl, S. V., Reynolds, C. F., III, Anderson, B., Zubenko, G. S., et al. (1995). Complicated grief and bereavement-related depression as distinct disorders: Preliminary empirical validation in elderly bereaved spouses. *American Journal of Psychiatry, 152,* 22–30.

Prigerson, H. G., Horowitz, M. J., Jacobs, S. C., Parkes, C. M., Aslan, M., Goodkin, K., et al. (2009). Prolonged grief disorder: Psychometric validation of criteria proposed for DSM-V and ICD-11. *PLoS Medicine, 6*(8), e1000121.

Prigerson, H. G., & Jacobs, S. C. (2001). Traumatic grief as a distinct disorder: A rationale, consensus criteria, and a preliminary empirical test. In M. S. Stroebe, R. O. Hansson, W. Stroebe, & H. Schut (Eds.), *Handbook of bereavement research: Consequences, coping, and care* (pp. 613–637). Washington, DC: American Psychological Association.

Prigerson, H. G., & Maciejewski, P. K. (2006). A call for sound empirical testing and evaluation of criteria for complicated grief proposed for DSM-V. *Omega, 52*(1), 9–19.

Prigerson, H. G., Vanderwerker, L. C., & Maciejewski, P. K. (2008). A case for inclusion of prolonged grief disorder in DSM-V. In M. S. Stroebe, R. O. Hansson, H. Schut, & W. Stroebe (Eds.), *Handbook of bereavement research and practice: Advances in theory and intervention* (pp. 165–186). Washington, DC: American Psychological Association.

Rando, T. A. (1988). *Grieving: How to go on living when someone you love dies.* Lexington, MA: Lexington Books.

Rando, T. A. (1993). *Treatment of complicated mourning.* Champaign, IL: Research Press.

Rando, T. A. (2000). On the experience of traumatic stress in anticipatory and post-death mourning. In T. A. Rando (Ed.), *Clinical dimensions of anticipatory mourning* (pp. 155–221). Champaign, IL: Research Press.

Raphael, B. (1978) Mourning and the prevention of melancholia. *British Journal of Medical Psychology, 51*(4), 303-310.

Raphael, B. (1983). *The anatomy of bereavement.* New York: Basic Books.

Raphael, B., & Martinek, N. (1997). Assessing traumatic bereavement and posttraumatic stress disorder. In J. P. Wilson & T. M Keane (Eds.), *Assessing psychological trauma and PTSD* (pp. 373–395). New York: Guilford Press.

Reed, M. L. (2000). *Grandparents cry twice.* Amityville, NY: Baywood.

Reed, M. L. (2003). Grandparents' grief: Who listens? *The Forum: The Association for Death Education and Counseling, 29*(1), 1–4.

Reid, F. T., Jr. (2010). *Pilgrims, paths and progress: Towards a comprehensive psychotherapy.* Leeds, England: We-Publish.

Reimer J. (Ed.). (1974). *Jewish reflections on death.* New York: Schocken Books.

Riesman, F. (1965). The "helper" therapy principle. *Social Work, 10,* 27–32.

Reyes, G., Elhai, J. D., & Ford, J. D. (Eds.). (2008). *The encyclopedia of psychological trauma.* Hoboken, NJ: Wiley & Sons.

Rogers, C. R. (1951). *Client-centered therapy.* Boston: Houghton Mifflin.

Rogers, C. R. (1957). The necessary and sufficient conditions of therapeutic personality change. *Journal of Consulting Psychology, 21*(2), 95–103.

Rosenblatt, P. (2005). Intimate relationship in bereavement. *Grief Matters,* Summer, 50–53.

Rosenblatt, P. C. (2008). Grief across cultures. In M. S. Stroebe, R. O. Hansson, H. Schut, & W. Stroebe (Eds.), *Handbook of bereavement research and practice: Advances in theory and intervention* (pp. 207–221). Washington, DC: American Psychological Association.

Rothenberg, A. (1984). Creativity and psychotherapy. *Psychoanalysis and Contemporary Thought, 7,* 233–268.

Rubin, S. (1981). A Two-Track Model of Bereavement: Theory and application in research. *American Journal of Orthopsychiatry, 51,* 101–109.

Rubin, S. S. (1984a). Maternal attachment and child death: On adjustment, relationship and resolution. *Omega, 15,* 347–352.

Rubin, S. S. (1984b). Mourning distinct from melancholia. *British Journal of Medical Psychology, 57,* 339–345.

Rubin, S. S. (1985). The resolution of bereavement: A clinical focus on the relationships to the deceased. *Psychotherapy: Theory, research, training and practice, 22,* 231–235.

Rubin, S. S. (1990). Treating the bereaved spouse: A focus on the loss process, the self and the other. *The Psychotherapy Patient, 6*(3/4), 189–205.

Rubin, S. S. (1992). Adult child loss and the Two-Track Model of Bereavement. *Omega, 24,* 183–202.

Rubin, S. S. (1993). The death of a child is forever: The life course impact of child loss. In M. S. Stroebe, W. Stroebe, & R. O. Hansson (Eds.), *Handbook of bereavement* (pp. 285–299). Cambridge, England: Cambridge University Press.

Rubin, S. S. (1996). The wounded family: Bereaved parents and the impact of adult child loss. In D. Klass, P. R. Silverman, & S. L. Nickman (Eds.), *Continuing bonds: New understandings of grief* (pp. 217–232). Washington, DC: Taylor & Francis.

Rubin S. S. (1999). The Two-Track Model of Bereavement: Overview, retrospect and prospect. *Death Studies, 23*(8), 681–714.

Rubin, S. S. (2000). Psychodynamic perspectives on treatment with the bereaved: Modifications of the therapeutic/transference paradigm. In R. Malkinson, S. Rubin, & E. Witztum (Eds.), *Traumatic and nontraumatic loss and bereavement: Clinical theory and practice* (pp. 117–141). Madison, CT: Psychosocial Press.

Rubin, S. S. (2010). Psychological ethics in Israel: Riding the winds of fashion to guide transformative changes. *Ethics and Behavior, 20* (3/4), 265-276

Rubin, S. S. (May, 2010). The ubiquitousness of the Holocaust for Jewish and Israeli people. Unpublished paper presented at the International Work Group Conference on Death, Dying and Bereavement in Cologne, Germany.

Rubin, S. S., & Ashkenazi, T. (2003). The implications of organ donation for parental adjustment and mourning following child loss. Unpublished grant request, Chief Scientist's Office, Ministry of Health, Israel.

Rubin, S. S., Bar Nadav, O., Malkinson, R., Koren, D., Gofer-Shnarch, M., & Michaeli, E. (2009). The Two-Track Model of Bereavement Questionnaire (TTBQ): Development and findings of a relational measure. *Death Studies, 33,* 1–29.

Rubin, S. S., & Katz-Dichterman, D. (1993). The contribution of attachment history and object relationship to bereavement outcome. In R. Malkinson, S. Rubin, & E. Witztum (Eds.), *Loss and bereavement in Jewish society in Israel* (pp. 51–67). Jerusalem: Canah/Ministry of Defense.

Rubin, S. S., & Malkinson, R. (2001). Parental response to child loss across the life-cycle: Clinical and research perspectives. In M. Stroebe, R. O. Hansson, W. Stroebe, & H. Schut (Eds.), *Handbook of bereavement research: Consequences, coping, and care* (pp. 219–240). Washington, DC: American Psychological Association.

Rubin, S. S., Malkinson, R., Koren, D., Mor-Yosef, S., & Witztum, E. (2011). Military bereavement and combat trauma. In S. Ringel & J. R. Brandell (Eds.), *Trauma: Contemporary Directions in Theory, Practice, and Research.* Thousand Oaks, CA: Sage, pp. 130–149.

Rubin, S. S., Malkinson, R., & Witztum, E. (2000). An overview of the field of loss. In R. Malkinson, S. Rubin, & E. Witztum (Eds.), *Traumatic and nontraumatic loss and bereavement: Clinical theory and practice* (pp. 5–40). Madison, CT: Psychosocial Press.

Rubin, S. S., Malkinson, R., & Witztum, E. (2003). Trauma and bereavement: Conceptual and clinical issues revolving around relationships. *Death Studies, 27,* 667–690.

Rubin, S. S., Malkinson, R., & Witztum, E. (2008). Clinical aspects of a DSM complicated grief diagnosis: Challenges, dilemmas, and opportunities. In M. S. Stroebe, R. O. Hansson, H. Schut, & W. Stroebe (Eds.), *Handbook of bereavement research and practice: Advances in theory and intervention* (pp. 187–206). Washington, DC: American Psychological Association.

Rubin, S. S., Malkinson, R., & Witztum, E. (2011). The Two-Track Model of Bereavement: The double helix of research and clinical practice. In R. Neimeyer, D. L. Harris, H. R. Winokuer, & G. F. Thornton (Eds.), *Grief and bereavement in contemporary society: Bridging research and practice.* New York: Routledge, pp. 47–56.

Rubin, S. S., & Nassar, H. Z. (1993). Psychotherapy and supervision with a bereaved Moslem family: An intervention that almost failed. *Psychiatry, 56,* 338–348.

Rubin, S. S., & Prigerson, H. G. (2008). Bereavement. In G. Reyes, J. D. Elhai, & J. D. Ford (Eds.), *The encyclopedia of psychological trauma* (pp. 73–75). Hoboken, NJ: Wiley & Sons.

Rubin, S. S., & Schechter, N. (1997). Exploring the social construction of bereavement: Perceptions of adjustment and recovery for bereaved men. *American Journal of Orthopsychiatry, 67,* 279–289.

Rubin, S. S., & Yasien-Esmael, H. (2004). Loss and bereavement among Israel's Muslims: Acceptance of God's will, grief, and the relationship to the deceased. *Omega, 49*(2), 149–162.

Ryff, C., & Singer, B. (1998) The contours of positive human health. *Psychological Inquiry, 9,* 1–28.

Rynearson, E. K. (2001). *Retelling violent death: Resilience and intervention beyond the crisis.* Philadelphia: Taylor & Francis.

Rynearson, E. K. (2006). (Ed.). *Violent death.* New York: Routledge.

Sacks, J. (2006). *Celebrating life: Finding happiness in unexpected places.* New York: Continuum.

Sadeh, A., Rubin, S., & Berman, E. (1993). Parental and relationship representations and experiences of depression in college students. *Journal of Personality Assessment, 60,* 192–204.

Saldinger, K., Porterfield, A., & Cain, A. C. (2004). Meeting the needs of parentally bereaved children: A framework for child-centered parenting. *Psychiatry, 67,* (4), 331–352.

Salzman, C., Glick, I., & Keshavan, M. S. (2010). The 7 sins of psychopharmacology. *Journal of Clinical Psychopharmacology, 30*(6), 1–3.

Salmon, P. (2001). Effects of physical exercise on anxiety, depression, and sensitivity to stress: A unifying theory. *Clinical Psychology Review, 21*(1), 33–61.

Sandler, I. N., Wolchik, S. A., Ayers, T. S., Tein, J., Coxe, S., & Chow, W. (2008). Linking theory and intervention to promote resilience in parentally bereaved children. In M. S. Stroebe, R. O. Hansson, H. Schut, & W. Stroebe (Eds.), *Handbook of bereavement research and practice: Advances in theory and intervention* (pp. 531–550). Washington, DC: American Psychological Association.

Sandler, J., Dare, C., & Holder, A. (1972). Frames of reference in psychoanalytic psychology. *British Journal of Medical Psychology, 45,* 127–131.

Sandler, J., & Sandler, A. M. (1978). On the development of object relationships and affects. *International Journal of Psychoanalysis, 59*, 285–296.

Schaal, S., Elbert, T., & Neuner, F. (2009). Prolonged grief disorder and depression in widows due to the Rwandan genocide. *Omega: Journal of Death and Dying, 59*, 203–219.

Schafer, R. (1992). *Retelling a life: Narration and dialogue in psychoanalysis*. New York: Basic Books.

Schermerhorn, R. A. (1978). *Comparative ethnic relations: A framework for theory and research*. Chicago: University of Chicago Press.

Schut, H. (2010). Grief counseling efficacy. *Bereavement Care, 29*, 8–9.

Schut, H. A. W., DeKeijser, J., van den Bout, J., & Stroebe, M. (1996). Posttraumatic stress symptoms in the first years of conjugal bereavement. *Anxiety Research, 4*, 225–234.

Schut, H., Stroebe, M. S., Van den Bout, J., & Terheggen, M. (2001). The efficacy of bereavement interventions: Determining who benefits. In M. S. Stroebe, W. Stroebe, R. O. Hansson , & H. Schut (Eds.), *Handbook of bereavement research: Consequences, coping and caring*. Washington, DC: American Psychological Association, pp. 705–737.

Segal, Z. V., Williams, J. M. G., & Teasdale, J. D. (2002). *Mindfulness-based cognitive therapy for depression: A new approach to preventing relapse*. New York: Guilford Press.

Seligman, M. E. P. (2006). Afterword: Breaking the 65 percent barrier. In M. Csikszentmihalyi & I. S. Csikszentmihalyi (Eds.), *A life worth living: Contributions to positive psychology*. New York: Oxford University Press.

Selvini-Palazzoli, M., Boscolo, L., Chechin, G., & Pratta, G. (1978). *Paradox and counterparadox*. New York: Jason Aronson.

Selvini-Palazzoli, M., Boscolo, L., Chechin, G., & Pratta, G. (1980). Hypothesizing-circularity and neutrality: Three guidelines for conductor of the session. *Family Process, 19*(1), 3–12.

Shalev, A. Y. (2002). Acute stress reactions in adults. *Biological Psychiatry, 51*, 532–543.

Shalev, R. (1999). *Comparison of war bereaved and motor vehicle accident bereaved parents*. Unpublished master's thesis, University of Haifa, Haifa, Israel.

Shalev, R. (2009). *Bereaved parents: Change of self, future orientation, functioning, and adaptation to loss*. Unpublished doctoral dissertation, University of Haifa, Haifa, Israel.

Shapiro, E. R. (1994). *Grief as a family process: A developmental approach to clinical practice*. New York: Guilford Press.

Shapiro, E. R. (1996). Family bereavement and cultural diversity. A social developmental approach. *Family Process, 35*, 313–332.

Shear, M. K., & Smith, K. (2002). Traumatic loss and the syndrome of complicated grief. *PTSD Research Quarterly, 13*, 1–6.

Shear, M. K., Simon, N., Wall, M., Zisook, S., Neimeyer, R., et al. (2011). Complicated grief and related bereavement issues for *DSM-5*. *Depression and Anxiety, 28*,103–117.

Shedler, J. (2010). The efficacy of psychodynamic therapy. *American Psychologist, 65*(2), 98–109.

Siggins, L. D. (1966). Mourning: A critical survey of the literature. *International Journal of Psychoanalysis, 47*, 14–25.

Silverman, G. K., Johnson, J. G., & Prigerson, H. G. (2001). Preliminary explorations of the effects of prior trauma and loss on risk for psychiatry disorders in recently widowed people. *Israel Journal of Psychiatry, 38*, 202–215.

Silverman, P. R. (2000a). Children as part of a family drama: An integrated view of childhood bereavement. In R. Malkinson, S. Rubin, & E. Witztum (Eds.), *Traumatic and nontraumatic loss and bereavement: Clinical theory and practice.* Madison, CT: Psychosocial Press.

Silverman, P. R. (2000b). *Never too young to know: Death in children's lives.* Oxford, England: Oxford University Press.

Silverman, P. R. (2004). *Widow to widow: How the bereaved help one another.* New York: Brunner-Routledge.

Silverman, P. R., Baker, J., Cait, C. A., & Boerner, K. (2003). The effects of negative legacies on children's adjustment after parental death. *Omega: Journal of Death and Dying, 64,* 359–376.

Silverman, P. R., Nickman, S., & Worden, J. W. (1992). Detachment revisited: The child's reconstruction of a dead parent. *American Journal of Orthopsychiatry, 62,* 494–503.

Silverman, P. R., & Worden, W. J. (1993). Children's reactions to the death of a parent. In M. S. Stroebe, W. Stroebe, &. R. O. Hansson, (Eds.), *Handbook of bereavement: Theory, research, and intervention.* Washington, DC: American Psychological Association, pp. 300–316.

Sirles, A., & Franke, P. J. (1989). Factors influencing mothers' reactions to intrafamily sexual abuse. *Child Abuse and Neglect, 13*(1), 131–139.

Skaff, M. M., & Chesla, C. A., Mycue, V. D., & Fisher, L. (2002). Lessons in cultural competence: Adapting research methodology for Latino participants. *Journal of Community Psychology, 1*(30), 305–323.

Smith, H. (1994). *The illustrated world's religions: A guide to our wisdom traditions.* New York: HarperCollins.

Smyth, J. M., Stone, A. A., Hureaitz, A., & Kael, A. (1999). Effects of writing about stressful experiences on symptom reduction in patients with asthma or rheumatoid arthritis. *Journal of American Medical Association, 281*(14), 1304–1309.

Spence, D. P. (1982). *Narrative truth and historical truth: Meaning and interpretation in psychoanalysis.* New York: W. W. Norton.

Spitz, E. K. (2000). *Does the soul survive? A Jewish journey to belief in afterlife, past lives & living with purpose.* Woodstock, VT: Jewish Lights.

Stein, M. B., Walker, J. R., Hazen, A. L., & Forde, D. R. (1997). Full and partial posttraumatic stress disorder: Findings from a community survey. *American Journal of Psychiatry, 154,* 1114–1119.

Stierlin, H. (1970). The function of inner objects. *International Journal of Psychoanalysis, 51,* 321–329.

Stroebe, M. S., Folkman, S., Hansson, R. O., & Schut, H. (2006). The prediction of bereavement outcome: Development of an integrative risk factor framework. *Social Science & Medicine, 63*(9), 2440–2451.

Stroebe, M. S., Gergen, M. M., Gergen, K. J., & Stroebe, W. (1992). Broken hearts or broken bonds. *American Psychologist, 47,* 1205–1212.

Stroebe, M. S., Hansson, R. O., Schut, H. A. W. & Stroebe, W. (2008). *Handbook of bereavement research and practice.* Washington, DC: American Psychological Association.

Stroebe, M. S., & Schut, H. A. W. (1999). The dual process model of coping with bereavement: Rationale and description. *Death Studies, 23*(3), 197–224.

Stroebe, M. S., Schut, H., & Finkenauer, C. (2001). The traumatization of grief? A conceptual framework for understanding the trauma-bereavement interface. *Israel Journal of Psychiatry, 38,* 185–201.

Stroebe, W., Schut, H. A. W., & Stroebe, M. S. (2005). Grief work, disclosure and counseling: Do they help the bereaved? *Clinical Psychology Review, 25,* 395–414.

Stroebe, W., & Stroebe, M. S. (1987). *Bereavement and health: The psychological and physical consequences of partner loss.* New York: Cambridge University Press, pp. 50–51.

Stroebe, W., Stroebe, M.S., Hansson, R. O., & Schut, H. (Eds.). (2001). *Handbook of bereavement research: Consequences, coping and caring.* Washington, DC: American Psychological Association.

Stroebe, W., Zech, E., Stroebe, M., & Abakoumkin, G. (2005). Does social support help in bereavement? Its impact on vulnerability and recovery. *Journal of Social and Clinical Psychology, 24,*(7), 1030–1050.

Sullivan, H. S. (1970). *The psychiatric interview.* New York: W. W. Norton.

Sveshnikov, S. (2010, June 7). *On the significance of the ritual of the Russian Orthodox Church surrounding death and dying for the grieving process of the bereaved.* Paper presented at the Pastoral Conference of the Western American Diocese of the Russian Orthodox Church, San Francisco, CA. Retrieved January 2, 2011, from http://frsergei.wordpress.com/2010/06/07/on-the-significance-of-the-ritual-of-the-russian-orthodox-church-surrounding-death-and-dying-for-the-grieving-process-of-the-bereaved

Tamir, G. (1987). *Functioning and attachment in war bereaved Israeli parents.* Unpublished master's thesis, University of Haifa, Haifa, Israel. (in Hebrew)

Tedeschi, R. G., & Calhoun, L. G. (2004). Posttraumatic growth: Conceptual foundations and empirical evidence. *Psychological Inquiry, 15,* 1–18.

Tessman, L. H. (1996). *Helping children cope with parting parents.* Northvale, NJ: Jason Aronson.

Telushkin, J. (2008). *Jewish literacy: The most important things to know about the Jewish religion, its people, and its history* (Rev. ed.). New York: HarperCollins.

Tsang H. W., Chan, E. P., & Cheung, W. M. (2008). Effects of mindful and non-mindful exercises on people with depression: A systematic review. *British Journal of Clinical Psychology, 47*(3), 303–322.

Van der Hart, O. (1983). *Rituals in psychotherapy.* New York: Irvington.

Van der Hart, O. (1986). (Ed.). *Coping with loss.* New York: Irvington.

Van der Hart, O. (1987). Leave-taking ritual in mourning therapy. *Society and Welfare, D.* (3), 267–279 (in Hebrew).

Van der Kolk, B. A., McFarlane, A. C., & Weisaeth, L. (Eds.). (1996). *Traumatic stress: The effects of overwhelming experience on mind, body, and society.* New York: Guilford Press.

Vanderwerker, L., & Prigerson, H. G. (2004). Social support and technological connectedness as protective factors of bereavement. *Journal of Loss and Trauma, 9,* 45–57.

Van Gennep, A. (1960). *The rites of passage.* London: Routledge. (Original work published 1908)

Volkan, V. D. (1972). The linking objects of pathological mourners. *Archives of General Psychiatry, 27,* 215–221.

Volkan, V. D. (1981). *Linking objects and linking phenomena.* New York: International Universities Press.

Walsh, F., & McGoldrick, M. (2004). *Living beyond loss: death in the family* (2nd ed.). New York: W. W. Norton.

Weathers, F. W., & Keane, T. M. (2008). Trauma, definition. In G. Reyes, J. D. Elhai, & J. D. Ford (Eds.), *The encyclopedia of psychological trauma.* Hoboken, NJ: Wiley & Sons, pp. 657–660.

Weiss, D. S., & Marmar, C. R. (1997). The Impact of Event Scale–Revised. In J. P. Wilson & T. M. Keane (Eds.), *Assessing psychological trauma and PTSD* (pp. 399–411). New York: Guilford Press.

Weiss, R. S. (2001). Grief, bonds, and relationships. In M. S. Stroebe, R. O. Hansson, W. Stroebe, & H. Schut (Eds.), *Handbook of bereavement research: Consequences, coping, and care.* Washington, DC: American Psychological Association, pp. 47–62.

Wells, A. (2005). Detached mindfulness in cognitive therapy: A metacognitive analysis and ten techniques. *Journal of Rational-Emotive & Cognitive-Behavior Therapy, 23*(4), 337–355.

Weston, D. (1998). The legacy of Sigmund Freud. *Psychological Bulletin, 124*, 331–371.

Weston, D., Novotny, C. M., & Thompson-Brenner, H. (2004). The empirical status of empirically supported psychotherapies: Assumptions, findings, and reporting in controlled clinical trials. *Psychological Bulletin, 130*(4), 631–663.

Wieseltier, L. (1998). *The Kaddish.* New York: Knopf.

Wijngaards-de Meij, L., Stroebe, M., Schut, H., Stroebe, W., Van den Bout, J., Van der Heijden, P., et al. (2007). Neuroticism and attachment insecurity as predictors of bereavement outcome. *Journal of Research in Personality, 41*, 498–505.

Wikan, U. (1988). Bereavement and loss in two Muslim communities: Egypt and Bali compared. *Social Science and Medicine, 27*, 451–460.

Williams, M., Teasdale, J., Segal, Z., & Kabat-Zinn, J. (2007). *The mindful way through depression: Freeing yourself from chronic unhappiness.* New York: Guilford Press.

Winnicott, D. W. (1965). *The maturational processes and the facilitating environment.* London: Hogarth.

Winnicott, D. W. (1971). *Playing and reality.* London: Routledge.

Wiseman, H., & Barber, J. P. (2008). *Echoes of the trauma: Relationship themes and emotions in the narratives of the children of Holocaust survivors.* New York: Cambridge University Press.

Wiseman, H., & Shefler, G. (2001). Experienced psychoanalytically oriented therapists' narrative accounts of their own personal therapy. *Psychotherapy, 38*(2), 129–141.

Wittouck, C., Van Autreve, S., De Jaegere, E., Portzky, G., & van Heeringen, K. (2011). The prevention and treatment of complicated grief: A meta-analysis. *Clinical Psychology Review, 31*(1), 69–78.

Witztum, E. (2004). *Spirit, loss and bereavement.* Tel Aviv, Israel: Ministry of Defense. (in Hebrew)

Witztum, E., & Kotler, M. (2000). Historical and cultural construction of PTSD in Israel. In A. Y. Shalev, R. Yehuda, & A. C. McFarlane (Eds.), *International handbook of human response to trauma* (pp. 103–114). New York: Plenum.

Witztum, E., & Lerner, V. (2008). *Genius and madness.* Tel Aviv, Israel: Arie Nir. (in Hebrew)

Witztum, E., Malkinson, R., & Rubin, S. (2001). Death, bereavement and traumatic loss in Israel: A historical and cultural perspective. *Israel Journal of Psychiatry, 38*(3/4), 157–170.

Witztum, E., Malkinson, R., & Rubin, S. (2005). Traumatic grief and bereavement resulting from terrorism: Israeli and American perspectives. In S. C. Heilman (Ed.), *Death, bereavement, and mourning.* New York: Transaction Books, pp. 105–120.

Witztum, E., & Roman, I. (2000). Psychotherapeutic intervention in complicated grief: Metaphor and leave-taking ritual with the bereaved. In R. Malkinson, S. Rubin, & E. Witztum (Eds.), *Traumatic and nontraumatic loss and bereavement: Clinical theory and practice* (pp. 143–171). Madison, CT: Psychosocial Press.

Witztum, E., Van der Hart, O., & Friedman, B. (1988). The use of metaphors in psychotherapy. *Journal of Contemporary Psychotherapy, 18*, 270–290.

Wolfenstein, M. (1969). How is mourning possible? *The Psychoanalytic Study of the Child, 21*, 93–123.

Worden, J. W. (1992). *Grief counseling and grief therapy: A handbook for the mental health practitioner* (2nd ed.). New York: Springer. (Original work published 1982)

Worden, J. W. (2008). *Grief counseling and grief therapy: A handbook for the mental health practitioner* (4th ed.). New York: Springer.

Worden, J. W., Davis, B., & McCown, D. (1999). Comparing parent loss with sibling loss. *Death Studies, 23*, 1–15.

Wortman, C. B., & Silver, R. C. (2001). The myths of coping with loss revisited. In M. S. Stroebe, R. O. Hansson, W. Stroebe, & H. Schut (Eds.), *Handbook of bereavement research: Consequences, coping, and care* (pp. 405–429). Washington, DC: American Psychological Association.

Yalom, I. (1980). *Existential psychotherapy*. New York: Basic Books.

Yasien-Esmael, H., & Rubin, S. (2005). The meaning structures of Muslim bereavements in Israel: Religious traditions, mourning practices, and human experiences. *Death Studies, 29*(6), 495–518.

Zisook, S., Chentsova-Dutton, Y., & Shuchter, S.R. (1998). PTSD following bereavement. *Annals of Clinical Psychiatry, 10*(4), 157–163.

Index